In this book, Mark Rowlands challenges the Cartesian view of the mind as a self-contained monadic entity, and offers in its place a radical externalist or environmentalist model of cognitive processes. Cognition is not something done exclusively in the head, but fundamentally something done in the world. Drawing on both evolutionary theory and a detailed examination of the processes involved in perception, memory, thought, and language use, Rowlands argues that cognition is, in part, a process whereby creatures manipulate and exploit relevant objects in their environment. It is not simply an internal process of information processing; equally significantly, it is an external process of information processing. This innovative book provides a foundation for an unorthodox but increasingly popular view of the nature of cognition.

CAMBRIDGE STUDIES IN PHILOSOPHY

The body in mind

CAMBRIDGE STUDIES IN PHILOSOPHY

General editor ERNEST SOSA

Advisory editors
JONATHAN DANCY University of Reading
JOHN HALDANE University of St Andrews
GILBERT HARMAN Princeton University
FRANK JACKSON Australian National University
WILLIAM G. LYCAN University of North Carolina, Chapel Hill
SYDNEY SHOEMAKER Cornell University
JUDITH J. THOMSON Massachusetts Institute of Technology

RECENT TITLES

The body in mind

Understanding cognitive processes

Mark Rowlands

University College, Cork

CAMBRIDGE
UNIVERSITY PRESS

PUBLISHED BY THE PRESS SYNDICATE OF THE UNIVERSITY OF CAMBRIDGE
The Pitt Building, Trumpington Street, Cambridge, United Kingdom

CAMBRIDGE UNIVERSITY PRESS
The Edinburgh Building, Cambridge CB2 2RU, UK   http://www.cup.cam.ac.uk
40 West 20th Street, New York, NY 10011-4211, USA   http://www.cup.org
10 Stamford Road, Oakleigh, Melbourne 3166, Australia

First published 1999

Printed in the United Kingdom at the University Press, Cambridge

Typeset in 10/12pt Monotype Bembo in QuarkXPress™   [SE]

A catalogue record for this book is available from the British Library

Library of Congress Cataloguing in Publication data

Rowlands, Mark.
The Body in Mind: Understanding Cognitive Processes / Mark Rowlands.
p.   cm. – (Cambridge Studies in Philosophy)
Includes bibliographical references and index.
ISBN 0 521 65274 X (hardback)
1. Philosophy of mind.   2. Mind and body.   3. Cognition.
4. Externalism (Philosophy of mind)   I. Title.   II. Series.
BD418.3.R78   1999
128′.2 – dc21   98-45620 CIP

ISBN 0 521 65274 X hardback

Contents

Preface

Philosophy since Kant has been, well, neo-Kantian. Indeed, neo-Kantianism in philosophy arguably predates Kant by a considerable time. Locke, Berkeley, and Hume were all neo-Kantians. Kant was a neo-Kantian. Hegel was a neo-Kantian, as was Marx (at least the Marx of the first and second Internationals). Nietzsche, that most professedly anti-Kantian of thinkers, was a neo-Kantian. The linguistic turn in philosophy is essentially a linguistic form of neo-Kantianism. Mainstream twentieth-century philosophy of science has been about as neo-Kantian as you can get. Structuralism is neo-Kantian. And anybody, but anybody, who writes about literary theory is neo-Kantian to their intellectual core. As you might have already gleaned, I am using the expression 'neo-Kantian' in a somewhat broad sense. Indeed, the way I am using the expression makes it difficult to imagine anyone who is not neo-Kantian. Neo-Kantianism is the view that there are activities of the mind whose function is to structure the world. At least some aspects of the world that is presented to us, therefore, are mind-dependent in that they depend for their existence or nature on the structuring activities of the mind. The significance of recent strands of thought that have been labelled *externalist*, or *anti-individualist* is that they effectively invert this picture of the relation of mind to world. What is essential to externalism, or, as I shall call it here, *environmentalism*, in all its forms, is the idea that the contents of the mind are, in some sense at least, *worldly*: they are environmentally constituted. This does not, of course, provide a *refutation* of neo-Kantianism, but it does, in effect, turn neo-Kantianism on its head.

This book was written over a period of time that straddled life both in the USA and in Ireland. My philosophical debts incurred on both sides of the Atlantic have been many and large. Colin McGinn first started me thinking about externalism. Max Hocutt helped me realize that commonalities between anti-Cartesian positions were more

ix

important than the differences. Of a more immediate nature, my thanks to Maeve Crowley, Eoin O'Kelly, and Paul Rothwell who read earlier versions of this book, and to staff and students at University College Cork, Trinity College Dublin, Queen's University at Belfast, and the University of Ulster at Coleraine where proto-versions of some of the individual chapters were presented. John Post and Pierre Jacob, as readers for Cambridge University Press, made several very useful suggestions which greatly improved the final version. Also at Cambridge, my thanks to Hilary Gaskin for her help and quiet efficiency, and to Gillian Maude for some outstanding copy-editing.

A much earlier version of chapter 5 appeared as 'Against methodological solipsism: the ecological approach', in *Philosophical Psychology*, 8, 1, 1995, 1–24. An earlier version of chapter 11 appeared as 'Teleological semantics', in *Mind*, 106, 422, 1997, 279–303.

Before his sad and untimely death, Edward Reed was kind enough to read, in its entirety, an earlier version of this book. His suggestions greatly improved the eventual result, particularly with regard to the chapter on memory. An abiding regret is that I never got to meet Ed, and so could not benefit from talking to him as I have benefited from reading him. This book is dedicated to his memory.

1

Introduction: 'A picture held us captive'

1.1 TWO PROJECTS AND A PICTURE

Any attempt to understand how minds work must address, at the very least, two questions. The first is essentially an engineering question. One way of putting the question would be: *how can one build a mind?* This project is an engineering one. And, adopting a neologism first coined by Colin McGinn (1989), I shall refer to it as the project of *psychotectonics*: 'psycho', here, pertaining to minds, and 'tectonics' deriving from the Latin verb for building. Psychotectonics, then, is the science of building minds. In order to begin the project of psychotectonics, one must first have a reasonably adequate grasp of the things a mind can do, a grasp of the various functions of the mind. Then, it is thought, one must proceed to show, firstly, how these functions can be broken down into component sub-functions and these sub-functions broken down into sub-sub-functions, and so on, and, secondly, how these progressively more and more simple functions can be realized in progressively more and more simple mechanisms. To understand how to build a mind, it is claimed, is to be able to effect this sort of functional and mechanistic decomposition. This is a standard account of what is involved in psychotectonics, an account enshrined in David Marr's (1982) famous tripartite distinction between *computational*, *algorithmic*, and *physical* levels of analysis; whose basic idea is reflected in Dennett's (1978b) distinction between *intentional, design*, and *physical* stances; whose ethos is captured in the general project, also endorsed by Dennett (1978b) among others, of *homuncular functionalism*. This, then, is a very orthodox picture of how to do psychotectonics, and, while the picture might be a little worn in places, it is, I think, broadly correct. I do not, therefore, propose to challenge it, although I shall try to show that many of its proponents work with an unduly narrow conception of what a computational specification of the mind

1

should look like, and, consequently, that their conception of the algorithmic and physical realizations of this specification is unrealistic. The general idea of psychotectonics as functional and mechanistic decomposition, however, I shall accept, indeed presuppose. Psychotectonics, the project of building minds, occupies Part I of this book.

In order to understand minds, it is also necessary to understand how they can do what they can do. That is, it is necessary to understand how they come to possess those features considered essential to them. In recent discussions of the mind, two of its features loom large: *consciousness* and *intentionality*. Of consciousness, I shall have nothing to say. My suspicion, for what it is worth, is that the problem of consciousness is one that needs dissolution rather than a constructive solution. *If* dissolving the problem of consciousness requires dissolving the picture of the mind upon which it is built, and *if* this book plays a role in dissolving that conception of the mind, then the arguments of this book might be considered relevant to the problem of consciousness. But that this is so is not something I shall assume. My concern, and the principal concern of Part II of this book, is with intentionality, with the aboutness or directedness of states of mind. It may ultimately turn out to be the case that one cannot understand intentionality independently of understanding consciousness, that the two are conceptually interlinked in such a way that forming an adequate conception of the one requires adequately conceptualizing the other (McGinn 1991). This may turn out to be the case, but I suspect not. And even if it does turn out to be so, there is no guarantee in advance of which will turn out to be conceptually prior. So, I shall assume that it is possible to understand intentionality, at least to some extent, without understanding consciousness. This assumption can be questioned, but it is by no means idiosyncratic. Indeed, the assumption is fairly standard.

Most recent discussions assume what Cummins (1989) calls a *representational theory of intentionality*; that is, they assume that the intentionality of mental states reduces to the representationality of mental representations. I, also, shall assume that this is the case, and, consequently, that the project of accounting for intentionality reduces to the project of accounting for how representations represent; how physical states can have semantic properties. This project I shall refer to as that of *psychosemantics*, employing another well-known neologism, but this time in a slightly different way from that intended by its author Jerry Fodor. Psychosemantics, as I shall understand it, is the project of accounting for the representationality of representations, for how representations represent, or possess semantic properties. Again, in common with most recent discussion, I shall assume that this is a reductionist project. Representation, or semanticity, is to be explained or accounted for in terms that are non-representational, non-semantic. Psychosemantics, in this sense, is the principal concern of Part II.

The projects of psychotectonics and psychosemantics are, of course, connected. The most straightforward connection is that the two accounts must cohere in that the functional/mechanistic decomposition of the mind yielded by the psychotectonic project, when combined with the reductionist, non-semantic account of representation identified by the psychosemantic project, must, together, be sufficient to add up to intentionality. Conversely, our account of representationality identified in the psychosemantic project must be consistent with what we know, or assume, to be the correct functional/mechanistic decomposition of the mind. What unites the two projects in this book, however, are not these fairly mundane connections but, rather, a conviction that both projects are hindered by a common conception of the mind. To use a phrase popularized by Wittgenstein, a picture of the mind holds us captive. And this picture prevents us from properly understanding what is required by the projects of psychotectonics and psychosemantics.

There is a view of the mind which began life as a controversial philosophical thesis and then evolved into common sense. The view is both widespread and tenacious, not only as an explicit doctrine but, more significantly, in the clandestine influence it has on explicit doctrines of the mind. The philosophical thesis from which the view is born is spelled out by Descartes, and its association with him is sufficiently robust for it to be called the *Cartesian conception*.

According to the Cartesian conception, minds are to be assimilated to the category of substance. That is, minds are objects which possess properties. Indeed, minds can, to some extent, be conceived of as relevantly similar to other bodily organs. Just as the heart circulates blood, the liver regulates metabolism, and the kidneys process waste products, the mind *thinks*. According to official Cartesian doctrine, the major difference between the mind and these other organs is that

3

the mind is a *non-physical* substance. The mind and brain are distinct entities, and, while the mind may receive input from the brain, and, in turn, send information back to the brain, the two are none the less distinct. The brain is a physical organ operating exclusively on mechanical principles; the mind is a non-physical organ operating according to principles of reason. And there is, Descartes thought, no prospect of deriving the former from the latter.

The Cartesian conception has been famously ridiculed as the myth of the *ghost in the machine*. And it has been Descartes' decision to make the mind ghostly (i.e., non-physical) that has drawn the principal fire from dissenters. The dissenters' case here has largely been successful, and not many philosophers or psychologists today would regard themselves as Cartesians in this sense. Ryle's expression, however, has another facet. Not only is Descartes' mind a ghost, but it is one that is *in* a machine. This was the principal source of Ryle's ire, of course. But, whereas the revolt against ghostly views of the mind has been overwhelmingly successful, criticism of the second aspect of Descartes' view has been comparatively muted. Most theorizing about the mind is now predicated on the assumption that the mind is physical; that is, that some sort of materialism is true. However, such theorizing has been, and largely still is, predicated on the view that the mind is an internal entity, i.e., located inside the skin of any organism that possesses it. The revolt against Cartesian views of the mind has been restricted to the first aspect of Descartes' view. The other aspect, Descartes' internalism, has, until recently, largely been ignored. Most forms of materialism are, thus, also forms of internalism.

Descartes' dualism and his internalism have, arguably, the same root: the rise of mechanism associated with the scientific revolution. This revolution reintroduced the classical concept of the atom in somewhat new attire as an essentially mathematical entity whose primary qualities could be precisely quantified as modes or aspects of Euclidean space. Macroscopic bodies were composed of atoms, and the generation and corruption of the former was explained in terms of the combination and recombination of the latter. Atomism is, then, mechanistic in the sense that it reduces all causal transactions to the translation, from point to point, of elementary particles, and regards the behaviour of any macroscopic body as explicable in terms of motions of the atoms that comprise it.

It is widely recognized that Descartes' dualism stems, at least in part, from his acceptance of mechanism. The physical world, for Descartes, is governed by purely mechanical principles. He was, however, unable to conceive of how such principles could be extended to the thinking activities constitutive of the human mind. Minds, for Descartes, are essentially thinking things and, as such, governed by principles of reason. But such principles, Descartes thought, are distinct from, and not reducible to, principles of mechanical combination and association. Rationality, for Descartes, cannot be mechanized. Each mind is, thus, a small corner of a foreign field, inherently non-mechanical, hence inherently non-physical. Descartes' dualism, in this way, stemmed quite directly from his mechanism.

Of equal significance, however, is the connection between mechanism and internalism. Mechanistic atomism is, we might say, methodologically individualist. A composite body is ontologically reducible to its simple constituents. And the behaviour of a composite body is reducible to the local motions of its constituents. Thus, if we want to explain the behaviour of a macroscopic body, we need focus only on local occurrences undergone by its parts. This methodological individualism would also have some purchase on the explanation of the behaviour of human beings, since we are also, in part, physical. It is, therefore, no surprise that minds became analogously and derivatively conceived of by Descartes, and his dualist descendants, in atomistic terms. A mind, for Descartes, is essentially a *psychic monad* (Callicott 1989). Each mind is a discrete substance insulated within an alien material cladding. Just like any other atom, the mind could interact with the physical atoms of the body. But, crucially, and again just like any other atom, the essential nature of the mind was not informed by this interaction. The rational nature of the mind is taken as an independent given, and its interaction with other atoms is extrinsic to this nature. The ghosts of this conception of the mind, and the mechanistic and individualistic conception of explanation that underwrites it, are very much with us today.

These ghosts occupy a house with many mansions. Ontological theses are entangled with epistemological ones, each giving support and succour to the other. It is genuinely unclear if any particular thesis precedes any of the others. It is more realistic to suppose, perhaps, that ontological and epistemological aspects of Cartesianism grew up, indeed, evolved, together. A close relative of Descartes' ontological internalism is epistemic internalism, a view which has its modern roots in Descartes. The central idea of epistemic internalism is that the difference between true belief and knowledge consists in some form of justification and, crucially, that justification consists in factors that are, in some sense, internal to the subject of the belief. The relevant notion of internality, however, is fundamentally epistemic. The activities of my heart, lungs, and liver are activities internal to me, but clearly these are not candidates for transformers of true belief into knowledge. Whatever transforms true belief into knowledge is, according to internalism, something of which the believing subject can be aware, something to which the subject has epistemic access. I can, however, be aware of many things, including whether or not it is presently raining, and the week's activity on the New York stock exchange. But this is not access of the relevant sort. Rather, epistemic internalism claims that justification consists in some sort of special access. According to Descartes, for example, the special access consists in the fact that the thinking subject can determine with certainty whether a belief has justification, and, consequently, whether a belief qualifies as knowledge. And, according to Chisholm (1966), a recent internalist descendant of Descartes, whether a belief has justification is something that can be determined by reflection alone. So, the central idea of epistemic internalism is that the factors that make a true belief justified, and, consequently, that transform a true belief into knowledge, are properties to which the believer has a special sort of epistemic access.

All these theses would be, if not straightforwardly undermined, then at least significantly threatened by the rejection of the Cartesian conception of the mind. If the mind is not self-contained in the relevant way, if the world enters into the very constitution of the mind so that the very identity of mental states involves something external, then it is not clear that this leaves any room for the special sort of epistemic access required by the internalist tradition. For the identity of the contents of one's mind would now, in part, consist of items to which one had no special epistemic access, and this threatens the epistemic relation one bears to the contents of one's mind as a whole. In this way, Descartes' ontological internalism is bound up with, supports and is supported by, his epistemic internalism.

Indeed, the content of internalism extends even beyond the ontological and epistemological spheres into the moral domain. This is because epistemic internalism is closely connected with the deontological notion of epistemic responsibility. The justification, or lack thereof, of my beliefs, is something for which I am responsible, something for which I can be praised or blamed. I may be victimized by a malevolent demon, I may be a brain in a vat, and so all or most of my beliefs may, in fact, be false. The truth of my beliefs depends on external factors and so is something beyond my control. But the justification of my beliefs depends only on internal factors, indeed, internal factors to which I have a special kind of access, and this is something that does lie within my control. Even though I may be hopelessly deceived about the truth of my beliefs, I can still do my epistemic duty with regard to their justification. Accordingly, the justification of my beliefs is something for which I can legitimately be praised or blamed; it is something for which I can be morally assessed. Thus, according to Descartes, epistemic justification is a form of deontological justification. If I do not have certainty but believe anyway, then I do not escape the blame of misusing my freedom. Ontological and epistemic forms of internalism, then, are also closely bound up with a certain view of the moral nature and responsibilities of human beings.

To speak of the Cartesian conception, therefore, is to speak of not just a single view of the mind, but of an array of interwoven views, each lending support to the others, and each being supported by the others. The strength of the Cartesian picture lies not merely in the strength of the individual theses – ontic, epistemic, ethical – that constitute it, but also, and perhaps even more importantly, in its scope. The Cartesian picture provides us with a sweeping and comprehensive vision of the nature of human beings. And the strength of the individual components of this vision derives, in an important sense, from the strength of the vision as a whole.

This book, in one clear sense, seeks to undermine the Cartesian picture of human beings. However, its primary concern is not with the picture as such, but with the influence it has exerted on subsequent theorizing about the mind. Moreover, the principal focus of the book will be restricted to a sub-set of mental phenomena that have proved particularly central to twentieth-century concerns. These phenomena comprise what are known as cognitive processes: processes such as perceiving, remembering, and reasoning whereby an organism gains and uses information about its environment. The Cartesian picture has bequeathed us a conception of such processes whose essence can be distilled into the following two principles. One is an ontological claim about the nature of cognitive processes, the other an epistemological corollary about how these processes are best studied or understood.

The Ontological Claim: Mental states and processes are located exclusively inside the skin of cognizing organisms.

The Epistemological Claim: It is possible to understand the nature of mental states and processes by focusing exclusively on what is occurring inside the skin of cognizing organisms.

These two assumptions constitute that particular version of the internalist picture of the mind with which this book is concerned. Cognitive processes are *essentially* internal items. They may stand in various relations to events, states, and processes occurring outside the skin of cognizers, and these external items may play an important, even essential, role in the facilitation or satisfaction of the internal processes themselves. Nevertheless, cognitive processes are, in essence, internal items. This internalist picture of cognition, I shall try to show, has greatly distorted our conception of what is required of us by the projects of psychotectonics and psychosemantics. And the principal task of this book is to unseat this conception of cognition, and outline, in broad strokes, the ramifications of this for the two projects.

1.2 PICTURE AS MYTHOLOGY

The task of this book is to unseat not a particular philosophical or psychological theory, but a certain pre-theoretical conception or picture of the mind. This picture is prior to theory in that it is what guides theory construction and thus lends coherence and unity to the experimental practices and procedures judged relevant to the conformation or falsification of particular theories within its domain. The notion of a pre-theoretical picture, then, corresponds largely to what Kuhn (1970) has, famously, labelled a *paradigm*.

In trying to unseat a pre-theoretical picture of a certain domain of inquiry, one's options are usually fairly restricted. One might try to attack the picture on grounds of internal incoherence. Many pictures, perhaps most, however, are not internally incoherent, and, certainly, I

8

would not want to suggest that the internalist picture of the mind suffers from this sort of defect. One might try to attack the picture on grounds of empirical inadequacy. As Wittgenstein, Kuhn, and others have pointed out, however, this sort of approach is unlikely to work. The problem is not so much that a pre-theoretical picture is at a further remove from the evidence, hence at a further remove from the possibility of experimental confirmation or falsification, than the theories predicated upon it (although this certainly might be a problem). The problem, rather, is that the very descriptions of the evidence employed for the purposes of experimental testing are based on, and thus presuppose, this pre-theoretical picture. It is very difficult to see how a pre-theoretical picture of a domain could be unseated solely on the basis of evidence whose very identification and conceptualization as evidence, presupposes the picture itself.

Kuhn, as is well known, sees the unseating of a pre-theoretical picture or paradigm as a matter of piecemeal accretions of problems unsolved within the framework of the picture gradually inducing a *crisis* within the picture itself. Such a crisis is likely to come to a head only when there is a competitor to the picture, an alternative paradigm that can play the same sort of role as the original. As Kuhn points out, however, the new picture, initially, is likely to be partial, restricted, and susceptible to all sorts of apparent refutations. This is because the evidence thought relevant to its truth or falsity is still conceptualized in terms of the old paradigm. It is only when the new paradigm becomes accepted that the relevant evidence can gradually be reconceptualized, and then the scope and coherence of the new paradigm can be progressively enhanced. Arguably, such a situation may today be occurring in cognitive science. Arguably, it may not. And, in any event, I would not want to predicate any argument upon such an essentially contestable claim.

The inspiration for the method I propose to adopt in this book derives from Wittgenstein rather than Kuhn. A pre-theoretical picture in the sense described above has the status of what Wittgenstein calls a *mythology*. To call something a mythology in this sense is not to cast, at least not directly, any aspersions at its truth or validity, although it may mean that, for it, questions of truth and validity do not arise. What Wittgenstein is getting at when he calls something a mythology is that it plays a certain role in organizing experience. More precisely, a mythology has the role of legislating that *this is how things must be*. One of the principal tasks of Wittgenstein's later philosophy is to show how certain pre-theoretical conceptions of the mind and its contents are mythologies in precisely this sense. And one of the principal methods employed by Wittgenstein in this context is to undermine a mythology by showing that we do not, in fact, have to think of things in the way the mythology tells us we do. Other ways of thinking about the mind and its contents, for example, are possible.

A good example of Wittgenstein's idea of mythology is to be found in his attitude toward Freud's concept of the unconscious. In his *Cambridge Lectures 1932–35*, Wittgenstein writes:

> What Freud says about the subconscious sounds like science, but in fact is just a *means of representation*. New regions of the soul have not been discovered, as his writings suggest. The display of elements of a dream, for example, a hat (which may mean practically anything) is a display of similes. As in aesthetics, things are placed side by side so as to exhibit certain features. (1979:40)

Wittgenstein is quite willing to allow that Freud has discovered certain psychological reactions of a hitherto unknown sort, but the apparatus he invokes to explain these is not a theory but simply a *means of representation*. That is, he has simply imposed, as Wittgenstein would say, a system of notation which allows him to redescribe these psychological reactions in these terms. Psychoanalysis, while presenting itself as an experimental discipline, does not, in fact, satisfy any of the conditions necessary to a discipline of this kind.

The comparison with aesthetics is indicative of Wittgenstein's attitude towards the unconscious. Consider the difference between the role of analogy ('simile') in fields like aesthetics and its role in the empirical sciences. An analogy of the first type might consist, for example, in comparing architecture with a language and, then, attempting to identify the vocabulary and grammar of this language. This type of analogy, however, does not generate hypotheses that can be tested in experiments, nor does it produce a theory that can be used to predict events. Thus, whatever understanding is occasioned by the use of such analogies is not the result of imparting new information, nor does it lead to new empirical discoveries. Furthermore, such understanding does not lead to the asking of fresh questions that can be answered by further empirical research. The analogy, rather, functions by making formal connections between architectural features and linguistic ones. The analogy yields new forms of comparison, changing our understanding of buildings and altering the way we look at things. We can then, for example, describe a piece of architecture in a new way: as making sense or not; as being rhetorical or bombastic; as being witty or ambiguous, and so on (Hacker 1987).

According to Wittgenstein, what Freud does is essentially offer us good analogies. But these analogies are of the sort employed by art historians and art critics, not the sort used by physicists. As Hacker (1987:487) puts it, the analogies employed by Freud are not *model-generating* but simply *aspect-seeing*. In presenting the hypothesis of the unconscious as a scientific hypothesis, then, Freud has misunderstood the type of illumination the hypothesis provides; he has misunderstood the status of the type of inquiry in which he is engaged.

In presenting the aspect-seeing analogy of the unconscious as if it were a model-generating scientific hypothesis, Freud has, in effect, introduced a new mythology into the study of the mind. For our purposes, the important feature of a mythology, in Wittgenstein's sense, is the role it plays in delimiting the acceptable forms of description and explanation applicable in the domain in which the mythology is operative. In the *Remarks on Colour*, Wittgenstein cites the Freudian idea of dreaming as disguised wish-fulfilment as an example of what he calls a *primary phenomenon*: 'The primary phenomenon is, e.g., what Freud thought he recognized in simple wish-fulfilment dreams. The primary phenomenon is a preconceived idea that takes possession of us' (no. 230). The primary phenomenon acts as a model or prototype that is to be used in the description of phenomena. And such a prototype, for Wittgenstein, 'characterizes the whole discussion and determines its form' (Wittgenstein 1978:14). In Freud, the model of dreams as disguised wish-fulfilment, a model whose legitimacy depends on the postulation of the unconscious, is presented as a scientific hypothesis, as a discovery about the real nature of dreaming. In fact, however, at least according to Wittgenstein, the model is something that determines the form of description and explanation of all phenomena considered relevant. It, therefore, applies to dreams not because it has been demonstrated by a scientific investigation of different kinds of dreams but because it has been granted a privileged place in discussion. The result is not simply that all evidence can now be described so as to confirm Freud's hypothesis, evidence that might prima facie just as easily disconfirm it. More importantly, with respect to the phenomena of interest, the *grammar* of any possible reason or explanation has been determined, and any competing reason or explanation that falls outside certain parameters cannot be accepted for consideration as the explanation or the reason of that phenomenon.

A mythology, for Wittgenstein, is essentially a pre-theoretical picture which has the function of delimiting, in advance, the form or grammar of all possible descriptions and explanations of the phenomena that fall within its scope. Thus, it has the function of making us see, or understand, the phenomena in a certain way rather than another. It makes us think *this is how things must be*, and initiate our explicit theorizing from this starting-point. Its efficacy in this role depends, to a considerable extent, on us, as in the case of Freud, not recognizing this mythology for what it is; on our mistaking it for something else, a scientific hypothesis, for example.

The central argument of this book is that our thinking about the mind has been guided by a mythology in roughly the sense described above; the myth is that of internalism. The goal of this book is to enable us to see this idea for the mythology that it is, and to thereby undermine the influence it has on our explicit theorizing about the mind and its contents.

1.3 SUBVERTING MYTHOLOGY

The aim of this book, then, is to unseat a certain pre-theoretical picture of the mind. The term *unseat* is not arbitrarily chosen. The aim of the book is *not* to *refute* this picture, but to unseat it. The aim, that is, is not to show that the picture is internally inconsistent, or lacking on empirical grounds. It may be either or both of those things, but I am not claiming that it is, and certainly not basing any argument on assumption that it is. The aim of the book is to unseat the picture in the Wittgensteinian sense of showing that this is not how we have to think about cognition. I shall argue that there is no theoretically respectable reason for separating the mind off from the world in the way the internalist picture tells us we should. There is, in other words, no theoretically respectable reason for thinking of cognitive processes as purely and exclusively internal items. And to say there is no theoretically respectable reason, here, simply means that there is no reason that can be derived from psychological theory as such. The parsing of the realm of cognition into, on the one hand, cognitive processes that are conceived of as purely internal items and, on the other, external causes, stimuli, or cues of these internal items is not something that is demanded by our theorizing about the mind, but an optional extra. It is a pre-theoretical picture we use to interpret our explicit theorizing, not something mandated by that theorizing. It is, in short, a mythology.

The aim of this book is to subvert or unseat this pre-theoretical picture. The strategy is to show that this is not how we have to think about the mind by outlining an alternative picture, and accumulating various sorts of evidence in favour of this picture. Thus, while I shall offer an alternative pre-theoretical picture of the mind, the rationale for offering this alternative is, to a considerable extent, negative: its primary aim is to unseat another picture, and only secondarily does it present a positive basis for new or additional theorizing. The project of psychotectonics, as developed in Part I of this book, firstly, acts as a palliative or antidote to a conception of the mind that has exerted a vice-like grip on our theorizing, and, secondly, indicates, in admittedly broad strokes, how our theorizing might change should we embrace this alternative conception.

Another feature of Wittgenstein's method is relevant to the approach adopted by this book. One of the more surprising features of Wittgenstein's approach is that he frequently seems to be attacking straw men. That is, he often appears to be attacking extremely simplified, indeed oversimplified, versions of the views he challenges. His attack on the Augustinian account of language acquisition in the first part of the *Philosophical Investigations* is a good example of this. Augustine's actual position is a lot more subtle and complex than one would suspect from a cursory reading of Wittgenstein, incorporating, in fact, many features with which Wittgenstein would, presumably, be in agreement. Moreover, more recent versions of the Augustinian account – into which category the *Tractatus Logico-Philosophicus* broadly falls – are certainly much more subtle, containing complexities Wittgenstein does not even begin to address. It may legitimately be wondered why Wittgenstein ignores the complexity of Augustine's view, or developments of the view, and attacks a version of it that is so simplified as to amount almost to parody. The answer is that Wittgenstein is concerned with unseating not any particular *theory* of meaning but, rather, the *picture* that lies behind it. And to get at the picture, one must strip away the details. The picture, for Wittgenstein, is a type of mythology in that it leads us to think that things must be a certain way. And the goal of Wittgenstein's method is simply to show that we do not have to think of things like this. Things do not, in fact, have to be this way at all. One unseats the picture by loosening its grip on us. And one way of doing this is to describe, in broad outline, another way of looking at things. And, for this task, the specific details of the various theoretical developments of the picture are irrelevant.

This procedure is also, to a considerable extent, adopted in this book. This is particularly true of Part I. The task of this part is to unseat the internalist picture of the mind described above. The strategy is to loosen the grip this picture has on us. And the method is to outline and defend an alternative way of looking at mental processes. Adopting this strategy leads me to describe various theoretical developments of the internalist picture in ways that are oversimplified. Nowhere, for example, is this more true than in the discussion of David Marr's theory of vision in chapter 5. Marr's theory is, in fact, a lot more subtle, complex, and indeed plausible, than would be apparent from a cursory reading of chapter 5. Indeed, Marr incorporates many ideas that are compatible with, even congenial to, the alternative environmentalist picture outlined in this part of the book (I am here thinking particularly of the theoretical role Marr gives to the notion of *assumptions* about the environment). There is a clear sense, I think, in which Marr's account is not straightforwardly in opposition to the Gibsonian account outlined in that chapter. A more accurate way of thinking about the relation between the two theories is, perhaps, to regard them as taking up positions on a spectrum. The poles of the spectrum are constituted by the internalist picture described above, and the alternative environmentalist picture outlined in the course of Part I. The difference between Marr's theory and that of Gibson, then, would be explained in terms of their relative positions on the spectrum. Marr, I think it is safe to say, is closer to the internalist end of the spectrum than Gibson. However, the precise position occupied by Marr, and indeed by Gibson, on this spectrum, is a question for the sort of detailed textual interpretation that is beyond the scope of this book. If you think, for example, that Marr ought to be located considerably more towards the environmentalist end of the spectrum than I have given him credit for, that is fine with me. My concern with Marr is restricted solely to his (as I see it) role as representative of the internalist position with respect to visual perception. My concern throughout Part I of the book, then, is not with the details of the specific theoretical developments of the internalist picture; it is with the picture itself. And this concern will, at certain points, lead me to overlook many of the details of its theoretical articulation, details which, in other contexts, and for other purposes, would be extremely important.

The central purpose of this book, then, is to unseat a certain pre-theoretical picture of the mind by loosening the grip it has on our thinking about the mind and mental processes. It attempts to do this by showing not that this picture is false or incoherent, but by showing that it is not necessary for our thinking about the mind; that we do not have to think about the mind and its contents in the way the picture requires. Failure to understand the strategy will almost certainly result in failure to understand the arguments. For example, in chapters 7 and 8 there is an extended discussion of connectionist approaches to the modelling of cognition in relation to the traditional symbolic approaches. This discussion is presented as one particular case in which the internalist picture has exerted a rather baleful influence on our theorizing. And, correspondingly, liberation from this picture can, I think, help us to understand more fully the merits of connectionism. However, nowhere in this discussion will one find the conclusion: connectionism is right and the symbolic approach is wrong. My concern in these chapters is not with connectionism or the symbolic approach as such, but with the pre-theoretical pictures that these programmes articulate. And, once again, the same tendency to oversimplification conspicuous in the discussion of Marr will also be evident. The purpose of the book is not to show that the internalist picture is false or incoherent. Therefore, neither is it to show that the theoretical articulations of this picture – as, I will argue, are the symbolic approach and associated language of thought hypothesis – are false or incoherent. The purpose, rather, is to loosen the grip that the dominant internalist picture has on us by showing that we do not have to think of things in this way. And this, I shall try to show, can shed new light on the dispute between connectionist and symbolic approaches. The aim of chapters 7 and 8, then, is not to show that the symbolic approach to understanding cognition, and the associated language of thought hypothesis, are false. The aim is to undermine them by removing, at least in part, their motivation.

To some extent already, the grip of the internalist picture is relaxing. In an excellent study, Andy Clark (1997) has shown how the internalist picture is, at best, dubiously compatible with recent development in artificial intelligence, in particular, development in the field of robotics and artificial life. I accept Clark's arguments, and the arguments to be developed in the following pages are, in an important sense, of a piece with his. However, there are differences of strategy. Firstly, while Clark focuses primarily on very recent work in the rather new fields of robotics and artificial intelligence, I shall focus primarily on older work in more traditional areas of psychology. This difference in strategy stems largely from my goal of unseating a certain picture of the mind, rather than of demonstrating its inadequacy. The goal of this book is as much persuasion as anything else; the goal is to persuade us that we do not have to think about the mind in this way, that other ways of looking at the mind are possible, indeed viable. And, a useful way of doing this is by showing that this is something we have always really known anyway, or, at least, something that is implicit in a quite familiar body of knowledge.

Paul Feyerabend (1975) has argued, plausibly, that this was the sort of strategy adopted by Galileo in his attempt to develop an alternative to Aristotelian cosmology. One of the key concepts required for this development was that of relative motion. The postulation of a moving earth, for example, was apparently quite clearly incompatible with certain uncontroversial facts of experience; for example, that rocks dropped off the top of towers hit the ground at the bottom of the tower, and not some distance away as might be expected if the earth were really moving. To undermine these apparently watertight experiential refutations, Galileo was obliged to develop the concept of relative motion. What is interesting is that his strategy here was to try and show that the concept of relative motion – a concept quite alien to Aristotelian cosmology – was something with which we were all quite familiar anyway. Feyerabend compares this to Plato's idea of *anamnesis*: the explicit remembering of something we have always implicitly known. This, at least to some extent, is the strategy that will be adopted in Part I of this book. The strategy, therefore, is to focus on work in psychology that is not particularly recent and is more or less traditional (with the possible exception of Gibson). And in this work,

16

it will be argued, we find no theoretically respectable reason for embracing internalist mythology.

In Part II, the focus switches from psychotectonics to psychosemantics. This is for two reasons. Firstly, the alternative picture of the mind developed in Part I relies, as we will see, quite heavily on the notion of mental representation. Thus, the completeness of the alternative anti-internalist, or as I shall call it, *environmentalist*, picture of cognitive processes requires an account of mental representation. If we can assume that the extent to which the environmentalist picture can be seen as a legitimate alternative to the internalist one depends in part on its completeness, then the success of the project of Part I requires the development of an account of mental representation. This is the project of Part II.

Just as importantly, however, it will be argued in Part II that recent discussions of the notion 'mental representation' have suffered considerably from a tacit adherence to the internalist mythology that Part I tries to undermine. Thus, it will be argued, replacing the internalist picture of cognition with the environmentalist account developed in Part I allows us to solve, or dissolve, some of the most troubling objections to naturalistic accounts of representation. Thus, the arguments of Part II serve a dual function. On the one hand, they complete the arguments begun in Part I. On the other hand, they give one important example of why those arguments were necessary.

PART I

Psychotectonics

2

Introduction to Part I:
'Don't work hard, work smart'

William of Occam is, of course, famous for his *razor*: a methodological injunction against multiplying entities beyond necessity. We might imagine, however, that if the great medieval logician had, perhaps, been of a less industrious nature, he might have ended up with another principle: 'Don't multiply *effort* beyond necessity.' And this prohibition has a well-known modern formulation: 'Don't work hard, work smart!' This slogan, I shall argue, is not, at least not in essence, a psychological crutch for those of shiftless character or slothful intent (although it certainly can be this too). Rather, the slogan, in fact, captures a fundamental principle of the natural world; one which has profound implications for the development of all living things. And one way of looking at this book is as an attempt to work out (some of) the consequences of this principle.

To be a little more precise, the following principle seems incontrovertible. Let us suppose you are faced with a given task that you are required to accomplish. And suppose the successful completion of this task requires that a certain amount of work be invested in it. Now, if you can get someone – or something – else to do part of this work for you, you will have correspondingly less to do yourself. At least, you will have less to do yourself as long as the work *you* do in getting this someone or something else to do the work for you is less than the work *they* then do for you. This principle is, of course, so obvious as scarcely to be deniable. Nevertheless, its ramifications are enormous. And one central concern of this book is the consequences the principle has for the development of human cognitive processes. And, I shall argue, there are consequences aplenty.

One of the principal claims of this book is that the injunction against multiplying effort beyond necessity, when its scope and power are properly understood, suggests a very radical view of the nature of cognitive processes. This view I label *environmentalism*, where this is understood as the conjunction of two claims, one ontological, the other an epistemological corollary.

The Ontological Claim: Cognitive processes are not located exclusively inside the skin of cognizing organisms.

The Epistemological Claim: It is not possible to understand the nature of cognitive processes by focusing exclusively on what is occurring inside the skin of cognizing organisms.

Environmentalism, understood simply as the conjunction of these two claims, can cover a wide variety of views. The principal work of chapter 3 is to clarify the nature of environmentalism by distinguishing it from other views with which it might be confused. Three such views will be discussed. The first is the view known as *externalism*, the view originally developed by, and largely associated with, Hilary Putnam and Tyler Burge (Putnam 1975; Burge 1979, 1982, 1986). This view has gained many adherents in recent years, and, in my view, is fundamentally correct. Certainly nothing that will be said in this book contradicts the central tenets of externalism; nevertheless, the position defended in the following pages is importantly distinct from it. In particular, the problem with externalism, as I see it, is not that it is incorrect, but that it just does not go far enough. One task of this book then, is to present a more radical alternative. The second view with which the one of this book is to be contrasted is *behaviourism*. The second part of chapter 3 is concerned with distinguishing the position defended in this book from behaviourism, at least as this is commonly understood. And, while there is nothing in this book which denies the reality of internal cognitive processes, there is, none the less, a clear sense in which the environmentalist position developed here is more radical than even behaviourism. The third position discussed is perhaps the closest to that defended in this book. This is the position defended by Ruth Millikan. While Millikan is, I think, the most radical and also the most consistent externalist around, I shall try to show that even Millikan's position may be infected with a residual internalism, and it is precisely at the point of infection that the arguments of this book have application.

In essence, the view to be defended in the following chapters claims that cognitive processes are not located exclusively inside the skin of cognizing organisms because such processes are, in part, made up of physical or bodily *manipulation* of structures in the environments of such organisms. The notion of manipulation, here, should be understood very broadly and, in particular, should not be restricted to its usual manual sense. When I make use of a pen and paper in working out the solution to a tricky long-division problem, this is one form of manipulation of an external structure. I am using an external or environmental structure, in this case an externally represented mathematical one. However, when, by moving my head, I transform the structure of the light around me – what Gibson (1966, 1979) refers to as the *optic array* – and thus make available to myself information contained in the light that would otherwise have remained hidden (specifically, *invariant* information), that also, as the term will be used in this book, is a form of manipulation. The external structure, in this case, is an ambient optic array, and I manipulate it in virtue of moving in it. In other words, the word *manipulation*, as used in this book does not strictly remain true to its derivation; it is not conceived as a purely manual form of interaction with the environment.

Furthermore, as used in this book, manipulation need *not* be understood as a necessarily intrusive activity, that is, as an activity that seeks to change the environment, or that inevitably results in such change. When a sponge exploits ambient water currents to assist the flow of water through it, thus facilitating its feeding activities, that also will be understood as a form of manipulation. The concept of manipulation, then, is understood broadly as any form of bodily interaction with the environment – manual or not, intrusive or otherwise – which makes use of the environment in order to accomplish a given task. And the principal thesis of Part I of this book is that cognitive processes are, in part, made up of the manipulation, in this extended sense, of environmental structures. And, for precisely this reason, cognitive processes are not located exclusively inside the skin of cognizing organisms and cannot, therefore, be understood by focusing exclusively on what is occurring inside the skin of such organisms.

So, the argument structure of Part I of the book – and Part I is essentially one long argument – runs something like this. Environmentalism, understood as the conjunction of the ontological and epistemological claims, is to be defended by way of the claim that cognitive processes are, in part, made up of manipulation of relevant structures in the cognizer's environment. Let us refer to this latter claim as the *manipulation thesis*. Then:

ENVIRONMENTALISM defended by appeal to MANIPULATION THESIS

The next question, quite obviously, is how the manipulation thesis is to be defended. This takes us back to the injunction, mentioned earlier, against multiplying effort beyond necessity. As suggested earlier, this injunction is a rough expression of a fundamental biological truth – incorporated, in different ways, into concepts as diverse as optimal foraging strategy, the red queen hypothesis, arms races, fitness, and so on. The basic idea is as follows.

An organism evolves because its environment (which can here include predators and species competing for the same niche) places it under a certain selection pressure. That is, the environment places certain demands on the organism, and meeting these demands is either a necessary condition of the survival of organisms of that lineage or, at very least, increases the probability of the lineage's survival. Let us say, then, that the environment presents the organism with various *tasks*, and successful accomplishment of such tasks increases the fitness of organisms of that lineage. Accomplishing a task requires an organism to adopt a particular *strategy*. And adopting a given strategy requires the investment of a certain quantity of the organism's genetic/energetic resources. The quantity of resources required to be invested in the strategy, I shall refer to as the *evolutionary cost* of the strategy. And, the crucial points here are, firstly, some strategies can be adopted at less evolutionary cost than others and, secondly, strategies of accomplishing an evolutionarily specified task which involve manipulating environmental structures can, typically, be purchased at less cost than those which refrain from such manipulation.

Therefore, I shall argue, all things being equal, an organism that has adopted a manipulative strategy in order to accomplish a given task is, with respect to that task, more fit than an organism that has adopted a non-manipulative one, even if both organisms are equally successful, in virtue of their adopted strategies, in the negotiation of the task in question. And this provides us with one reason for believing the *manipulation thesis* advanced above. All that is needed to apply the above considerations to cognitive processes is the assumption that

24

the mechanisms which underwrite such processes have evolved in order to allow the organism to accomplish evolutionarily determined tasks. And if this is so, and if we have adopted the most efficient strategies for accomplishing these tasks, then the cognitive mechanisms we have evolved should be designed to function in conjunction with environmental structures. Then, the cognitive processes realized by these mechanisms would have to be understood as straddling both internal processes and those external processes whereby the organism interacts with these environmental structures. This, at least, is the central argument of chapter 4.

The argument of chapter 4, if correct, provides one reason for thinking that cognitive processes are essentially hybrid in character, made up of both internal processes and bodily manipulation of external structures. However, while powerful, these considerations can scarcely be regarded as conclusive. They would be conclusive only if it could be assumed that the development of our cognitive capacities followed the most efficient evolutionary path. And without some essentially adaptationist assumptions, assumptions which will be granted by many but by no means all, it is not clear how to demonstrate this. Nevertheless, what the arguments of chapter 4, if correct, do show is that *if* development of our cognitive capacities has followed the most efficient evolutionary path *then* we should expect our cognitive processes to be an essentially hybrid combination of internal and external processes. The remaining chapters of Part I argue that this is, in fact, the case. And they do this by way of a detailed examination of four pretty central cases of cognitive processes, namely those involved in visual perception (chapter 5), memory (chapter 6), thought (chapter 7), and language use (chapter 8). In each chapter, it is argued that the relevant cognitive process is best understood as a combination of internal processes and bodily manipulation of environmental structures. And the arguments developed in each of these chapters are completely independent of the general biological arguments developed in chapter 4. One is, thus, at liberty to accept the arguments of the later chapters while rejecting those of chapter 4, and vice versa. However, much like a jigsaw, the arguments do, I think, acquire more power and coherence when combined. And this is the way they are presented in the following chapters. While the arguments are logically independent of each other, then, practically they have a mutually reinforcing role. Viewed in this way, Part I becomes, in essence, one long argument; an argument whose basic structure looks something like this:

ENVIRONMENTALISM defended by appeal to MANIPULATION THESIS

MANIPULATION THESIS supported by:

I. GENERAL BIOLOGICAL ARGUMENTS
(chapter 4)

II. EXAMINATION OF SPECIFIC COGNITIVE PROCESSES
PERCEPTION (chapter 5)
MEMORY (chapter 6)
THOUGHT (chapter 7)
LANGUAGE USE (chapter 8)

Chapter 5 argues that visual perception is constituted, in part, by the manipulation, by the perceiving organism, of the structure of light around it. This structure of light – the *optic array* – is a *locus* of information for any organism capable of appropriating it. By way of certain types of action, the organism is able to effect transformations in the optic array, and by doing so identify and appropriate information that would otherwise have remained hidden. Manipulation of the optic array, then, is, in effect, a form of information processing; a processing of information relevant to the task of visual perception. And, therefore, in the case of such perception, at least some of the information processing involved occurs by way of an organism's manipulation of a structure external to it. What is essential in the above account are the following:

(i) The presence of a structure, external to the organism, which is a *locus* of information.
(ii) The ability of the organism to identify and appropriate this information through manipulation of the structure.

This pattern is found to be repeated in the discussions, in later chapters, of other types of cognitive process. This manipulation of external structures, it will be argued, can legitimately be seen as a form of information processing. It is, moreover, a form at least as important in the accomplishing of visual perception tasks as whatever information processing is occurring inside the organism.

Chapter 6 discusses the process of remembering. In common with the previous chapter, it is argued that there are certain structures in the environment of rememberers and these structures carry information relevant to the solution of the memory task in question. The rememberer is able to identify and appropriate information necessary for the successful accomplishment of a memory task by manipulating these structures. And, therefore, not all the information processing relevant to remembering need occur inside the skin of remembering organisms. Some of the relevant information processing can be constituted by bodily manipulation, on the part of the remembering organism, of relevant environmental structures. This, at least, is the central contention of chapter 6.

In chapter 7, the focus switches from memory to thought; to thinking in a fairly broad sense. Several claims will be defended. Firstly, it is argued that *reasoning* – in particular, of the sequential logical and mathematical type – is, in many cases, partly constituted by manipulation of external information-bearing structures. Logical and mathematical reasoning are, therefore, hybrid processes, having both an internal and external character, in the same sort of way that, if earlier chapters are correct, visual perception and memory are hybrid processes.

The second theme of chapter 7 concerns the nature of thought, understood, as is common in philosophical contexts, as made up of a variety of *propositional attitudes*. It is a fairly commonplace idea that thought, in this sense, has several constitutive features; in particular, generativity, systematicity, and inferential coherence. Generativity refers to the capacity of the thinker to think any randomly selected number of grammatically well-formed thoughts, selected from an infinite set of such thoughts. Systematicity refers to the capacity of the thinker to think any thought that is systematically (or grammatically) related to a thought she does in fact entertain. Inferential coherence refers to the capacity of the thinker to draw inferences based on the structure of the thought she entertains. These features have often been taken to show that thoughts must have syntactic or grammatical structure; that it must be essentially linguistic in nature. This, in part, is what motivates the *language of thought hypothesis* (Fodor 1975). However, the environmentalist position defended in this book suggests a different approach. Roughly, the idea is this. Generativity, systematicity, and inferential coherence are features of the external linguistic milieu; a milieu in which all generative, systematic, and inferentially coherent thinkers operate. For a thinker's thoughts to exhibit these features, what is required is not that she should have within her internally instantiated linguistic structures, and internally instantiated rules of linguistic composition, but that she should have the ability to manipulate and exploit the surrounding linguistic milieu in ways that respect its grammatical rules, and, hence, respect its generativity, systematicity, and inferential coherence. And what has to be internally instantiated in the thinker which enables her to do this need not be essentially linguistic in nature.

This brings us to the third theme of chapter 7. The sort of internal system which allows the organism to manipulate and exploit the linguistic environment in appropriate ways (i.e., in generative, systematic, and inferentially coherent ways) may best be captured by the *connectionist* approach to modelling cognition. Connectionist networks provide what is probably the best way of modelling the sort of procedural knowledge – or knowing *how* – that allows the organism to manipulate and exploit its linguistic milieu in relevant ways. The idea that the environmentalist view of cognitive processes defended here is best supplemented by a connectionist account of the internal component of those processes is an idea that will be further developed in chapter 8.

The eighth, and final, chapter of Part I discusses how the environmentalist approach can be applied to the processes involved in language acquisition. Language acquisition is often regarded as something of a test case for connectionism since the sort of processes it seems to require are of precisely the sort that are most difficult to model by connectionist means. In particular the sort of recursive rules necessary to account for the grammatical structure of language have proved extremely difficult to account for by way of standard neural networks. The reasons for this are well known and derive, ultimately, from Chomsky's claim that no finite state or statistical inference engine is capable of modelling or accounting for (the right sort of) grammatical rules (Chomsky 1957, 1968). Chapter 8, however, argues that connectionist systems are capable of modelling grammaticality if, and probably only if, we take into account the ways in which such systems can interact with relevant environmental structures. The point of departure, here, is provided by some recent work of Elman (1991a, 1991b, 1991c), who argues that what is crucial for the connectionist modelling of grammatical rules is that the system should be able to adopt a *hierarchical* approach to such modelling. That is, the system must be able to model the simplest rules first, and then use the simplest rules to build up models of progressively more complex rules. If Elman is correct, a connectionist system that is able to do this is capable of modelling at least certain sorts of grammatical rules. It will be argued in chapter 8 that interaction with certain relevant environmental structures will naturally lead a connectionist network to adopt this sort of hierarchical problem-solving approach. Thus, through appropriate interaction with environmental structures, a connectionist net of the Elman sort might naturally acquire the capacity to model grammatical rules. Perhaps the central conclusion of chapter 8, then, is that, at least in the case of the cognitive processes involved in language acquisition, the environmentalist is the connectionist's best friend.

There are essentially two distinct conclusions defended by Part I, one metaphysical, the other methodological, corresponding to the ontological and epistemological claims that constitute the definition of environmentalism.

The metaphysical claim is that not all cognitive processes occur inside the head or skin of cognizing organisms. Therefore, if we assume that the mind of a cognizing organism such as a human being is made up, at least in part, of cognitive processes, the central metaphysical assertion of this book is that the mind is not, exclusively, inside the head. Minds are not purely internal things; they are, in part, *worldly* in character. That is, minds are hybrid entities, made up in part of what is going on inside the skin of creatures who have them, but also made up in part of what is going on in the environment of those creatures. And this claim locates the book within a tradition of dissent to orthodox Cartesian internalism; a tradition made up of thinkers as diverse as Heidegger, Wittgenstein, Ryle, Putnam, and Gibson, among others.

The other central conclusion of Part I is a methodological one. To use the neologism coined by Colin McGinn, the central methodological claim of this book concerns the project of *psychotectonics*. As mentioned in the opening chapter, psychotectonics is the study of how to build minds. And, at an extremely abstract level, building minds is precisely what this book is about. If the environmentalist position defended in the following pages is correct, then the project of building a cognizing mind requires one to focus not just on what you put into the cognizer's head, but also, and with equal importance, on what you put into the cognizer's environment, and on the ways in which the cognizer is able to interact with this environment. Very roughly, to build a mind it is not sufficient that one build a *computer*, one must build a *robot*. The environment, by way of its contained structures, is a *locus* or store of information for the cognizing organism. In exploring its environment, and in manipulating its contained structures, the organism processes this information. But, in performing any given cognitive task, the more information the organism can process *externally*, through manipulation of the environment, the less information it has to process internally. The more external information processing one is able to effect, the less internal information processing one is required to perform. In this way, one can substantially reduce the demand on the internal processing that a system must perform by giving it an ability to manipulate relevant structures in its environment and, by doing so, process the information contained in them.

3

Environmentalism and what it is not

3.1 INTERNALISM, EXTERNALISM, AND ENVIRONMENTALISM

The concept of *externalism* has figured prominently in recent philosophical reflections on the nature of the mind (Putnam 1975; Burge 1979, 1982, 1986; Woodfield 1982; Pettit & McDowell 1986; McGinn 1989). The aim of this book is to defend a view which is, in effect, a cousin of externalism, although a quite distant and very radical cousin. This view I shall call *environmentalism*.

The concept of externalism, as employed by philosophers, is, in fact, broad enough to subsume a variety of views, and to be motivated by a variety of considerations. These views can be more or less radical in both scope and nature, and the considerations that motivate them correspondingly diverse. And it is extremely difficult to develop a blanket formulation of the concept of externalism that is adequate to capture all these forms and reflect all these motivations. In contrast, the environmentalist view of the mind can be understood quite easily as a conjunction of two claims, one ontological, the other epistemological:

The Ontological Claim: Cognitive processes are not located exclusively inside the skins of cognizing organisms.

The Epistemological Claim: It is not possible to understand the nature of cognitive processes by focusing exclusively on what is occurring inside the skins of cognizing organisms.

The epistemological claim is, of course, a corollary of the ontological one. The ontological claim, however, is not entailed by the epistemological one. In fact, many philosophers who describe themselves as externalists would balk at the ontological claim. Their externalism is based not on the external *location* of mental states but on what is

31

referred to as their external *individuation* (Macdonald 1990). It can be argued that the external individuation of mental states does not entail their external location. Therefore, any form of externalism that is predicated on the notion of external individuation is not a form of externalism that involves, or necessarily involves, the ontological claim. So, it is possible, at least in principle, to be some form of externalist while denying the ontological claim. The distinction between external individuation and external location will be discussed in a lot more detail shortly. For now, let me make it clear that the environmentalist position to be defended in this book claims that cognitive processes are not just externally individuated, they are also, and perhaps much more importantly, externally located. The ontological claim is an essential part of the position to be developed in this book.

Given the definition of environmentalism in terms of the ontological and epistemological claims listed above, it is possible to understand what I shall call *internalism* as constituted by the denial of the above claims. That is, internalism, as I shall use the term, is the view that cognitive processes *are* located exclusively inside the skins of cognizing organisms and that, therefore, it *is* possible to understand the nature of cognitive processes by focusing exclusively on what is occurring inside the skins of cognizing organisms.

This book, then, seeks to defend both the epistemological and the ontological claims listed above. And, while the conjunction of these claims delineates a concept broad enough to subsume a variety of views, the specific form of environmentalism to be developed and defended in the following pages differs markedly from most views commonly identified as externalist. And the considerations that motivate the environmentalist position to be defended here also differ significantly from those which motivate these other views. So, in order to make clearer the precise nature of the view to be developed in this book, I propose to spend most of this chapter comparing it with other views that either embrace, or have been viewed as embracing, one or both of the ontological and epistemological claims.

3.2 PHILOSOPHICAL EXTERNALISM

In philosophical circles, at least, the concept of externalism is associated largely with the work of Hilary Putnam (1975) and Tyler Burge

(1979, 1982, 1986), and also with certain views on the nature of indexicals (Perry 1977, 1979; Kaplan 1980).

Putnam's twin earth case

We are to imagine a near duplicate of our planet earth; call it *twin earth*. Except for certain features about to be noted, twin earth duplicates earth in every detail. Many inhabitants of earth have duplicate counterparts on twin earth, and these counterparts are type-identical with their corresponding earthlings in point of neurophysiological constitution, and in terms of functional, behavioural, and experiential histories, where all of these are specified *solipsistically*, that is, identified in a way that presupposes the existence of no entities external to the subjects of those states. The key difference between the two planets is that the liquid on twin earth that runs in rivers and taps, although identical, with respect to observational properties, with the liquid that we, on earth, refer to with the term 'water', and although referred to by twin earthlings with the linguistic form 'water', is not, in fact, water. It is not the substance whose chemical structure consists of two parts of hydrogen to one part of oxygen. Rather, the liquid on twin earth has a radically different chemical structure – XYZ. Thus, despite being identical with respect to the observational properties they present to the observer, water, and what goes by that name on twin earth – call it the substance *retaw* – are distinct substances.

Suppose Herbert$_1$ is an English speaker of earth, and Herbert$_2$ is his counterpart on twin earth. Neither knows the structure of the substance that he calls 'water'. We can assume that the two Herberts are identical in point of (solipsistically specified) physical constitution, functional profile, behavioural dispositions, and experiential history. As Putnam points out, the form of words 'water is wet' means something different in the mouth of Herbert$_1$ than it does in the mouth of Herbert$_2$. The former's utterances of 'water' refer to water. The latter's utterances of the same phonetic form refer to retaw. Hence, the utterances differ in meaning because they differ in reference. And the form of words 'water is wet' has a different meaning on the two planets because its truth-conditions vary from planet to planet. This indicates that the physical and, solipsistically specified, functional, phenomenological, and behavioural properties of a speaker do not suffice to determine speaker meaning.

Furthermore, as Putnam does not in fact point out, the differences in meaning affect oblique occurrences in *that*-clauses which specify the contents of mental states. Herbert₁ believes that water is wet whereas Herbert₂ believes that retaw is wet. The contents of Herbert₁'s and Herbert₂'s beliefs differ, while every feature of their solipsistically described physical, functional, and experiential histories remains the same. The differences between the contents of their beliefs, and hence between their beliefs, seem to be a product of differences in their physical environments.

Burge's counterfactual case

We are to imagine a person, call her Margaret, who has a number of psychological states which are commonly attributed with content clauses containing the term 'arthritis' in oblique occurrence. For example, she believes that she has had arthritis for years, that arthritis can be very painful, that it is better to have arthritis than lung cancer, etc. In addition to these beliefs, she also believes that she has developed arthritis in her thigh. But arthritis, in fact, is an ailment which affects only the joints. Therefore, this latter belief is false. What is important is that, despite her misapprehension, we still regard Margaret's belief as a belief about arthritis. It is simply a false belief about arthritis. The principle underlying our intuition in this case seems to be the following: if other people in her language community can bear attitude A towards the proposition X is F, then it seems we are committed to interpreting Margaret's belief in this way. That is, given the fact that Margaret would allow herself to be corrected by members of her language community, then, given plausible constraints on interpretation, not only *can* we interpret Margaret's belief this way, it seems we *must* do so.

We now imagine Margaret in a counterfactual situation. Counterfactual Margaret is type-identical with actual Margaret in point of physical constitution, functional profile, behavioural dispositions, and experiential history (where all of these are solipsistically specified). The counterfactuality in the situation touches only on Margaret's linguistic environment. In the counterfactual situation, the phonetic or syntactic form 'arthritis' – as used by physicians, lexicographers, and competent laymen – applies not only to an affliction of the joints but also to various other rheumatoid ailments. That is, the standard counterfactual use of the term encompasses Margaret's actual misuse. In this case, our intuition tells us that Margaret, in the counterfactual situation, does not have arthritis attitudes. That is, counterfactual Margaret lacks the attitudes that we, in the actual world, attribute with content clauses containing the term 'arthritis' in oblique occurrence. For Margaret in the counterfactual situation, unlike Margaret in the actual situation, does not have the concept of arthritis; she has the concept of counterfactual arthritis (= arthritis + rheumatism, as we might say).

The difference in the content of the attitudes involved stems from differences in linguistic usage. The differences are again the result of differences in the reference of the terms used in the expression of the content, but in this case the difference in reference stems from a difference in linguistic use, not from a difference in the physical environment. What is also interesting here is the range of application of Burge's argument. Putnam's argument (arguably) turned on the natural kind status of water. But Burge's argument has no such restriction. Indeed, Burge claims that relevantly similar arguments can be constructed for 'any notion that applies to public types of objects, properties or events that are typically known by empirical means' (1986:6).

Indexicals

In addition to classical indexical beliefs, the category of relevant mental states here includes demonstrative thoughts and *de re* thoughts about individuals. On certain treatments of indexicality it is recognized that indexical beliefs can be ascribed by content sentences which have, in Kaplan's terminology, the same *character* but which differ in referential truth-conditions (Kaplan 1980). For example, the sentence 'today is fine', while expressing the same character on each occasion of use, differs in point of referential truth-conditions on each day on which it is used. Similarly, the utterance 'I am tired' possesses the same character on each occasion of use but differs in referential truth-conditions depending on the utterer and time of utterance. Thus, suppose that I and my twin earth *doppelgänger* both have a belief specified by the content sentence 'I am tired.' Again, even if we assume identity of non-intentionally specified physical, functional, behavioural, and experiential properties, then my twin and I

35

still do not share the same belief. The truth-conditions of my belief are that I am tired, the truth-conditions of his belief are that he is tired. Thus, our beliefs share the same character, but the contents of our beliefs, and hence our beliefs, differ.

The view of mental states developed by Putnam and Burge, and suggested by such work on indexicals as that of Kaplan and Perry, I shall call *philosophical externalism*. Philosophical externalism is very different from the environmentalist position to be developed and defended in this book. There is a clear sense, I think, in which philosophical externalism is a much weaker view than the one developed in this book. Indeed, it is not clear that the arguments described above establish either the ontological claim or even the epistemological claim; and these claims are constitutive of the environmentalist position. In the interests, then, of elucidating the concept of environmentalism, it will be useful to examine why philosophical externalism is compatible with the denial of the ontological and epistemological claims.

3.3 PHILOSOPHICAL EXTERNALISM AND THE EPISTEMOLOGICAL CLAIM

The first point to note about the arguments for philosophical externalism is that they centre around the *content* of mental states. That is, if they apply to a given class of mental states then this is in virtue of the fact that those mental states possess semantic content. In fact, in order for the arguments to go through as presented, one must suppose not only that mental states possess semantic content but that they possess such content *essentially*. That is, one must suppose that this semantic content enters into the identity conditions of mental states. For, if not, then all the above arguments would show is that certain of the inessential features of mental states are not determined exclusively by what occurs inside the skin of any given individual but depend on the nature of the physical and/or linguistic environment of that individual. But that is very different from showing that mental states themselves are, in this sense, environmentally dependent. The inference to this latter claim will go through only if we assume that the content of mental states is essential to them. The upshot is, of course, that the arguments for philosophical externalism will work only for *propositional attitudes*. And then only if we assume that propositional attitudes possess their contents essentially. This provides the first point of contrast between the arguments for philosophical externalism and the arguments to be developed in this book. The arguments developed in the following pages do not centre around the content of mental states. Hence they are not restricted in scope to propositional attitudes.

It is the issue of content, in fact, that provides the pivotal distinction between the arguments for philosophical externalism and the arguments for environmentalism developed in this book. A distinction which will help clarify matters here is a distinction between two fundamentally different types of project, two crucially distinct approaches to understanding the mind. The distinction is between what I shall call *psychotectonics* and *psychosemantics*.

> *Psychotectonics*: the project of working out how to build a system capable of cognition.

Psychotectonics is an engineering project. It is an investigation into how psychological systems are constructed, by what design principles cognitive capacities are forged. Since a system that is capable of cognition is a system to which intentional or semantic content can be attributed (or at least we can assume this is so for the sake of argument), psychotectonics is simultaneously the project of working out how to build a system that can sustain the attribution to it of semantic content. This project, however, should be clearly distinguished from the project of psychosemantics:

> *Psychosemantics*: the project of working out the conditions under which the attribution of semantic content to a system is warranted.

In engaging in psychosemantics one would, presumably, have to pay attention to how the system in question is constructed, what design principles are followed, etc. This is because whether the attribution of content to the system is warranted depends, in part, on such matters. Nevertheless, an investigation into the principles involved in building a system capable of sustaining the attribution to it of semantic content is not the same as an investigation into the conditions under which the attribution of semantic content to that system is warranted. The former is an engineering project, concerned with how the edifice of the mind is erected from the ground up, so to speak. The latter is, for want of a better word, an interpretive project, concerned with the conditions under which it is legitimate to employ a particular sort of interpretation of the behaviour of a system.

This distinction is important because the arguments for philosophical externalism can show only that the project of *psychosemantics* must be environment-involving. The arguments show that we cannot know whether a given attribution of semantic content to a system is warranted unless we focus, at least in part, on the environment of that system, specifically, on the objects, properties, events, and so on, to which that system is causally or environmentally related. Even if this is true, however, given the distinction between psychosemantics and psychotectonics, it implies nothing whatsoever about the nature of the internal mechanisms which, in part, underwrite the attribution of content to cognizing systems. If externalism about content is true, and if (certain sorts of) mental states have their contents essentially, it follows that (philosophical) externalism about mental states is true also. However, this is perfectly compatible with the claim that an organism to which the attribution of content is warranted also possesses purely internal states and mechanisms that, in part, underwrite this content attribution. The internal states and mechanisms would then form the internal structural basis of mental states. And the arguments for philosophical externalism in no way impugn the possibility of mental states possessing this sort of internal structural basis. Thus, a psychotectonic investigation of these structural bases can afford to focus purely on what is internal to the cognizing system. And this is true even if the project of psychosemantics is essentially environment involving.

On certain interpretations of philosophical externalism, this point is especially clear. One interpretation of the arguments for philosophical externalism lies in what is known as the *dual component theory* of mental properties (Field 1978; Loar 1981; McGinn 1982; Block 1986; Rowlands 1991a). An extended quotation from McGinn captures this theory quite nicely:

> our intuitive conception of belief-content combines two separable components, answering to two distinct interests we have in ascriptions of belief. One component consists in a mode of representation of things in the world; the other concerns itself with properly semantic relations between such representations and the things represented. I want to suggest that the former component is constitutive of the causal–explan-

atory role of belief, while the latter is bound up in our taking beliefs as bearers of truth. We view beliefs *both* as states of the head explanatory of behaviour, and as items possessed of referential truth-conditions.

(McGinn 1982:210)

When I believe that water is wet, and my twin has a belief ascribable with a sentence of the same syntactic or phonetic form, we have distinct beliefs. Nevertheless, we will still be functionally identical and disposed to the same behaviour (solipsistically specified). This has suggested to many that we ought to regard beliefs, and other propositional mental states, as being made up of separable components. One component, often called the *internal* component, consists in the properties of a mental state in virtue of which it occupies a certain causal or functional role. This component is identical with what many have called the mental state *narrowly individuated* or the *narrow mental state*. The other component, the *external* component, consists in the properties possessed by a mental state in virtue of which it represents a portion of the world. This component is, according to the dual component theory, irrelevant to that state's causal or functional role. The combination of internal and external components makes up the state *widely individuated* or the *wide mental state*.

Given the basic apparatus of internal and external components, and the consequent idea that mental states are hybrid entities composed of both, we can give the following characterization of the dual component theory:

DC1. Inside the head of cognizing organisms are various mental representations.

DC2. Outside the head of cognizing organisms are various environmental objects, properties, events etc.

DC3. Specification of the identity conditions of certain sorts of mental states involves essential reference to these environmental objects, properties and events. That is, certain sorts of mental states are hybrid entities that straddle both internal representations and external objects, properties and events.

DC1 is intended exclusively. That is, mental representations are viewed as exclusively and purely internal items. Thus, according to the dual component theory, being in a mental state M cannot consist in standing in a particular relation to a mental representation M*, since the latter is a purely internal item whereas the former incorporates environmental objects and properties. Nevertheless, the dual component theory is consistent with the view that mental representations are the internal structural bases of mental states. That is, a mental representation M* can, when appropriately connected to certain environmental objects, properties, or events, constitute mental state M.

The crucial assumption here is that mental representations are purely and exclusively internal items. One of the principal objectives of this book is to undermine this claim. The claim leads to a corollary which is just about constitutive of recent cognitivist theorizing in psychology: the capacity of an organism to process the information it needs to successfully interact with the environment can be explained solely in terms of operations defined over representations. Since these representations are viewed as exclusively internal items, the operations defined over them are viewed as exclusively internal operations. Of course, according to the dual component theory, such an explanation of an organism's information processing capacity is not strictly a mentalistic explanation; it does not invoke mental states or processes as such, but only their internal structural bases, i.e., mental representations. Nevertheless, the apparatus of internal and external components invoked by the dual component theory effectively guarantees that this sort of internalist account of information processing capacity can be given. That is, when properly understood, the dual component theory entails the following corollary:

DC4. The capacity of an organism to process the information it needs to interact successfully with the environment can be explained purely in terms of internal representations and internal operations defined over those representations.

Such an account of the information processing capacity of an organism is, of course, an engineering account, a psychotectonic account. Since semantic content can arise only in the context of organism–environment relations, and since the arguments for philosophical externalism turn on the semantic content of mental states, the arguments for philosophical externalism are perfectly compatible with this sort of internalist psychotectonic account of the mind.

The epistemological claim listed earlier as partly definitive of the form of externalism to be developed in this book claimed that it is not possible to understand the nature of cognitive processes by focusing exclusively on what is occurring inside the skin of cognizing organisms. However, we now see that philosophical externalism, by itself, is perfectly compatible with one sort of internalist understanding of mental processes, a psychotectonic understanding of cognition. That is, philosophical externalism is perfectly compatible with the claim that it is possible to understand the ability of the an organism to process the information it needs in order to interact successfully with its environment in terms of structures and processes that are purely internal to that organism. It is this claim which constitutes the principal focus of attack in the coming chapters. It will be argued that there can be no purely internalist psychotectonic account of mental processing. Even if we confine ourselves to the level of psychotectonics, and bracket the semantic properties instantiated by representations, still we cannot hope to develop a purely internalist account. Thus, one of the things this book attempts to do is show why DC4 should be rejected. The project of psychotectonics, it will be argued, is externalist (i.e., environmentalist) to its core.

There are, of course, other ways of interpreting the import of the arguments for philosophical externalism. The dual component theory is based on the assumption that it is possible to identify two conceptually distinct parts of any given propositional mental state. The internal component is regarded as the *locus* of the causal–explanatory powers of the state *vis-à-vis* the production of behaviour. The external component consists in the representational properties of the mental state. Sometimes it is thought that the internal component can be identified by way of a certain type of content that it possesses in isolation from the external component. This sort of content − *narrow content* − is claimed to be distinct from ordinary semantic content and thus forms the basis for identifying the internal component as a separable part of the mental state as a whole (LePore & Loewer 1986; Fodor 1987; Rowlands 1991b). Another suggestion involves denying that the internal component possesses content, at least essentially, but claiming that it can none the less be identified by way of its *syntactic* properties (Field 1978; Stich 1983). My aim is not to evaluate these suggestions at this point. If the arguments developed in the remainder of this book are correct, this will entail the rejection of both of these views. Indeed, it will entail rejection of any version of the dual component theory. For present purposes, the important point to note is that the dual component theory, as an interpretation of externalism, can work only if it is possible to identify two separable components of a mental state.

More radical versions of philosophical externalism deny that there are two separable components (Pettit & McDowell 1986). That is, a more radical form of externalism will deny that it is possible to conceptually separate the internal from the external component of any given propositional mental state. And this more radical form of externalism will not, by itself, entail the possibility of a purely internalist approach to psychotectonics. The position to be developed in this book is much more compatible with this radicalized version of externalism. However, there is still a fundamental difference between the two positions.

Philosophical externalism, even in its more radical form, is still a view which is centred around the content of mental states. The dual component theory would claim that there is a separable part of any given propositional mental state, namely the contentful part, the part constituted by semantic relations, and that it is this part which is externally individuated or externally located. The more radical form of externalism would deny that it is correct to speak of separable parts of mental states in this context, however the notion of a part is understood. Thus, it is the mental state taken as a whole which must be regarded as externally individuated or located. Nevertheless, the more radical form would still maintain that the mental state, taken as a whole, is externally individuated or externally located *in virtue of* its content. Philosophical externalism, in either of its forms, claims that mental states are externally individuated because, and only because, they have content.

In contrast, the environmentalist position developed in this book does not, in any way, turn on the content of mental states. The arguments to be developed in the following pages will, if correct, establish both the epistemological and ontological claims listed earlier. However, there is no suggestion that these principles are true because mental states possess semantic content. The arguments are motivated by fundamentally different considerations than those which motivate philosophical externalism.

3.4 PHILOSOPHICAL EXTERNALISM AND THE
ONTOLOGICAL CLAIM

According to the ontological claim, cognitive processes are not located exclusively inside the skins of cognizing organisms. It is important to realize that this is a claim about the location of cognitive processes. For it is not clear that the arguments for philosophical externalism are, by themselves, sufficient to secure this claim.

One way of interpreting the arguments for philosophical externalism is in terms of the notion of *individuation dependence*, a notion which derives from the work of Strawson (1959). Following Strawson, then, we can identify four aspects to a claim of individuation-dependence: linguistic, epistemological, metaphysical, and conceptual. Suppose Fs are individuation-dependent on Gs. Then we can say the following: (i) reference to Fs requires prior reference to Gs, (ii) knowledge of the properties of Fs requires prior knowledge of the properties of Gs, (iii) it is of the essence of Fs that they be related to Gs, and (iv) possessing the concept of an F requires prior possession of the concept of a G.

As Colin McGinn (1989) has pointed out, philosophical externalism seems to follow this general schema quite closely. Let the Fs be beliefs and the Gs be objects and properties environmentally related to the subject of those beliefs. Then the claim that beliefs are individuation dependent on the environment is the claim that the following four conditions hold: (i) reference to beliefs requires reference to appropriate environmental entities – there is no way of specifying what beliefs a subject has except by reference to the worldly entities that those beliefs are about; (ii) knowledge of beliefs requires knowledge of appropriate environmental entities – we cannot know what someone believes in a particular case without knowledge of the worldly entities that his belief is about; (iii) it is of the essence of a particular belief that it be related to environmental entities – it simply is not possible for a belief to be held by a subject unless his environment or world contains the appropriate entities; and (iv) one could not master the concept of a belief without having mastered concepts for the worldly entities that beliefs are about. These four conditions, then, express the content of the claim that beliefs are individuation-dependent upon environmental objects and properties.

Armed with this idea of individuation dependence, we can define the notion of *external individuation* thus:

> Mental state M, possessed by subject S, is *externally individuated* if and only if M is individuation-dependent on objects and properties that are external to S.

What I propose to call *weak externalism* is the view that (some, but not all) mental states are externally individuated in the above sense.

Weak externalism, based on the notion of external individuation, seems to capture what many have understood to be the content of externalism (for example, Macdonald 1989, 1990). It is important to realize, therefore, that weak externalism does not entail the ontological claim. That is, to say that mental states are externally *individuated* does not, by itself, entail that they are externally *located*. It does not entail, that is, that mental states are located in part outside the skins of organisms that have them. The external individuation of mental states must be clearly distinguished from the external location of mental states.

To see this, consider an analogy (Macdonald 1990). The property of being a planet is an externally individuated property in the sense that, (i) specification of what it is to be a planet involves reference to such things as stars and orbits, (ii) one cannot know what a planet is unless one knows what stars and orbits are, (iii) it is of the essence of a planet that it be related to stars and orbits, and (iv) one could not master the concept of a planet unless one had also mastered the concepts of a star and orbit. Nevertheless, even though the property of being a planet is externally individuated in the sense described above, this does *not* mean that a token of this type, an individual planet, is located, even partly, where its orbit and sun are located. The property of being a planet can be individuation-dependent upon stars and orbits without planets sharing the same location as stars and orbits. In a similar vein, mental states can be individuation-dependent upon environmental objects and properties, hence be externally individuated in the above sense, without being located, even in part, where those environmental objects and properties are located. Weak externalism, then, based on the notion of external individuation, does not establish the ontological claim.

Weak externalism, however, does not seem to capture everyone's concept of externalism. McGinn (1989:42ff.), for example, seems to have something much stronger in mind. Consider, again, condition (iii) as applied to mental states. Condition (iii) claims that it is of the essence of a particular belief that it be related to appropriate environmental entities; it is not possible for a subject to hold a given belief unless his environment contains the appropriate entities. McGinn, in fact, interprets this condition in terms of the idea of environmental *constitution*. The reason it is impossible for a subject to hold a given belief without his environment containing appropriate entities is, McGinn thinks, because the environmental entities are *constituents* of the belief. Thus, the individuation dependence of a belief upon environmental entities is grounded, on McGinn's view, by the fact that these environmental entities form the very constituents of the belief. On this view, mental state types must be understood as relational entities, entities that are composed of internal state types of a subject, environmental object types or properties, and appropriate types of connecting relations. Along these lines, then, we can define the idea of *external constitution* as follows:

> Mental state M, possessed by subject S, is *externally constituted* if and only if it is composed not only of an internal state of S but also of an object, property, or event in the environment of S together with an appropriate relation connecting the two.

Strong externalism, as I shall use that term, is the view that (certain sorts of) mental states are externally constituted. Strong externalism, it should be fairly clear, *does* entail the ontological claim; it entails that mental states are located, at least in part, outside the skins of organisms that possess them.

Therefore, the situation is this. Weak externalism does not entail the ontological claim, but strong externalism does. However, the arguments for philosophical externalism, *by themselves*, seem to establish only weak externalism. They show that contentful mental states are externally individuated but do not, at least by themselves, show that they are externally located. Therefore, the arguments for philosophical externalism, by themselves, do not establish the ontological claim.

That the arguments for philosophical externalism are not sufficient to establish strong externalism can be seen easily from the fact that supporters of strong externalism feel obliged to back up their interpretation with arguments *in addition* to the usual arguments for philosophical externalism (McGinn 1989; Rowlands 1995a, 1995b).

McGinn's strategy, for example, consists essentially in placing the burden of proof on anybody who would deny the external constitution interpretation. Thus, McGinn points out that any hostility to the external constitution interpretation of philosophical externalism cannot be based on hostility to regarding mental states as having constituents *per se*. Many internalist views of mental states are perfectly happy to regard mental states as having constituents; images, bits of cerebral syntax, and so on, depending on the type of internalism in question. But, once it is allowed that mental states have constituents, and once the arguments for philosophical externalism are accepted, then on what grounds could it be denied that they have external constituents? The only grounds there could be, McGinn argues, is a lingering attraction to internalism. That is, the only grounds for denying the external constitution interpretation, once the arguments for philosophical externalism have been accepted, would be a residual internalist bias.

Whether or not McGinn is correct on this point is not germane to the present issue. The important point, however, is that McGinn has to resort to additional argument in order to support his strong interpretation of externalism. If the arguments for philosophical externalism were sufficient to establish the strong interpretation, then such additional argument would be unnecessary. Therefore, it is fairly clear that the arguments for philosophical externalism do not, by themselves, secure the strong interpretation of externalism. At most, they show only that mental states are externally individuated, not that they are externally located.

To sum up the main points of the discussion so far. The environmentalist position to be defended in this book is characterized by two principles that I have labelled the ontological claim and the epistemological claim. Philosophical externalism, the view deriving from the work of Putnam, Burge, and others, is compatible with the denial of the ontological claim. Only the strong form of philosophical externalism, characterized by the claim that mental states are externally constituted, establishes the ontological claim. However, the usual arguments for philosophical externalism do not establish the strong, but only the weak, form, according to which mental states are externally individuated but not externally located. Therefore, the usual arguments for philosophical externalism do not establish the ontological claim. With regard to the epistemological claim, the position is not so straightforward. The important distinction here is between two ways of understanding cognitive processes, psychotectonic approaches, and psychosemantic approaches. The arguments for philosophical externalism are sufficient to establish that, at the level of psychosemantics, it is not possible to understand cognitive states and processes without focusing on relations between cognizing subjects and their environment. However, the arguments for philosophical externalism are compatible with a purely internalist psychotectonic understanding of cognitive states and processes. Thus, philosophical externalism is compatible with the claim that it is possible, at least in one sense, to understand cognitive processes by focusing purely on what is going on inside the skin of cognizing subjects.

The environmentalist position developed in this book, then, diverges from philosophical externalism in two important and connected ways. Firstly, it entails the ontological claim. If the environmentalist position to be developed here is correct, then cognitive processes are located, in part, outside the skins of cognizing organisms. Secondly, it entails the epistemological claim, and this is true even when it is psychotectonic accounts of cognitive processes that are at issue. That is, environmentalism entails, and this is one of its constitutive features, that there can be *no* understanding of cognitive processes – whether psychosemantic *or* psychotectonic – achieved by focusing purely on what is going on inside the skin of cognizing organisms.

3.5 ENVIRONMENTALISM AND BEHAVIOURISM

Philosophical externalism is one source of opposition to the Cartesian conception of the mind. Philosophical externalism is currently quite popular. Another source of opposition to the Cartesian conception is provided by *behaviourism*. Behaviourism is currently very unpopular. In fact, so unpopular has behaviourism become that anyone who is attempting to develop a theory of mind which seems to have some elements in common with behaviourist programs in psychology is faced with a major tactical decision: whether to draw attention to this fact. While the position defended in this book is not a form of behaviourism, there are elements of it which are *behaviouristic*, although I must qualify this by saying that I am not sure what behaviourism is.

One thing is clear: whatever behaviourist programmes in psychology are, they have very little in common with the view presented to philosophy undergraduates and refuted within the space of a lecture. So, in the following sections I shall try to outline which elements of the position to be developed in this book are behaviouristic, and why. And to do this it will, at the same time, be necessary to dispel a few unhelpful myths concerning behaviourism.

Behaviourism and reductionism

The most pervasive, tenacious, and unhelpful of the philosopher's myths about behaviourism is that it is committed to the view that mental state or process types can be reduced to types of behavioural dispositions. Such a reduction, it is alleged, can take one of two forms. Firstly, it could be a *definitional reduction*, that is a redefinition of mental terms or expressions by way of behavioural terms or expressions. Secondly, it could be a *nomological reduction*, a reduction which is effected by way of a necessary coextension between any given mental property and a given behavioural property. Any version of behaviourism, it is commonly thought, is committed to the possibility of reducing, in one or both of these senses, mental items to behavioural ones. And, as any undergraduate student will tell you, there is a major problem with this sort of project. The behaviour to which an organism is disposed depends not just on any single mental state but on a conglomeration of such states. This fact is variously referred to as the *belief–desire–perception cycle*, or, sometimes, the *holism of the mental*. And, it is commonly thought to be a fatal blow to behaviourism. It precludes any possibility of the definitional reduction of mental expressions to behavioural expressions. Any attempted definition of a mental expression in terms of a behavioural one would have to make essential – that is, ineliminable – reference to other mental terms or expressions. Secondly, it rules out the possibility of a nomological reduction of mental properties to behavioural properties. Dispositions to behaviour are a function not of any single mental state but of multiple mental states acting together. It is, therefore, impossible to effect any one-to-one mapping of mental properties onto behavioural properties.

The first point which should be made about this objection is that it simply does not apply to the sort of behaviourism practised by behavioural psychologists. Most psychologists, of course, confined their behaviourism to the methodological level, and would have no interest whatsoever in the definitional or nomological reduction of mental terms or properties to behavioural terms or properties. The concern with reduction, in either of its forms, seems to be a peculiarly philosophical concern, that is a concern constructed from philosophical reflections on what behavioural psychologists are, or should be, doing. And, as Zuriff (1987) has argued, the reason philosophers were inclined to gloss behaviourist programmes in this way was probably because of the undue influence that logical empiricism had on them at the time.

The main problem, however, is that the above sort of objection is not very compelling even when restricted to philosophical versions of behaviourism. What proves illuminating here, I think, is a comparison of the belief–desire–perception cycle objection with certain objections which used to be raised against mind–brain identity theories.

It was not so long ago that any form of the mind–brain identity theory was thought to be refuted by the following sort of objection. Consider a mental state, for example, pain. According to the mind–brain identity theory, pains are identical with brain states or processes. Now a pain can be intense or weak, long-lived or brief, intermittent or continuous, sharp or dull, throbbing or constant, etc. However, it was argued, it makes no sense at all to say that a pain is of high or low voltage, or has a certain electro-chemical composition, or a certain location, size, shape, etc. So, the idea that a person can have a two-inch long, octagonal, low-voltage pain makes no sense. But these are all descriptions that might justifiably be applied to brain states. Therefore, it was argued, this shows that pains and brain states belong to different categories, and to confuse categories is to talk nonsense. We arrive at the same results whatever physical states we choose to equate with pain. And what holds for pain holds for mental states quite generally. So mental states cannot be identical with brain states. Or so the argument goes.

The materialist response to this lies, in effect, in the distinction between *connotation* and *denotation*. The identity of mental and physical is to be understood as an identity of denotation, not an identity of connotation. A mental term such as 'pain' and a physical expression such as 'C-fibre stimulation' can refer to the same property, i.e., have the same denotation, even if they express distinct connotations. The correct model for mental–physical identities is provided by well-known examples of scientific a posteriori identities, such as 'Water = H_2O', and 'Heat = molecular motion'. The term 'water' and the expression 'H_2O' have the same denotation, i.e., they refer to the same thing, even though they have distinct connotations. Anti-materialist arguments of the above sort, therefore, can show only that mental and physical terms or expressions differ in connotation. And this in no way precludes identity of their denotations. An identity statement such as 'pain = C-fibre stimulation' should be understood as expressing an a posteriori identity of denotation, not an a priori identity of connotation.

The behaviourist, however, can adopt essentially the same line of argument. Thus, if the philosophical, as opposed to methodological, behaviourist wished to assert the identity of mental items with behavioural ones, then he could assert that this is an a posteriori identity of denotation, not an a priori identity of connotation. That is, the behaviourist could assert that mental and behavioural terms or expressions denote or refer to the same thing but, none the less, express distinct and irreducible connotations. He can, therefore, assert the identity of mental properties with behavioural properties while denying the possibility of defining mental idioms in behavioural terms. The impossibility of a definitional reduction of the mental to the behavioural need not trouble even the philosophical behaviourist, since he is committed to no such thing.

The second major distinction that has shaped the development of mind–brain identity theories is that between types and tokens. The mind–brain identity theory was seen as committed to type–type identity claims; that is, to statements of the form:

Pain = C-fibre stimulation

where both pain and C-fibre stimulation are here viewed as types or properties.

This conception of the identity theory has now largely been rejected. This was largely the result of what is known as the problem of *multiple realization*, first discussed by Putnam (1967). The possibility of multiple realization is the possibility that the same mental property may, in different creatures, or in the same creature at different times, be realized by distinct physical properties. It seems extremely implausible to suppose that a single physical property will be found to be responsible for a single mental property across *all* organisms. How can the type–type identity theorist justify dismissing the possibility that silicon-based Martians could feel pain, assuming the silicon is properly organized? And so forth.

The identity theorist's response to this problem has been to move from a type–type to a token–token version of the identity theory (Hocutt 1966; Davidson 1970; Fodor 1974). Such a theory claims that mental event tokens, conceived of as dated, unrepeatable, concrete particulars are identical with neurophysiological event tokens, similarly conceived. And this identity of event tokens is thought to imply nothing about the relation between mental and neurophysiological event types. What is typically overlooked, however, is the similarity between the multiple-realization objection and the objection to behaviourism based on the belief–desire–perception cycle. The similarity amounts to this: the problem of multiple realization rules out the possibility of a *nomological* reduction of mental properties to neurophysiological properties in exactly the same way, and for analogous reasons, that the belief–desire–perception cycle rules out the possibility of a nomological reduction of mental properties to behavioural ones.

The major consequence of the belief–desire–perception cycle is that any given mental property cannot be correlated with any one behavioural property. Instead, any given mental property might be associated with any number of distinct behavioural properties, depending on what other mental properties are instantiated by its subject. That is, the position the behaviourist now finds himself in corresponds exactly with the position faced by the type–type identity theorist in the face of the problem of multiple realization. For the major consequence of the belief–desire–perception cycle is that mental properties can have different behavioural realizations. Once this parallel is recognized, however, it quickly becomes apparent that, far from being a fatal objection to behaviourism, the problem posed by the belief–desire–perception cycle can be easily resolved. It can be resolved along precisely the same lines as those adopted by the identity theorist in the face of the problem of multiple realization. The behaviourist can abandon type–type behaviourism in favour of token–token behaviourism. Interpreted in this way, behaviourism is the view that mental state tokens are identical with behavioural state tokens. This position, however, entails nothing whatsoever about the relation between mental state types and behavioural state types. In particular, it does not entail that mental state types are reducible – either definitionally or nomologically – to behavioural state types and, crucially, it does not entail that there is any sort of one-to-one correlation between mental state types and behavioural state types.

According to the position developed in this book, cognitive processes are, in part, constituted by behaviour. This claim is restricted to the level of token cognitive processes. Thus, according to the position developed in this book, cognitive process tokens should be viewed as being made up of constituent parts, and, in many cases at least, one of these parts will be a behavioural token; an individual, concrete-particular, instance of a behavioural type. This is the extent, and this is the only extent, to which the position developed here is behaviouristic. But, and this cannot be emphasized too much, there is no attempt here to reduce, either definitionally, or nomologically, cognitive processes to behaviour. The view developed here is not in any way reductionist. Furthermore, the view developed here is not even a version of token–token behaviourism in the sense explained above. There is no claim that cognitive process tokens are identical with behavioural tokens. The claim is, rather, that cognitive process tokens are, *in part*, made up of, or constituted by, behavioural tokens. This brings us to the second major contrast with behaviourism as it is usually understood.

Behaviourism and inner processes

Behaviourism is usually understood as involving some sort of hostility to inner processes, specifically hostility to the idea that inner processes can be relevant to our understanding of cognition. Such hostility, however, plays no role whatsoever in this book. I shall argue that many token cognitive processes are constituted, in part, by tokens of certain types of behaviour. However, the qualification *in part* is crucial. There is no suggestion that cognitive processes are exhaustively constituted by behaviour. That is, there is no suggestion that cognitive process tokens can be *identified* with behavioural tokens. Rather, the claim is that cognitive process tokens are, *in part*, constituted by behavioural tokens. That is, many cognitive process tokens are hybrid entities: they straddle, or incorporate, not only behavioural tokens of certain types but, in addition, inner process tokens of certain appropriate types, and also environmental objects of various sorts. Cognitive processes are made up of behaviour, inner processes, and environmental objects.

Wide and narrow behaviour

When the great philosophical behaviourist Gilbert Ryle talked about behaviour, he had in mind such descriptions of a person's actions as these: 'telling oneself and others that the ice is thin, skating warily, shuddering, dwelling in imagination on possible disasters, warning other skaters, keeping to the edge of the pond' (Ryle 1949:129). The contrast between this conception of behaviour and that exemplified in the following passage from Jaegwon Kim could not be more profound:

> [An] action of turning on the burner, in so far as this is thought to involve the burner going on, is not an action that it is the proper business of psychological theory to explain or predict. . . . It is not part of the object of *psychological* explanation to explain why the burner went on. . . . The job of psychological explanation is done once [psychological theory] has explained the bodily action of turning on a knob; whether or not this action results in my also turning on the stove, my starting cooking the dinner . . . is dependent on facts quite outside the province of psychology, [which] are not the proper concern of psychological theory.
>
> (1982:64)

There are two important differences here between Ryle's and Kim's conceptions of behaviour. Firstly, in his descriptions of behaviour, Ryle makes reference to things beyond the agent's body; Kim thinks such reference is psychologically irrelevant or, worse, misguided. Secondly, Ryle's behavioural items are actions, that is, events of people doing things such as moving their bodies. Kim's behavioural items do not seem to be actions, in this sense, at all but, rather, movements of a person's body. Behaviour in Ryle's sense we can call *wide* behaviour. Behaviour in Kim's sense we can call *narrow* behaviour.

Many philosophical reflections on psychology suggest that the sort of behaviour relevant to psychological theorizing, and susceptible to psychological explanation, is narrow behaviour. The reasoning behind this is quite simple, and, very roughly, looks like this. Suppose Larry turns a knob and turns on the burner. A psychological theory attempting to explain this piece of Larry's behaviour might invoke internal states of Larry (such as a desire to cook dinner and the belief that turning on the burner was the best way of going about this). Would such internal states have explained Larry's turning on the burner. Not really, so the argument goes, because suppose someone had, unbeknownst to Larry, removed his burner and replaced it with a skilfully constructed burner façade, together with its own knob. Then Larry would not have turned on the burner at all, but only turned the knob of the burner façade. None the less, so the argument goes, the psychological explanation would be the same in either case. Therefore, what the internal states explain is not the turning on of the burner as such, but what the turning on of the burner and the manipulation of the façade have in common, namely the turning of a knob. The moral of the story, so it is claimed, is that the sort of behaviour relevant to psychological explanation is behaviour described in such a way that it presupposes the existence of no items external to the agent.

There is much, I think, that is questionable about this argument. In particular, a pressing problem for the proponent of narrow behaviour is demarcating how narrow the province of psychological explanation would become if the argument were wholeheartedly endorsed. Kim, for example, speaks as if *turning a knob*, unlike *turning on the burner*, were an admissible object of psychological explanation. However, *turning a knob* also involves the existence of an item external to the agent. And if someone replaces the knob with a skilfully constructed knob façade, the same argument could be run again. Furthermore, it is not clear why Kim's argument does not also rule out psychological explanations even of bodily actions – of why Larry moved his finger, for example. If, unbeknownst to Larry, his finger had been surgically removed and, under the influence of pain killers he fails to remember this, he may certainly *try* to move his finger. And, presumably, the same internal states will be involved in this as in the straightforward case of his moving his finger. So, it could be argued, what the internal states explain is not the moving of his fingers but what the moving of his fingers and the trying to move of his non-existent fingers have in common (Hornsby 1986).

Whether this sort of problem is fatal to the claim that there is such a thing as narrow behaviour is, again, beyond the scope of this book. At this point, I should just like to emphasize that the concept of behaviour that is relevant to the arguments of this book is very definitely *wide* behaviour. When it is argued that cognitive processes are partly constituted by behaviour, the sort of behaviour in question is emphatically not narrow. Far from it. I shall argue that the type of behaviour constitutive of cognitive processes is essentially behaviour which involves the manipulation or exploitation of (certain sorts of) structures in the environment of the agent. Without reference to these environmental structures, what is distinctive about this behaviour, from the point of view of cognition, is lost. Hence, the behaviour in question must be understood as *wide* behaviour; behaviour identified by way of the environmental structures that it essentially involves. And these structures, it will be argued, can be constituents of cognitive processes.

3.6 MILLIKAN'S THEORY

Of all contemporary philosophical approaches to the mind, the one that most closely resembles the position advocated in this book is that of Ruth Millikan. Millikan's theory incorporates both the project of psychosemantics and that of psychotectonics. It is for her approach to the former that she is, perhaps, best known; and Millikanian psychosemantics will constitute a sizeable proportion of the subject-matter of Part II of this book. At present, I shall be concerned solely with the implications of Millikan's theory for the project of psychotectonics. In what follows, I choose to emphasize the differences between Millikan's position and that defended in this book (what follows would be a rather pedestrian discussion if I chose otherwise). This emphasis, however, should not be allowed to blind us to the enormous amount of common ground between Millikan's position and my own.

Millikan defends two theses, both of which bear more than a passing resemblance to the ontological and epistemological claims outlined earlier. Both theses are ontological claims that possess clear epistemological corollaries, corollaries strongly advocated by Millikan. The first is a thesis about the nature of behaviour, the second about the nature of organisms.

According to Millikan, any occurrence that qualifies as behaviour involves at least the following three elements:

1. It is an external change or activity exhibited by an organism or external part of an organism.
2. It has a function in the biological sense.
3. This function is or would be normally fulfilled via mediation of the environment or via resulting alterations in the organism's relation to the environment (1993:137).

Claim 2 is, here, the central one. Millikan's argument for this claim goes essentially as follows. Any organism exhibits an uncountable number of outputs, each of which can be described in an uncountable number of ways. It is not possible to differentiate relevant from irrelevant output, or relevant from irrelevant description of that output by any of the traditional means. One traditional suggestion, for example, is that what marks the difference between relevant and irrelevant output, between genuine behaviour and somatic 'noise', is that the former but not the latter instantiate repeated patterns. This suggestion is inadequate for, as Millikan points out, there are repeated patterns of output that are clearly psychologically and behaviourally irrelevant. Every mouse eyeblink is a momentary movement of its eyelashes away from its eyebrows, and, thus, 'movement of eyelash away from eyebrows' designates a repeated pattern of output just as much as 'eyeblink'. But this is pretty clearly not an output that the behavioural scientist has an obligation to explain. Similarly, Millikan argues, the traditional appeal to nomologicality is not sufficient to differentiate relevant from irrelevant output. The chameleon has a disposition to turn brown when placed in a brown box, and one might be tempted to think of this as a law of chameleon behaviour. But the mouse has a disposition to turn brown when placed in a suitably hot oven, and this disposition is as nomic as that of the chameleon. But the disposition of the mouse is, again, not something that the behavioural scientist is in the business of explaining. Indeed, Millikan argues plausibly that any temptation to accept nomologicality as the demarcation criterion depends, for whatever plausibility it possesses, on a confusion of law with proper biological function. Thus Millikan argues, essentially by elimination, that the only output forms of interest for the study of organisms as living systems are those forms that have biological functions. Behaviour, as Millikan would put it, is a teleofunctional or biological category.

The assimilation of behaviour to a teleofunctional category is one of enormous significance. The functions constitutive of behaviour are, by definition, functions performed through mediation of the environment. Indeed, the functions that define behaviours often extend very far out into the environment. Thus, the entire process of building a beaver dam is part of beaver behaviour. 'What the beaver does is not just to move its muscles or put sticks down where water trickles but also to build a dam and create a pond' (1993:163). This is the ontological claim with respect to behaviour. Behaviour incorporates as one of its constituents the environmental objects and structures that it is the function of the beaver to mediate. All genuine behaviour is, in the terminology of the previous section, essentially *wide* behaviour. And this ontological claim has a clear epistemological corollary. 'To understand beaver behaviour is to understand how this entire process is accomplished, not just how the muscles happen to become contracted' (1993:163). We cannot understand the beaver's behaviour by focusing on the beaver alone, a fortiori, by focusing on what is going on inside the beaver. We must also concentrate on the environment in which the beaver is situated, more precisely on the environmental structures it is the proper function of the beaver to mediate. Thus, Millikan, in effect, defends, for the case of behaviour, versions of the ontological and epistemological claims outlined at the beginning of this chapter. One cannot understand behaviour in isolation from the environment because the latter is literally a constituent of the former. As should perhaps be clear by now, the position defended in this book concurs wholeheartedly with both these claims.

Millikan also defends an ontological claim, and its epistemological corollary, about the nature of organisms. According to Millikan, 'the line between organism and environment, as it is customarily drawn, is useless so far as the study of the organismic system is concerned' (1993:158). This is not to say that one cannot draw any distinction between organism and environment; clearly one can. The point is, rather, that the distinction is not principled: not theoretically useful for understanding the nature and behaviour of organisms. Rather, the only principled way of differentiating organism and environment makes this distinction a matter of degree, specifically the 'degree of control that the system as a whole has over the production and maintenance of normal structure and normal states for its various portions' (1993:159).

The basic idea underlying this claim runs as follows. Consider the lungs. These are an organismic sub-system and, as such, have a normal environment in the absence of which they cannot perform their normal functions. They cannot, that is, perform their function of supplying tissue with oxygen unless they are encased in an airtight chest cavity, are displaced periodically by certain muscles, are next to a heart pumping blood through the relevant vessels, and unless the wider system of which they are a part (i.e., the organism) is surrounded by an atmosphere containing oxygen. The crucial point is that as we move closer to the spatial centre of any organism we find a greater proportion of systems whose normal conditions for proper functioning are maintained by some other connected system. Presence of a functioning heart, for example, is an essential condition for the normal functioning of the lungs, and there are numerous organs and systems within the body that help maintain a functioning heart as part of their jobs. Towards the spatial periphery of the organism, however, conditions necessary for proper functioning of the organism's sub-systems tend to be less under the organism's control. The proper functioning of the lungs requires that the organism be situated in an environment containing oxygen, and whether the organism is so situated depends on factors over which the organism does not always have control. It is true that, if an organism finds itself in an atmosphere bereft of oxygen, it might be able to move into a more oxygen-rich one, but, as we move from the spatial centre of the organism, the tendency is for the method of maintaining normal conditions to become 'less a making and more a seeking or a fitting in' (1993:161). At the outer limit, normal conditions for portions of the organismic system are simply there or not there, maintenance of these conditions being completely beyond the organism's control.

Thus, Millikan is, in effect, putting forward an ontological claim about the nature of organisms. There is no theoretically salient reason for absolutely distinguishing organisms from environments. To the extent that there is a theoretically principled distinction here at all, the distinction is one of degree, not of kind. The environment of an organism is, to a degree at least, a constituent of that organism, part of the organism's nature. And, once again, this has an epistemological corollary. We cannot hope to understand the nature of organisms by focusing on what is spatially located inside that organism's skin. Proper understanding of any organism requires our focus to extend from what is in the organism to what the organism is in. Indeed, these claims about the nature of organisms reinforce the earlier claims about behaviour. Once we have done away with the absolute distinction between organisms and environments, Millikan argues, behaviour emerges as the 'functional form of the wider organismic process' (1993:163). Functional changes occurring in non-bodily parts of the organism have exactly the same status as changes in bodily parts. 'What the organism maintains, modifies, or puts in place through the activity of its body is just part of the developing wider organismic system. Behaviour, then, is just the functional form of the widest organismic processes' (1993:163).

Thus Millikan defends two sets of very radical claims about the nature of organisms and of their behaviour. Both organisms and behaviour are, in an important sense, environmentally constituted: they contain environmental structures and processes as proper parts. This is the ontological aspect of Millikan's externalism. Therefore, also, we can understand neither organisms nor their behaviour by focusing purely on what is going on inside organisms or at their spatial periphery. This is the epistemological aspect of Millikan's externalism.

These claims are ones with which I wholeheartedly agree. Indeed, Millikan's position is, to this extent, of a piece with the position to be defended in this book. There are differences, however. Firstly, although I agree with Millikan on the nature and status of both behaviour and organisms, the position I develop does not depend on the truth of these claims. I presuppose neither her ontological nor her epistemological claim about the nature of organisms. And, while Millikan's account of the nature of behaviour might be entailed by the position defended in this book, her account is not presupposed in the arguments I shall develop for this position. Secondly, the conceptual centrepiece of Millikan's position is her theory of proper functions (a theory which has not been sufficiently emphasized in the foregoing discussion, but see Part II). All her major arguments, I think, derive more or less directly from this theory. Again, I accept Millikan's theory of proper functions but will not presuppose it in the arguments to follow. The arguments developed in this book, then, are quite distinct from those of Millikan.

Most importantly, however, the position developed in the following pages is, at least in one crucial respect, more radical even than that of Millikan. Indeed, if the position defended in this book is correct,

Millikan's position might actually contain a residual element of internalism. Millikan, as we have seen, makes two very radical sets of claims about the nature of organisms and behaviour. But the principal concern of Part I of this book is with neither of these things, but with cognitive processes, with the mechanisms of behaviour production. And while Millikan's claims about organisms and behaviour are impressively radical, her view of the mechanisms of behaviour production is curiously traditional.

According to Millikan, the mechanisms of behaviour production take the form of representations which can be indicative or imperative in character. Indicative representations, associated with beliefs, are conceived of as maps of how the world is. Imperative representations, associated with desires, are conceived of as blueprints for how the world could be. These maps and blueprints are connected to the world by way of normatively constituted projection rules, and these are explained in terms of the theory of proper functions (1984, 1993). Therefore, while Millikan endorses a thoroughgoing externalism with regard to both behaviour and organisms, she also adopts an essentially internalist (specifically 'Ramseyesque') account of the mechanisms of behaviour production. And it is precisely with the mechanisms of behaviour production that this book is concerned.

According to the position developed in Part I of this book, behaviour-producing mechanisms – cognitive processes in the broadest sense of the expression – do not necessarily or even always take the form of maps or blueprints. It would be more accurate to describe them as *partial* maps or blueprints. The complete map is, in many cases, obtained only when the internal mechanism is combined, in appropriate ways, with suitable environmental objects. If we want to think of cognitive processes as maps or blueprints, then it would be better to think of such maps as being both internally and externally constituted. Suppose, as in the stereotypical pirate film one might remember from childhood Saturday cinema, we have a treasure map divided into two halves. It is a condition of the intelligibility of the second half of the map that we locate a certain environmental structure – say the skull-shaped mountain – and orient the map in a certain way to this structure. We might use the first half of the map to locate the structure, but only when we have located it, and oriented the second half of the map towards it in the correct way, does this half become usable by us. There are no projection rules, evolutionarily constituted or not, that connect the second half of the map with the world independently of the skull-shaped mountain. Or, more precisely, what projection rules there are have been designed, as part of their proper function, to work only in connection with the environmental structure, the skull-shaped mountain. In this case, we should regard the mountain as an essential feature of the map. The map is not simply the paper, it is the combination of the paper and the world.

According to the position defended in this book, then, if we want to think of the mechanisms of behaviour production as cognitive maps, then these maps straddle both internal and external structures. And, from this point of view, regarding such maps as purely internal items is a last (hopefully) vestige of internalism. Development of a properly environmental conception of cognition requires letting go this final ghost of Descartes.

3.7 THE VIEW

I have spent most of this chapter explaining what the view developed in this book is not; that is, differentiating it from other views with which it is, or might be, superficially similar. It is now time to spell out, with some admittedly broad strokes, what the view to be developed in this book actually is.

Essentially, the position to be developed in the following pages can be stated thus: cognitive processes are fundamentally hybrid in character, made up of three distinct types of thing. They are partly constituted by certain sorts of internal process instantiated in the brain, partly by certain forms of behaviour, specifically, behaviour that involves manipulating, or exploiting, certain types of structure in the environment of the cognizer, and partly by these external structures themselves.

Consider, first, the internal processes involved in cognition. It is not, actually, within the scope of this book to argue for one sort of internal process over others. And none of the arguments developed in the following pages will aim at demonstrating that a certain type of internal process is the only one that could possibly be responsible for cognition. However, the arguments of chapters 7 and 8 do point to a hitherto unsuspected role for *pattern mapping* (i.e., matching, completing, associating, or transforming) operations. The concept

61

of representation also figures quite prominently, but discussion of this will be postponed until Part II.

The external processes that are partly constitutive of cognition are behavioural in character. The behaviour in question is of a quite specific kind, and consists in a manipulation, or exploitation, of structures existing in the environment of the cognizing organism. What is crucial about these structures, which are also partly constitutive of cognitive processes, is that they are bearers, or containers, of *information*. And manipulating or exploiting these structures is a means of *processing* the information embodied therein. Thus, when a given cognitive task requires the processing of information, this processing can, at least in part, be achieved through the manipulation of *external* information-bearing structures. And to this extent the need for the manipulation of *internal* information-bearing structures – mental representations, for example, is correspondingly reduced. This is really the central message of the book. Many, if not all, cognitive tasks require, for their solution, the processing of information. Processing of information is almost always conceived of as an internal process, involving the manipulation and transformation of internal information-bearing structures – mental representations – according to internally implemented rules. I shall argue that information processing does not purely, and perhaps not even largely, consist in internal processes of this sort. Information processing can take the form of manipulation and transformation of external information-bearing structures. The consequence of this, of course, is that any cognitive system that, in the performance of a given cognitive task, is capable of manipulating and transforming relevant external information-bearing structures is under correspondingly less of a burden to accomplish this task through the manipulation and transformation of internal information-bearing structures. The demands placed on a system to perform cognitive tasks through internal information processing can be reduced by giving that system an ability to engage in external information processing. And I shall argue that, in the case of human beings at least, much of the information processing necessary to the performance of many cognitive tasks takes the form of a manipulation and transformation of external information-bearing structures.

Commitment to this, as I have called it, *environmentalist* model of cognition entails, I shall argue, commitment to both the epistemological and the ontological claims described earlier. We cannot understand the nature of cognitive processes without understanding the ways in which cognizing organisms are able to manipulate information bearing structures in their environment. And this is because cognitive processes are, in part, constituted by the manipulation of such structures.

4

Environmentalism and evolution

In this anti–behaviourist age, anyone who wishes to argue that cognitive processes might, in part, be constituted by physical manipulation of the environment must be prepared for the following sort of retort: *And pigs might fly!* This provides a rather contrived *segue*. Pigs do not fly, of course, because they do not have wings. But why is this? It is tempting to think that, from an evolutionary point of view, wings would be selectively advantageous, allowing one to escape one's most dangerous predators, to spot suitable food items, habitats, etc. So, one might be led to suppose that there would be a significant selection pressure towards the evolution of wings by pigs and other ground–based vertebrates. Why, then, have pigs not developed wings?

In the case of pigs, the answer is almost certainly that the necessary genetic variation has never been available (Lewontin 1979). And the reason for this, again almost certainly, has to do with the nature of evolution. There are pressing historical facts that constrain any straightforward development towards optimality. In evolution, there is no *tabula rasa*. To use an analogy developed by Dawkins, imagine the designers of the first jet engine being obliged to develop (to 'evolve') their product from an existing propeller engine, changing one component at a time, nut by nut, screw by screw, etc. Furthermore, imagine that not only the end product of the development, but also each successive intermediate stage, must provide a viable form of propulsion for an aircraft. In fact, not only must each successive intermediate stage provide a viable form of propulsion, it must provide a form of propulsion that is superior to the one that preceded it. If you can imagine this, then you will have some idea of the sort of design constraints involved in evolutionary development (Dawkins 1982:38). Evidence of these sorts of constraints is readily visible in many evolved organisms. Consider, for example, the twisted construction of the face of a flat-fish such as a sole. Or, again, the fact that the retina of the vertebrate eye appears to have been installed backwards. Because evolutionary development is subject to these sorts of constraints, then, it is quite natural to suppose that, once a lineage has begun to evolve in a given direction, this may itself close off genetic options that were formerly available. At some time in the evolutionary past of pigs, the necessary genetic variation may well have been available for the development of wings. But, once the pig's ancestors started developing in a certain way, this development automatically closed down this variation.

The reason for the wingless state of pigs, then, seems to lie in the absence of the necessary genetic variation which, in turn, seems to derive from the pig's evolutionary history. However, in other cases, the explanation seems to be rather different. Consider the case of wingless ants as opposed to wingless pigs. Female ants can sprout wings if they happen to be nurtured as queens. However, if nurtured as workers, they do not express this developmental capacity. Furthermore, in many species of ant the queen will use her wings only once – for her nuptial flight – and will then proceed to bite or break them off at the roots (Dawkins 1982:42). Why should this be? One might be tempted to suppose that, from an evolutionary point of view, wings would be selectively advantageous. So, since the necessary genetic variation clearly is available, why would not all ants have developed wings?

Examples of this sort can easily be multiplied. Some aphids, for example, have wings, while others of the same species do not. Moreover, the class of examples can be extended to include other, seemingly advantageous, body parts. The juvenile sea squirt spends its days navigating its way along the ocean floor. To facilitate such navigation it possesses a rudimentary brain and nervous system. However, upon reaching maturity it fastens itself to a rock where it spends the rest of its life. Having done this, it then proceeds to eat its own brain. As the neuroscientist Rodolfo Llinas observes, it is much like getting tenure really! Why should the sea squirt do this? It is tempting to suppose that if any bodily part or organ can confer selective advantage on a creature that possesses it, then it is the brain. So why dispense with such an advantageous feature?

The answer seems to lie in a concept that it absolutely central to the argument of this chapter – the concept of *evolutionary cost*.

4.1 THE CONCEPT OF EVOLUTIONARY COST

The idea that will be developed and defended in this section is quite simple. Any evolutionary development involves an investment of *resources*. If, for example, a lineage has evolved wings, then such evolution will use up a certain quantity of resources. These resources are then not available for use elsewhere in the biological economy of the organisms of that lineage. Given that any organism of this lineage has at its disposal only a finite quantity of resources, then any investment of resources in a particular evolved feature will necessarily show up as a deficit elsewhere in the organism's biological economy. The answer to the questions posed by the earlier examples, then, is that wings, and brains, have their costs as well as their benefits. If the selection pressures that might lead to the development of a given feature F are not sufficiently important, then the cost of developing F might be greater than the benefits that accrue from possession of F.

Every evolutionary adaptation must cost something. That is, every adaptation involves the utilization of resources which cannot then be utilized for other purposes. In the case of aphids, for example, even within a species winged aphids are less fertile than wingless aphids (Dawkins 1982:47). Resources that have been invested in wing development are then not available to be invested elsewhere – in this case, in reproductive processes. In evolution, there really is no such thing as a free lunch. Evolutionary development is a constant process of balancing costs and selective advantages. Any evolutionary development takes place only against a background of compromises and trade-offs. For a bird, for example, resources that are invested in making breast muscles for powering wings are resources that could have been spent on making eggs. For mammals, resources that have been spent on a larger brain have similarly been bought at a cost that will be felt somewhere else in the creature's economy. Moreover, it is in the nature of costs to multiply. An enlarged brain comes at the cost of an enlarged head. This means extra weight at the front of the body, and this, in turn, will necessitate a larger tail for aerodynamic stability. This, presumably, will necessitate stronger, hence larger, leg muscles to carry the extra weight, and so on. Each point in the evolutionary development of a lineage becomes a balancing of costs and benefits. In this sense, each point in evolutionary development is a 'solution' to this balancing problem (Dawkins 1982:47). Since the concept of evolutionary cost will play such a prominent role in this chapter, the task of this section is to explicate, as precisely as possible, the content of this concept.

In order to understand the notion of evolutionary cost, we must first understand the concept of *fitness*. Since fitness is, among evolutionary processes at least, associated only with natural selection, it is, therefore, reasonable to suppose that fitness is what natural selection maximizes. And this is indeed a common view. The problem, however, comes in when we try to non-trivially specify what it is that natural selection maximizes. Population genetics says that selection maximizes the number of individuals in the next generation. Thoday (1953) thought it maximizes the probability of any descendants after a long period of time. Carson (1961) thought it maximizes biomass. Lewontin (1961) thought it maximizes the lowest possibility of survival of any offspring after one generation. Later (1968) he thought it maximizes stability. MacArthur (1962) and Slobodkin (1972) thought it maximizes efficiency (although they meant very different things by this). Claringbold and Barker (1961) thought it maximizes competitive ability. And these are a mere sampling of the diversity of views available.

Happily, there emerged in the 1970s a way of unifying these diverse views while, at the same time, developing a much more theoretically penetrating account of evolutionary fitness. The crucial concept, here, is the concept of *energy*. In the development of the concept of evolutionary cost to follow, I shall, therefore, assume that the concept of energy is central to, or constitutive of, the concept of fitness, and shall try to explain the relation between these two. I do so largely because, I think, articulation of the concept of evolutionary cost can proceed much more readily if we have a particular concept of fitness with which to work. Moreover, game–theoretical approaches to understanding evolution emphasize the centrality of energy to the concept of fitness. Therefore, my assumption is by no means idiosyncratic. However, it is important to realize that the focus on energy in the following discussion is largely for expository purposes. Nothing much turns on this choice of concept. In particular, if you feel that the notion of fitness should be cashed out in terms of a concept or concepts distinct from that of energy, that is fine. The considerations developed below will work for any concept of fitness. What is crucial is the view of evolution as a zero-sum competition for (regulatory) resources, whether or not all these resources ultimately reduce to energy.

If we assume that energy is the key conceptual constituent of the notion of fitness, we can develop the following account of the notion of evolutionary cost. First, let us define the notion of a *regulatory resource* (Van Valen 1976, 1980) as follows:

> A resource R is *regulatory* if and only if (i) the available quantity of R is limited (i.e., finite) and (ii) the use of a certain quantity q of R by organism O precludes the use of q by any other organism.

Energy is clearly a regulatory resource in this sense. The reason there is competition in the first place is that most of the resources essential to organisms are regulatory resources. The crucial feature of regulatory resources is this: for any regulatory resource, what one organism gains the rest lose. The result is a zero–sum competition where each organism seeks to maximize its control of its essential regulatory resources (Van Valen 1976).

Not only are most resources available to organisms regulatory in this sense, most are also *surrogate regulatory resources*:

> A resource R is a *surrogate regulatory resource* if and only if (i) R is a regulatory resource, and (ii) the control of resource R by organism O maximizes O's fitness only to the extent that it enables O to control another resource R_1 that is distinct from R.

From the point of view of the life processes, the only resource that is not surrogate in this sense is energy. Competition for surrogate resources is effective only to the extent that it permits greater control of trophic energy. Competition for surrogate resources reduces to competition for energy (Van Valen 1976).

If this is not already clear, then consider a particular essential resource. Phosphorus is sometimes thought to be essential to some aquatic communities. The brachiopod *Lingula*, for example, has a phosphatic shell, and so must compete for phosphorus with algae and other organisms. However, this degree of control of phosphorus is not selected for *per se*; any other suitable material would do equally well, and many shelled organisms use other materials. However, this is not true of potential energy in the form of reduced carbon. Any organism that can effectively obtain and exploit it will do so. Control of phosphorus for *Lingula* is useful only to the extent that it facilitates control of potential energy. Similarly, a plant in a desert, where energy from sunlight is in great excess, still maximizes its control of energy. It does so by maximizing its control of water (or, of whatever happens to regulate its population density). If gaining more water didn't give it more usable energy, then it would not gain more water.

Many kinds of surrogate regulatory resources exist, for different organisms and habitats, but the extent of their direct control is in every case subsidiary to, and dependent upon, their ultimate effect on the control of trophic energy. Energy is the only non-surrogate regulatory resource.

Since competition between organisms is competition to control regulatory resources, then the fitness of an organism is going to be a function of its capacity to control the regulatory resources that are essential to it. And, since energy is the only non-surrogate regulatory resource, it seems most useful to characterize the fitness of an organism in terms of its capacity to control trophic energy.

Therefore, as a first approximation, we can formulate the notion of the *realized absolute fitness* of an organism as follows (adopted, with minor modifications, from Van Valen 1976):

The absolute fitness of an organism O is directly proportional to the quantity of trophic energy controlled by O   (1)

The trophic energy controlled by an organism per unit time, however, can be broken down into (i) structural energy, (ii) maintenance energy, (iii) expansive energy, and (iv) reserve energy (Van Valen 1976, 1980).

Structural energy (E_s) is the energy contained in the materials of the organism's body. This is unavailable for growth and reproduction, but some of it is usually available for maintenance. Maintenance energy (E_m) is the energy required to maintain the organism in a viable state. Expansive energy (E_e) is the energy available to the organism for reproduction. Reserve energy (E_r) is external energy that is unavailable to competitors because it is defended, as by territoriality or allelopathy, but is not now being used by the organism. Strictly, one should also introduce the category of waste energy (E_w) as the energy contained in the egesta and excreta of the organism. However, for our purposes, this category proves relatively unimportant, and I propose to ignore it. Therefore, developing (1), we can say:

Absolute fitness of O = (Total trophic energy controlled by
O) − (E$_s$ + E$_m$ + E$_r$)   (2)

where E$_s$, E$_m$, and E$_r$ are all understood to be controlled by O and are measured per unit time; they are effectively rates. Thus, the absolute fitness of O is identified with the expansive energy controlled by O. If O is, for example, sterile, it will control no expansive energy; hence its absolute fitness will be zero.

What is important for our purposes, however, is not the notion of the absolute fitness of an organism, but what I shall refer to as *differential fitness*. The first point to note is that it makes sense to speak of not only the absolute fitness of an organism, but also its fitness in a particular respect. What underwrites this sort of talk are the following considerations. On the view advanced above, a positive adaptation to the environment is one which increases the adapted organism's control of trophic energy. Adapting to the environment in this sense, then, is a task: the task of increasing one's control of trophic energy. It is, moreover, a task that can be broken down into subsidiary tasks. Thus, the desert plant's task of controlling trophic energy breaks down, in part, into the task of controlling water. When an organism adapts positively to its environment, it is always by way of accomplishing some or other task. Accomplishing this task, however, necessarily involves some or other strategy. The strategy evolved by a desert plant, for example, might involve the development of longer roots so as to facilitate acquisition of ground water.

Given that this is so, it makes sense to speak not only of the absolute fitness of an organism but, also, of the effect that adopting a particular adaptative strategy has on that absolute fitness. That is, it makes sense to talk of whether adoption of a particular strategy of adaptation will increase or decrease a particular organism's realized absolute fitness. This change in an organism's realized absolute fitness brought about by adoption of a strategy of adaptation I shall call differential fitness. Since differential fitness is brought about by the adoption of a particular strategy of adaptation, differential fitness is always a function of, and therefore indexed to, a particular adaptative strategy. It will, therefore, be referred to by way of the expression *differential fitness*$_{(S)}$, where the subscript (S) denotes the relevant strategy.

Suppose an organism adapts to the environment through accomplishing a task T via a strategy S. The differential fitness engendered by adoption of S can, then, be represented as follows:

Differential Fitness$_{(S)}$ = Energy Assimilated$_{(S)}$ −
Energy Expended$_{(S)}$ (3)

where, Differential Fitness$_{(S)}$ is the change in realized absolute fitness
of the organism brought about by adoption of strategy S; Energy
Assimilated$_{(S)}$ is the energy that the adoption of S allows the organism
to assimilate or control; and Energy Expended$_{(S)}$ is the energy the
organism is obliged to invest in the adoption and performance of S.
When Differential Fitness$_{(S)}$ takes a positive value, then there has been
a positive adaptation to the environment and hence an increase in the
realized absolute fitness of the organism. Conversely, when
Differential Fitness$_{(S)}$ takes a negative value, there has been a negative
adaptation (or maladaptation) to the environment and a decrease in
the organism's realized absolute fitness.

The notion of evolutionary cost, as I shall use that expression, is to
be equated with the energy expended part of equation (3). That is, the
cost associated with adoption of a given evolutionary strategy by an
organism is the energy that must be expended (and, hence, which is
no longer controlled) by that organism. Conversely, the notion of the
evolutionary benefit that accrues to an organism through the successful pursuance of a given strategy is the energy that the organism is now
able to assimilate, or, more precisely, the additional energy that the
successful adoption of the strategy allows the organism to control.
Evolutionary development, as was stated earlier, is a process of balancing costs and benefits of this sort.

Suppose an organism O adopts a strategy S in order to accomplish
adaptive task T. What are the costs associated with the adoption of
S? To answer this, we must distinguish broadly between two types of
cost. On the one hand, there are what I shall call *implementational*
costs; on the other, there are *performance* costs. A desert plant that specializes in deep roots, for example, will incur the implementational
cost of investing certain genetic resources in the production of large
roots, and it will incur the performance cost of diverting extra energetic resources into the maintenance of such roots. Both these costs
are ultimately energetic costs − costs in the quantity of energy controlled by the organism, since possession and maintenance of genetic
material requires a certain expenditure of energy, and this is the quantity of energy embodied in the genetic material.

Therefore, when one is assessing the costs involved in the adoption
of a certain adaptative strategy, one must be careful to assess both

implementational and performance costs associated with that strategy. Suppose we have two organisms, O_1 and O_2, both of which need to be able to accomplish a certain adaptative task T. O_1 adopts a particular strategy S_1 in the performance of T, but O_2 adopts a distinct strategy S_2. Suppose that through the adoption of S_1 and S_2 respectively, O_1 and O_2 are able to accomplish T at an equal level of competence. That is, the benefits in the form of energy assimilation or control that accrue to O_1 and O_2 through the performance of S_1 and S_2 respectively, are identical. Even if we assume identity in the quantity of energy controlled resulting from adoption of S_1 and S_2, this does not mean, of course, that differential fitness$_{(S1)}$ is identical to differential fitness$_{(S2)}$. This would be so only if the costs incurred through the adoption of S_1 and S_2 were identical. And this is obviously not necessarily the case.

When assessing the relative costs of each strategy one must include both implementational and performance costs in the assessment. Consider, first, implementational costs. Suppose O_1 and O_2 each have the same (partial) string of genetic material which we can represent as:

A–B–C–D–E

The genetic string is, we shall suppose, the same for each organism, and, thus, in each organism embodies the same amount of free energy. Suppose that strategy S_1, adopted by O_1, involves investment of the genetic material A-B-C; that is, investment of genetic material A-B-C is necessary and sufficient for the implementation of strategy S_1. On the other hand, the implementation of strategy S_2, adopted by O_2, requires only the investment of genetic material –B–. That is, genetic material –B– is sufficient for implementation of strategy S_2. Then, if through the implementation of S_1 and S_2, O_1 and O_2 respectively are able to accomplish T at an equal level of competence (and, therefore, S_1 and S_2 bestow equal benefits from the point of view of energy control) it does not follow that differential fitness$_{(S1)}$ is identical with differential fitness$_{(S2)}$. And this is true even if we assume that the performance costs of S_1 and S_2 are the same. That is, it is not true that S_1 and S_2 are equally selectively advantageous adaptative strategies. The reason is that adoption of S_2 requires less investment of genetic resources than does adoption of S_1. That is, S_2 can be adopted at less implementational cost than S_1. Therefore, all other things being equal, the differential fitness associated with adoption of S_2 would be greater than the differential fitness associated with adoption of S_1. All other things (i.e., selective benefits and performance costs) being equal, adoption of S_2 would be more selectively advantageous than adoption of S_1.

One can give the same sort of account for the performance costs associated with a given strategy. Suppose that O_1's adoption of S_1, and O_2's adoption of S_2 involve the same investment of genetic resources, i.e., the same implementational costs. Then, if the performance costs associated with S_2 are less than those associated with S_1, then, once again, S_2 can be implemented at less cost than S_1 (O_2 catches flies by flicking out its tongue, O_1 leaps into the air and intercepts them). Again, the differential fitness associated with the adoption of S_2 would be greater than the differential fitness associated with S_1. All other things being equal, adoption of S_2 would be more selectively advantageous than adoption of S_1.

Therefore, with regard to the 'energy expended' part of equation (3), we can say that:

$$\text{Energy Expended}_{(S)} = \text{Implementational Costs}_{(S)} + \text{Performance Costs}_{(S)} \qquad (4)$$

where, energy expended$_{(S)}$ is the energy expended in the adoption of S; implementational costs$_{(S)}$ are the genetic–energetic resources invested in the adoption of S; and performance costs$_{(S)}$ are the day-to-day running costs of strategy S.

The energy assimilated part of (3) consists in the benefits which accrue to an organism through successful adoption of S. These benefits consist in the energy which the adoption of S allows the organism to control, and will primarily take the form of an increase in the expansive energy – the energy available for growth and reproduction – that is controlled by the organism. In certain circumstances, specifically when the energy controlled by the organism lies in structures that remain external to that organism, then the energy assimilated will take the form of what I have called reserve energy.

To summarize: evolutionary development involves adapting to the environment. Such adaptation is achieved through the accomplishment of certain tasks. Such tasks are accomplished by way of the adoption of certain strategies. And these strategies will bring with them both costs and benefits. The costs associated with adoption of a certain adaptative strategy comprise implementational and performance costs. Implementational costs are primarily made up of the genetic–energetic resources that must be invested in the strategy. Performance costs are primarily made up of the day-to-day energetic running costs of the strategy. The benefits associated with a given strategy comprise the expansive energy and (sometimes) the reserve energy that the strategy allows the organism to control.

In the next section I shall argue that the above sort of cost–benefit analysis of evolutionary development favours certain kinds of strategies over others. In particular, strategies that involve the manipulation by organisms of structures in their environment typically (but not necessarily, and perhaps not even always) have a more favourable cost–benefit analysis than strategies which do not. Strategies of the former sort are, therefore, typically more selectively advantageous than those of the latter sort. The former sort of strategy, then, is to be favoured on evolutionary grounds.

4.2 EVOLUTIONARY COST AND ENVIRONMENTAL MANIPULATION

Beavers build dams. The explanation of this dam-building behaviour goes something like this. A dam results in the creation of a miniature lake. The presence of the lake increases the distance the beaver is able to travel by water, and this is both safer than travelling by land and easier for transporting food. If a beaver lived on a stream only, then the supply of food trees lying along the stream bank would be quickly exhausted. By building a dam, the beaver creates a large shoreline that affords easy foraging without the beaver having to make long and hazardous overland journeys. So, the building of dams became incorporated into the beaver's evolution (Dawkins 1982:200). Things, of course, could have happened differently. Instead of investing in dam-building behaviour, the evolution of the beaver might have involved investing in ways which facilitated the beaver's ability to travel overland. Suppose that in the dim and distant evolutionary past the ancestor of the beaver had started evolving in two alternative ways. The first of these ways involved adopting the dam-building strategy and culminated in the sort of beaver with which we are familiar today. We will suppose, however, that the second evolutionary strategy completely eschewed dam-building behaviour and, instead, concentrated on making the beaver stronger, quicker, and more intelligent, thus increasing its efficiency in evading predators and transporting food on the long overland journeys it was obliged to make. This sort of strategy, therefore, involved investing in such features as increased muscle mass, larger brain, more powerful legs and torso, etc. So, in this thought experiment, evolution results in two very different types of beaver: the ordinary dam-building beaver, and the stronger, smarter, speedier super beaver.

The task, or rather tasks, that the beaver's ancestor had to accomplish were (i) the location/transport of food, and (ii) the evasion of predators. Let us refer to the conjunction of these tasks as 'T'. The ordinary beaver and the super beaver have attempted to accomplish T through the adoption of two alternative strategies. Let us refer to these as S_O (the strategy adopted by the ordinary beaver) and S_S (the strategy adopted by the super beaver). Let us suppose that the ordinary beaver and the super beaver are equally competent in the performance of T. That is, statistically speaking, the ability of the ordinary beaver to transport food and evade predators by way of strategy S_O is equal to the ability of the super beaver to transport food and evade predators by way of strategy S_S. That is, the benefits which accrue to the ordinary beaver and the super beaver through the adoption of S_O and S_S respectively, are the same. Or, to put the point in the idiom of the previous section, adoption of S_O and S_S allows the ordinary and super beaver respectively to control the same amount of trophic energy.

Does the fact that the ordinary and super beaver are equally competent (in the above sense) in the performance of T entail that the differential fitness associated with adoption of S_O is identical with the differential fitness associated with the adoption of S_S? In fact, it does not. It would entail this only if it could be shown that the cost of adopting S_S was equal to the cost of adopting S_O. However, this does not, in fact, seem to be the case. On the contrary, it would seem that the ability of the super beaver to transport food and evade predators has been bought at a greater cost than the corresponding ability of the ordinary beaver.

When assessing costs in this context, it is important to recognize both the implementational and the performance costs inherent in the adoption of a given strategy. Consider, first, how the implementational costs of the two strategies compare. The implementational costs of the ordinary beaver's strategy comprise largely the genetic resources necessary for the development and maintenance of the structures which allow the ordinary beaver to pursue its adaptive strategy. The primary structures, here, will be large, flat, powerful teeth and a flat tail, together with the musculatures that surround these structures. Compare these to the implementational costs of the super beaver's strategy. Firstly, the super beaver will require more powerful muscles for dragging its food on the long overland journeys it must make. Thus its limbs and torso must become more powerful (i.e., larger). Secondly, it must also possess the capacity to escape from the predators it will inevitably meet on these long overland journeys. Thus, it might have to become quicker, which might in turn generate the need for longer limbs, etc. It might also have to become more intelligent, thus creating a need for brain encephalization. At the very least, its sensory modalities would have to improve, allowing it earlier and more reliable detection of predators. This would again require some sort of encephalization. Moreover, should encephalization occur, then costs might start to multiply dramatically. Encephalization entails a larger brain, which, in turn, requires a larger head, which in turn leads to more weight at the front of the body. This must be balanced by added weight elsewhere, which, in turn, requires stronger, i.e., larger, muscles, and so on. Given that this is so, it seems reasonably clear that the implementational costs of the super beaver strategy are greater than those of the ordinary beaver strategy.

When we turn to performance costs, the disparity seems even greater. The performance cost of dragging food trees overland, perhaps long distances, remembering to run away from the predators one is likely to encounter, and making sure one's attention is constantly tuned to the possibility of predators, seems to be far greater than the cost of depositing the food trees in the lake and letting the lake do most of the work for you, particularly when this procedure also removes the risk of predation. Of course, in terms of performance costs, the ordinary beaver's strategy requires a significant initial outlay in the form of building a dam. However, when you compare this outlay with the alternative of daily overland journeys dragging heavy food trees, then it seems fairly clear that this outlay would soon be compensated for. The situation is very much like catching a horse and then using it. There is a significant initial outlay in the energetic costs of catching the horse, but this outlay is soon outweighed by the benefits of getting the horse to do much of your work for you. If this was not the case, then there would have been no future in the horse-catching strategy. Or compare the initial outlay involved in building a bicycle with the benefits that arise from its completion. The latter outweigh the former. This is, of course, why our ancestors' strategy of building tools has been so successful.

Therefore, both the implementational and performance costs of the ordinary beaver strategy seem to be less than those of the super beaver strategy. That is, the resources that the super beaver has invested in its ability to transport food and avoid predators are greater than the resources that the ordinary beaver has invested in the corresponding ability. Therefore, if we assume that each strategy is equally effective in the performance of T – the conjunction of the tasks of transporting food and avoiding predators – then the differential fitness associated with S_O (the ordinary beaver strategy) is greater than the differential fitness associated with S_S (the super beaver strategy). The super beaver has invested more resources in the performance of T than has the ordinary beaver. And if this is so, the super beaver will have less resources to invest in the possession of other capacities, and this deficit must be felt somewhere else in the super beaver's biological economy. It is because the (ultimately energetic) resources available to an organism are strictly finite, and, thus, that investing a certain quantity of resources in one strategy makes those resources unavailable for investment in other strategies, that the notion of differential fitness ultimately makes sense.

Therefore, the differential fitness associated with S_O is, it seems, greater than the differential fitness associated with S_S. This is because S_O can be adopted at less cost (in terms of energy expended) than S_S. Therefore, all other things being equal, it seems that the quicker, stronger, smarter super beaver would, in fact, be less fit than the ordinary dam-building beaver.

It is important, I think, to be clear on the status and role of the *ceteris paribus* clause, here. And to do this, it is necessary to be clear on the distinction between absolute fitness and differential fitness introduced earlier. The claim is not, of course, that the ordinary beaver would be fitter in an absolute sense than the super beaver. The absolute fitness of the two types of beaver obviously depends on a lot more than their performance with respect to a single task, or small number of tasks. It depends, at the very least, on how they respond to the whole gamut of tasks set them by evolution. The central claim made above is that, with respect to task T, and the strategies, S_O and

S_S, the ordinary beaver and the super beaver have respectively adopted for accomplishing T, the differential fitness of the ordinary beaver is greater than that of the super beaver. This claim is *not* qualified by a *ceteris paribus* clause. If we assume, however, that the differential fitness the beaver and the super beaver possess with respect to all the other tasks set them by evolution are equal, that is, if we assume they accomplish these other tasks equally effectively and with the investment of an equal amount of resources, then, in virtue of the difference in their differential fitness with respect to the conjunctive task of finding food and evading predators, the ordinary beaver would be more fit, in an absolute sense, than the super beaver. Thus, in the above discussion, talk of all things being equal simply refers to an imagined equality in the ratio of task effectiveness to resource investment possessed by the two types of beaver with respect to all the other tasks evolution sets them. Insertion of a *ceteris paribus* clause, then, does not introduce some vague, open-ended, and indeterminate list of conditions. Its meaning is reasonably precise, and its extension relatively circumscribed. Therefore, the claim defended above is really a conjunction of claims: (i) with respect to task T (finding food and evading predators) the differential fitness of the ordinary beaver would be greater than that of the super beaver, and (ii) *ceteris paribus*, the absolute fitness of the ordinary beaver is greater than that of the super beaver. The *ceteris paribus* clause is to be understood in the sense described above; that is, as denoting an assumption that with respect to all the other tasks evolution sets them, the ordinary beaver and the super beaver accomplish these tasks with equal effectiveness and with an equal investment of resources.

The above remarks may prompt the following question: how do we know, in any given case, whether the *ceteris paribus* conditions are satisfied? The answer to this is, of course, that, at least in many cases, we do not know. Happily, however, this is completely irrelevant to the concerns of this chapter. The central claim defended in this chapter is that, with respect to a given task T, a manipulative strategy for accomplishing T results in greater *differential* fitness than a non-manipulative one. Other than pointing out the connection between differential fitness and absolute fitness, this chapter makes no claims about the absolute fitness of organisms. The argument to be developed with regard to cognitive processes does not rely on, or in any way require, the notion of absolute fitness. Thus, I am not, as some might think, exhibiting undue confidence that things are equal (often enough). The question of whether other things are, in fact, equal is simply irrelevant to the concerns of this chapter. These concerns are with differential fitness, not absolute fitness; and so the question of undue reliance on *ceteris paribus* clauses, simply does not arise.

Therefore, there is *no* claim – explicit or implicit – in the above argument that creatures that employ, for a given task, a manipulative strategy are thereby fitter in an absolute sense than those that do not. A beaver is *not* more fit than, for example, an otter, just because it builds dams while the otter does not. Nor, to anticipate a future example, are cuckoos more fit in an absolute sense than other birds simply because they implement a manipulative strategy with respect to the task of raising their offspring while other birds do not. The arguments of this chapter require, and therefore focus upon, the notion of differential fitness. And the claim defended above is that, with respect to a given evolutionary task, a manipulative strategy is productive of more differential fitness than a non-manipulative one.

4.3 BARKING DOGS AND THE NOT SO OBVIOUS

Reflections of the above sort suggest the following very general principle: for the purposes of performing a given task, do not evolve internal mechanisms which are sufficient for performing that task when it is possible to perform it by way of manipulation of the environment. That is, from the standpoint of evolutionary fitness, it is in general more *differentially selectively advantageous* to accomplish a given task, or solve a particular problem (transporting food, avoiding predators etc.) through the development of capacities to manipulate the environment rather than through the development of internal structures or mechanisms. And this is because, generally speaking, the ability of an organism to manipulate its environment in the performance of a given task can be purchased at less evolutionary cost than can any internal structures which, by themselves, are sufficient for performing that task.

There is an old adage that seems to capture the import of this principle quite nicely: *why keep a dog if you are going to bark yourself.* Or, closer to the present point, if you do have a dog, then you do not have to bark yourself. And getting your dog to do your barking for you will save you considerable investment of resources (i.e., energy). We can call this the *barking dog principle* (BD), and give it a more precise formulation as follows:

> BD: If it is necessary for an organism to be able to perform a given adaptive task T, then it is differentially selectively *dis*advantageous for that organism to develop internal mechanisms sufficient for the performance of T when it is possible for the organism to perform T by way of a combination of internal mechanisms and manipulation of the external environment.

That is, given the 'option' of two evolutionary strategies, (1) developing internal mechanisms $m_1, m_2 \ldots m_n$ which, by themselves, provide sufficient conditions for an organisms's possessing a capacity to perform a given task T, and (2) developing internal mechanisms $m_1^\star$, $m_2^\star \ldots m_n^\star$ which, when combined with a certain type of environmental manipulation, provide sufficient conditions for the organism's possessing the capacity to perform T, then the second type of strategy is differentially selectively advantageous relative to the first. That is, the differential fitness associated with adoption of the latter strategy is greater than that associated with adoption of the first. This is because, I shall argue, in general, the second type of strategy can be adopted at less evolutionary cost (understood as the algebraic sum of implementational and performance costs) than strategies of the first sort. The second strategy involves less investment of resources which are, therefore, available for employment elsewhere in the organism's economy.

There is another extremely important point that emerges from the example of the beaver. In manipulating the environment, *some* internal structures or mechanisms must be developed. The (ordinary) beaver, in order to implement its particular adaptive strategy, must have evolved structures such as large flat teeth suitable for cutting through wood, powerful jaws, large flat tail, etc. And the strategy adopted by the beaver will, implementationally speaking, be selectively advantageous *vis-à-vis* the alternative strategy of the super beaver only if the resources which must be invested in the development of these structures (teeth, tail, etc.) are less than the resources which must be invested in implementing the alternative super beaver strategy, that is, the resources which go into developing more powerful leg muscles, larger brain, etc. So, the claim that the beaver can perform a given task, for example, transporting food, through manipulation of the environment is not only compatible with, but, in fact, *requires*, the postulation of various appropriate internal structures and mechanisms. However, and this point is crucial, the structures and mechanisms developed in conjunction with the manipulation of the environment may be not at all obvious ones given the nature of the task or problem at hand. One does not need a precise criterion of obviousness to appreciate this point. If we were told that the adaptive task in question was one of enabling a smallish furry creature to transport food and/or avoid predators, then the inference to the development of big flat teeth, useful for cutting through wood but not much else, and a big flat tail is by no means obvious. The importance of this point cannot be overemphasized. Once we allow that the performance of a given task can involve, in part, manipulation of the environment, then the internal mechanisms which are necessary for the execution of this particular strategy may be very different from what we might initially expect.

I shall call this the *principle of the non-obvious character of evolved internal mechanisms* (NOC):

NOC: For the performance of a given task T, and for any internal mechanism M which has evolved in organism O and which, when combined with suitable environmental manipulation on the part of O, allows O to perform T, the nature of M is not always obvious on the basis of T.

The non-obvious character of evolved internal mechanisms derives from the fact that it is not the mechanisms alone which perform the relevant task but the mechanisms in conjunction with suitable environmental manipulation on the part of the organism. In the case where internal mechanisms alone are sufficient for performing a given task T there would, perhaps, be a fairly perspicuous connection between the nature of these mechanisms and the nature of T. The more that environmental manipulation plays a role in the performance of T, however, the less perspicuous the connection between the task and the internal mechanisms becomes.

The remainder of this chapter will try to do two things. Firstly, the principles BD and NOC will be defended. Secondly, I shall argue that BD and NOC can legitimately be extended into the cognitive domain; that is, BD and NOC also apply to cognition and the structures and mechanisms that subserve cognitive processes. The next couple of sections will be concerned with defence of BD and NOC.

In the next section I shall amass an array of biological examples to show not only that the *manipulate the environment* strategy favoured by the beaver is a pervasive biological phenomenon, but also that the BD and NOC principles clearly apply to these cases, and thereby explain why it is such a pervasive biological phenomenon. The section following that will consider, and hopefully rebuff, some objections to BD and NOC.

4.4 THE 'MANIPULATE THE ENVIRONMENT' STRATEGY AT WORK

Cases similar to that of the beaver are easy to find. Not all ways of manipulating the environment, however, need be so obviously intrusive. Consider, for example, how a sponge 'manipulates' its environment in order to ingest food (Clark 1989). Sponges feed by filtering water, and thus require water to pass through them. This is partially achieved by way of small flagella that are capable of pumping water at a rate of one bodily volume every five seconds. However, sponges also exploit the structure of their environment to reduce the amount of pumping involved. Various adapted features – incurrent openings facing upstream, valves closing incurrent pores lateral and downstream, suction from large distal excurrent openings, and so on – make it possible for sponges to exploit ambient water currents to aid the flow of water through them. It is easy to see how such exploitation would reduce the resources the sponge needs to invest in its feeding activities. More precisely, the performance costs of adopting this sort of strategy are obviously lower than those that would be involved in a pumping strategy alone. The implementational costs are more ambiguous. However, if a sponge relied on pumping alone, and did not seek to exploit the ambient water currents, then it would need either a larger or a more efficient pumping apparatus in order to process water at the same rate as a sponge that did exploit the ambient currents. Developing a larger or more efficient pumping apparatus would require greater genetic investment, and this would raise the implementational costs. Therefore, the implementational costs of the strategy which eschews exploitation of ambient currents are at least as high as, and very probably higher, than those of the strategy that incorporates environmental exploitation. Therefore, the *differential* fitness associated with the exploitation of the environment strategy is greater than the differential fitness associated with the non-exploitative strategy. That is, the strategy that involves exploitation of the water currents is differentially selectively advantageous relative to the strategy which does not. Therefore, also, *all things being equal*, a sponge which exploited the environment in this way would be at an *absolute* selective advantage over a sponge that did not, even if the latter had a larger pumping apparatus which allowed it to process food at the same rate. The extra (genetic cum energetic) resources which would inevitably be invested in the pumping apparatus would not be available for incorporation elsewhere in the sponge's economy.

In this case, the sponge's manipulation of its environment is a lot less intrusive than the kind of manipulation employed by the beaver. The beaver changes its environment, the sponge does not, or does so only minimally. In fact, 'exploitation' seems a better word for what the sponge does to its environment. In practice, I think, manipulation and exploitation are two sides of the same coin; each shades by degree into the other. The barking dog principle advanced above should be understood as enjoining against the development of internal structures or mechanisms for the performance of a particular task when that task can be performed through either manipulation *or* exploitation of the environment. The case of the sponge, then provides a good example of the barking dog principle at work.

The environment that an organism can exploit or manipulate includes not just inanimate structures or objects but also other creatures. Sometimes this is true in the quite dramatic sense that one organism, a parasite for example, is spatially located inside another host organism. The environment of the parasite is thus made up of nothing but a living organism. And there is impressive documented evidence of the way in which parasites can survive by exploiting or manipulating their hosts. And the notion of manipulation, here, includes manipulation of both the structure and behaviour of host organisms.

Parasites that have a life cycle involving an intermediate host, from which they have to move to a definitive host, often manipulate the behaviour of the intermediate host to make it more likely to be consumed by the definitive host. For example, there are two species of acanthocephalan worm, *Polymorphus paradoxus* and *P. marilis* which both use a freshwater shrimp, *Gammarus lacustris*, as an intermediate host, and which both use ducks as their definitive host. The definitive host of *P. paradoxus*, however, is generally a mallard which is a surface-dabbling duck. *P. marilis*, on the other hand, specializes in diving ducks. *P. paradoxus*, then, should benefit from making its shrimps swim to the surface, while *P. marilis* would benefit from its shrimps avoiding the surface. Uninfected shrimps tend to avoid the light, and, therefore, stay close to the lake bottom. However, when a *G. lacustris* becomes infected with *paradoxus* it behaves very differently. It then stays close to the surface, often clinging stubbornly to surface plants. This behaviour presumably makes it vulnerable to predation by mallards (Holmes & Bethel 1972; Bethel & Holmes 1973, 1977).

Polymorphus paradoxus, no doubt, might have evolved in a different way. That is, it might have adopted a different evolutionary strategy. Instead of developing a capacity to manipulate the behaviour of its intermediate host, it might instead have developed structures and mechanisms which enabled it to make its way to its definitive host under its own steam, as it were. But think of what successful adoption of this alternative strategy would involve. Firstly, *P. paradoxus* would have to develop structures which enabled it to break out of its inter-mediate host. Secondly, it would require structures which enabled it to move, under its own power, to the region where its definitive host is to be found. Thirdly, since it is now obliged to journey from its intermediate to definitive host, it would also perhaps have to develop some means of evading any predators which are not suitable hosts. It seems fairly clear that this alternative strategy can be bought only at a considerably higher cost than the actual strategy of *P. paradoxus*. The performance costs of fighting your way out of your host, making your own way to the surface, avoiding any non-suitable hosts you might happen to meet on the way, and so on, are clearly greater than those of a strategy which lets your intermediate host do all this work for you. The implementational costs are also almost certainly lower. The actual strategy of *P. paradoxus* involves producing a chemical that alters the behaviour of *G. lacustris*. Thus, certain genetic resources will have to be invested in the production of this chemical. However, these resources seem small compared to those which would have to be invested in the alternative strategy. The imagined counterfactual strategy requires production not only of new structures for breaking out of *G. lacustris*, but also of structures necessary for making one's way to the surface, avoiding predators, etc. It seems fairly clear that this strategy would require greater implementational resources than the actual strategy of *P. paradoxus*.

Therefore, at least intuitively, the costs – both performance and implementational – of the manipulate the shrimp strategy are lower than those of the alternative non-manipulative strategy. This is because in the manipulative strategy it is the shrimp, *G. lacustris*, that does most of the necessary work for *P. paradoxus*. Therefore, without too much precision being required, it is fairly safe to say that, all things being equal, greater differential fitness would accrue to the organism which manipulates the shrimp than one which does not, even if both were equally competent at finding their way into their definitive hosts. The greater investment of resources required by the worm which does not manipulate the shrimp would inevitably show up as a relative loss somewhere else in the worm's biological economy. Relative to the strategy of manipulating the behaviour of the shrimp, the strategy of developing suitable internal structures or mechanisms sufficient for the transition to the definitive host would be *differentially* selectively disadvantageous. Therefore, also, *ceteris paribus*, adopting the non-manipulative strategy would result in the shrimp being at an *absolute* selective disadvantage relative to the shrimp with the manipulative strategy. Once again, however, I must reiterate that the arguments developed here concern only, and require only, the notion of differential fitness, not that of absolute fitness. The claim is that manipulative strategies place their employers at a differential selective advantage over the users of non-manipulative strategies, not that they place the former at an absolute selective advantage over the latter. The ultimate purpose of this chapter is to develop an argument pertaining to cognitive processes. And, for this purpose, it is only the notion of differential fitness, and not that of absolute fitness, that is required.

There is, in fact, nothing very different between the case of the worm manipulating the shrimp and that of the beaver manipulating the world around it. Both are cases of an organism manipulating its environment in order to secure a selectively advantageous state of affairs. For the acanthocephalan worm, its environment *is* the shrimp. The barking dog principle applies equally in both cases.

The case of the acanthocephalan worm manipulating the behaviour of its host is by no means isolated or unusual. Indeed, it seems to be a fairly common evolutionary strategy. The case of the fluke, or 'brainworm' *Dicrocoelium dendriticum* provides another useful example of this sort of strategy. The definitive host of the fluke is an ungulate such as a sheep, and the intermediate hosts are first a snail and then an ant. The normal life cycle requires the ant to be eaten by the sheep. It seems that the fluke achieves this by burrowing into the brain (specifically, the sub-oesophageal ganglion) of the ant and, thereby, changing the ant's behaviour. And the difference in behaviour is quite noticeable. For example, whereas an uninfected ant would normally retreat into the nest when it becomes cold, infected ants climb to the top of grass stems. Here they are vulnerable to being eaten by the sheep. Note also that the changes in ant behaviour are not indiscriminate. The infected ant, like the normal ant, does retreat down the grass stem to avoid death from the midday heat, since this would be bad for the parasite also. Nevertheless, the ant returns to its elevated resting position when the sun has cooled sufficiently during the course of the afternoon (Wickler 1976; Love 1980).

Once again, the 'manipulate the ant' strategy adopted by *D. dendriticum* seems to be procurable at less evolutionary cost than any alternative non-manipulative strategy. A strategy of the latter sort would require investment in structures or mechanisms which enable the fluke not only to escape from the ant, but also to survive in the 'wild' until ingested by a suitable itinerant ungulate. It is fairly clear that this is a much more complex, hence more difficult, strategy to execute than the actual strategy employed by *D. dendriticum*. Hence, it would require a correspondingly greater investment of genetic–energetic resources than the 'manipulate the ant' strategy. Once again, the reason why the manipulative strategy involves less investment of resources than its non-manipulative alternative is because, in the former strategy but not the latter, much of the necessary work is done by the outside world, in this case another organism.

In the above examples, the imagined alternatives to *P. paradoxus* and *D. dendriticum* are, of course, purely heuristic devices. Indeed, given the constraints of evolutionary processes outlined at the beginning of this chapter, there are good reasons for thinking that not only do the parasites *not* exist, but also that they *could not* exist. This, however, does not detract from the central point of the above examples. This is that manipulative strategies for accomplishing tasks can be implemented at less overall cost than non-manipulative ones, hence that successful manipulative strategies bring with them greater differential fitness than successful non-manipulative ones. This is clearly distinct from the claim, which I do *not* endorse, that non-manipulative strategies would not evolve because they could never work. Clearly, non-manipulative strategies for accomplishing tasks have evolved, and clearly they do work. My point is simply that where we have a successful non-manipulative strategy for accomplishing a task and also an equally successful manipulative strategy, the latter will bring with it greater differential fitness than the former.

Many parasites live inside the body of their hosts. However, this is not true of all parasites. Indeed, some parasites may seldom come into contact with their hosts. A cuckoo is a parasite in much the same way as *P. paradoxus* or *D. dendriticum*. This second form of parasitism, extraneous parasitism, if you like, provides us with another way in which one organism can exploit or manipulate another so as to minimize the utilization of its own resources.

Brood parasitism provides a very good example of the extraneous manipulation of one organism by another. A parent bird, such as a reed-warbler, transports a large supply of food from a relatively large catchment area back to its nest. Brood parasites such as the cuckoo make a living by intercepting this flow of food. The reed-warbler, of course, is not a natural altruist. The cuckoo must not only have its body inserted in the host's nest; it must also have the means of manipulating its supplier. And to this end it has evolved various features which allow it to manipulate the reed-warbler's nervous system. By way of key stimuli, the cuckoo is able to manipulate – to engage and employ for its own purposes – the host's parental care mechanisms (Wickler 1968; Dawkins 1982:67). Most importantly, the young cuckoo, with its huge gape and loud begging call, has evolved, in a grossly exaggerated form, the stimuli which elicit the feeding response of parent birds. In fact, so much is this so that there are many records of adult birds feeding a fledged young cuckoo raised by a different host species. This demonstrates successful exploitation or manipulation by means of a *supernormal* stimulus. The cuckoo achieves the task of feeding and raising its offspring not by the sweat of its own brow, but through the manipulation of others (Dawkins 1982:67).

Therefore, relative to the task of raising its young, this strategy of the cuckoo obviously involves a huge reduction in performance costs. In fact the performance costs are reduced to just about zero: after the cuckoo has laid its eggs it can then completely forget about them.

Some genetic resources will have been invested in development of the supernormal stimulus. But it is surely clear that, whatever small increase in implementational costs there might be (and it is not even clear that there must be an increase here), this is more than offset by the virtual elimination of performance costs. Therefore, all other things being equal, the cuckoo's strategy of manipulation is selectively advantageous relative to the more traditional approach of other birds.

Again, one must be clear about what is being claimed here. Most importantly, there is nothing here which entails that cuckoos are more fit than birds that raise their young by more orthodox means. We must be careful to distinguish differential from absolute fitness. The claim is that the manipulative strategy adopted by the cuckoo brings with it more differential fitness than more orthodox non-manipulative strategies. Therefore, it places the cuckoo at what I have called a differential selective advantage over other birds with respect to the task of raising offspring. However, it does not follow from this that cuckoos are at an absolute selective advantage over other birds. This would depend on a variety of factors including, most importantly, how well the cuckoo responds to and accomplishes, relative to other birds, the whole spectrum of tasks set it by evolution. The concerns of this chapter are purely with the differential fitness associated with particular tasks, not with absolute fitness.

The extraneous manipulation of one organism by another is not restricted to brood parasitism. For example, the angler fish, in effect, manipulates the nervous system of its prey. An angler fish sits on the sea bottom and is highly camouflaged except for a long rod projecting from the top of its head. On the end of the rod is the *lure*, a piece of tissue which resembles some appetizing morsel such as a worm. Small fish are attracted by the lure which resembles their own prey. When they approach it, the angler entices them into the vicinity of its mouth, which it then suddenly opens causing the prey to be swept in by the inrush of water (Dawkins 1982:60). Instead of using massive body and tail muscles, the angler uses the small economical muscles controlling his rod. It is the prey's own muscles that the angler uses to close the gap between them. The difference in performance costs between this manipulative strategy and a non-manipulative alternative is, of course, extremely significant. The implementational costs are less clear cut. Genetic resources have to be invested in the rod and lure, of course. However, there seems to be no reason why these costs would be any greater than those which would have to have been invested in larger body and tail muscles should the angler have adopted a non-manipulative strategy. Therefore, once again, it seems that the manipulative strategy of the angler fish can be adopted at less evolutionary cost than non-manipulative alternatives. Relative to those non-manipulative alternatives, this *manipulate the environment* strategy is, again, differentially selectively advantageous.

Examples of this sort could be multiplied indefinitely. Similar principles emerge, for example, when we switch the focus from predatory to reproductive behaviour. Male crickets do not physically drag their female partners along the ground and into their burrows. Instead, they sit and sing, and the females come to them under their own power (Dawkins & Krebs 1978; Dawkins 1982:59–64). From the point of view of performance costs, this type of communication is much more efficient than trying to take a partner by force. In a similar vein, male canaries have not developed the means of injecting gonadotrophins or oestrogens into female canaries, thus bringing them into reproductive condition. Instead they sing. The male does not have to synthesize and inject gonadotrophins, he makes the female's pituitary do the work for him (Dawkins 1982:63–4). Evolution, presumably, could have done it differently. Male canaries might have evolved structures for the production of gonadotrophins and their injection into females. But, once we appreciate the concept of evolutionary cost, it is clear that this strategy, relative to the actual one, would be selectively disadvantageous: it would almost certainly be more costly than the actual one, from the point of view of both implementational and performance costs.

These examples merely scratch the surface of manipulative behaviour in the animal kingdom. It would be possible to devote a whole book to the behaviour of ants alone in this regard. These examples, however, are presumably sufficient to show that, in the performance of some adaptive tasks at least, the *manipulate the environment* strategy is widespread, incorporating such behaviours as diverse as predation, evasion of predators, reproduction, rearing of young, feeding and gaining access to food, locating suitable habitats, etc. Moreover, the examples also indicate why the strategy should be widespread. In each of the cases described above, it is fairly clear that the strategy of manipulating the environment can be adopted at less evolutionary cost – either implementational or performance or both – than strategies that do not involve such manipulation. That the sponge should allow ambient currents to feed water through it rather than pump the water by its own efforts is an obvious saving in performance costs at no extra implementational cost. That the acanthocephalan worm *P. paradoxus* should manipulate the shrimp to facilitate its ingestion by its definitive host the mallard is, again, a clear saving in performance cost at no extra, indeed almost certainly less, implementational cost. That *D. dendriticum* should manipulate the ant in order to facilitate ingestion by its definitive host is, again, a clear saving in performance cost at no extra, indeed almost certainly less, implementational cost. And so on. The *manipulate the environment* strategy is, from an evolutionary point of view, an extremely cost-effective method of accomplishing a given evolutionary task. Thus, typically, a strategy which involves manipulating the environment in order to accomplish some adaptively specified task is more *differentially* selectively advantageous than a strategy which eschews such manipulation. The crucial point is that, when an organism adopts a manipulative strategy, the organism can get the environment to do much of the necessary work for it, and this is what reduces the evolutionary cost of the strategy.

The cases described above, then, provide clear examples of BD, the barking dog principle. How about NOC, the principle of the non-obvious character of evolved characteristics? Again, most of the above cases provide good illustrations of this also. That, when faced with the adaptive task of moving from its intermediate host, *P. paradoxus* should have evolved the capacity to produce a certain chemical is by no means obvious, unless we know about the possibilities for manipulation of *G. lacustris*. That, when faced with the adaptive task of persuading a female to copulate with it, the male canary should have evolved the capacity to sing is, again, by no means obvious unless we know about the possibilities for manipulation of the female's pituitary. That, when faced with the adaptive task of raising their offspring, the cuckoo should have evolved a huge gape and loud begging call is, once again, by no means obvious unless we understand the possibilities for the manipulation of passerine birds. This is the principal message of NOC. If we focus on the single organism alone, and neglect the relations, in particular manipulative relations, that the organism enters into with its environment, and with objects in its environment, then the structures, mechanisms, and methods by which the organism accomplishes various adaptive tasks will be by no means obvious ones. Focusing on the individual organism alone will inevitably lead to our failure to understand how the organism accomplishes many of its adaptive tasks. For the structures, mechanisms, and methods employed by organisms in performing adaptive tasks only make sense when seen in the wider context of how the organism is able to manipulate structures in its environment in order to facilitate their performance of these tasks.

In conclusion, then, *manipulate the environment* strategies seem to be widespread in the biological domain. The barking dog principle, BD, explains why this should be so. And NOC, the principle of the non-obvious character of evolved characteristics, is a corollary of them.

4.5 OBJECTIONS AND REPLIES

One important objection to the line of argument developed above might run as follows: 'How do we know, in specific cases, whether it is in fact more costly to develop an internal mechanism in order to accomplish a given adaptive task than to find a way to exploit or manipulate a feature of the environment? The danger is that we might identify some of the costs that enable us to defend the story we want to tell, but fail to notice others that would point in the opposite direction.' We might call this the *hidden costs* objection.

This is, I think, a legitimate concern. However, one must be careful not to push it too far. Firstly, a methodological point. The question of costs versus benefits involved in any adaptive strategy is, of course, an empirical question which can be answered only by a detailed empirical investigation. This book is, of course, not such an investigation, and it would be hubris of the highest order to present the arguments of this chapter in such a way. The purpose of this book, and the arguments of this chapter in particular, is to create a *presumption* in favour of the *manipulate the environment* strategy. And it attempts to do this by showing that it *seems very likely* that the costs of the *manipulate the environment* strategy are less than those of alternative non-manipulative strategies, or that *as far as we can tell* the costs of manipulative strategies are less than those of non-manipulative strategies. The cases described in the preceding sections are, thus, intended to create a presumption in favour of the manipulate the environment strategy, not to demonstrate conclusively that the *manipulate the environment* strategy can be adopted at less evolutionary cost.

Secondly, and most importantly, there seems to be something fundamentally unsound, at the methodological level at least, with the hidden costs objection. The essential idea underlying the argument developed in the preceding pages is as follows. *If you can get someone or something else to do some of your work for you, you will have less to do yourself.* That is, if you are faced with a certain task which you must accomplish, and if this task requires a certain quantity of work be put into it for its successful completion, then the more you can get someone or something else to put in this work, the less work you will have to put in yourself. This, ultimately, is a principle of mechanics, not biology, governing the behaviour of any system that is required to do work. And, as such, it seems scarcely contestable. However, it is also true that we must add an important qualification to the above principle. That is, it is also true that getting someone or something else to do some of your work for you requires you to invest some work – in persuasion, manipulation, or whatever. And the whole procedure will result in a net saving of work for you if, and only if, the amount of work you have to put in to getting this someone or something else to do some of your work for you is less than the amount of work they or it actually contribute to the task at hand. It is this qualification that is seized upon by the hidden costs objection.

What motivates the objection is the possibility of costs that were not recognized or noticed in the identification of the costs involved in manipulative strategies. Such hidden costs are, of course, perfectly possible. However, the appeal to them in this context is methodologically suspect. The reason is that hidden costs can cut both ways. Suppose you attach your car to your neighbour's car, thus getting a *free ride*. Your performance costs are thus substantially reduced. It could be objected, of course, that hooking up your car in this way involves a certain (implementational) investment – towing hitches, welding, etc. And the obvious reply here is that the extra implementational costs are outweighed by the reduction in performance costs. However, it could then be objected: 'How do you know there are not any hidden costs, ones which you have not even thought of, in the hooking up of your car to your neighbours?' This sort of introduction of hidden costs would be methodologically dubious. The answer to the question, in brief, is that we do not know that there are no hidden costs. However, we do not have any reason to suppose there are hidden costs. And, crucially, we have just as much reason to suppose there are hidden costs that we have not thought of with *not* hooking the car up; i.e., hidden costs in the normal running of our car. This is the reason why the raising of the possibility of hidden costs against the manipulative strategy is methodologically suspect: there is as much reason to suppose that non-manipulative strategies have hidden costs, as to suppose that manipulative strategies have them. In other words, the possibility of hidden costs cuts both ways, and, therefore, cannot be used as objection specifically to manipulative strategies. The methodological moral seems to be this. Hidden costs are possible, but, since they cut both ways, it is better, in arguments of this sort, to bracket them off and focus on manifest costs. The possibility of hidden costs cannot be allowed to function as a sort of general and nebulous methodological *angst*. Costs should be considered only when they become manifest.

Another possible objection to the arguments of this chapter focuses on the longer-term benefits of internalist, non-manipulative, strategies: 'Why, in the long run, can't non-manipulative strategies be more beneficial, having a pay-off which manipulative strategies do not have?' This objection acknowledges that, in the short term, manipulative strategies can be achieved at less cost, but claims that the long-term benefits which accrue to organisms that have adopted non-manipulative strategies can outweigh this reduction in cost. Therefore, in the long run, manipulative strategies could be less selectively advantageous than non-manipulative strategies even though they can be implemented at less evolutionary cost. This is, in effect, a *hidden benefits* objection.

The reasoning behind this objection goes something like this. Suppose we have a certain task, T, say lifting a weight. A manipulative strategy for performing this task might involve getting somebody else to lift the weight for you. A non-manipulative strategy might involve engaging in a programme of body-building until you are capable of lifting the weight yourself. Now, clearly, in the short term, for the accomplishment of particular token task T, the manipulative strategy involves a substantial reduction in performance costs (assuming that it is not too difficult getting the other person to do the work for you). However, it could be argued, the non-manipulative strategy has ramifications not only for the present task but also for your future abilities. After engaging in the body-building programme you are now able to perform many tasks of which you were not physically capable before. Thus, it could be argued, in the long run, implementing the non-manipulative strategy would be more beneficial, hence more selectively advantageous.

It is this sort of argument, I think, which underlies much of the resistance to the implications of the *manipulate the environment* strategy. The feeling is that, while developing dedicated internal structures and mechanisms may be more difficult, and, hence, require a greater investment of resources, nevertheless, this greater investment of resources will be more than outweighed by the fact that these internal structures will endow one with the ability to perform many other sorts of tasks, tasks beyond the original one for which the structures were evolved in the first place.

There are at least two major problems with this line of reasoning, however. Firstly, as with hidden costs, hidden benefits cut both ways. Just as a non-manipulative strategy might produce unexpected long-term benefits, so, also, might a manipulative strategy. The strategy of the beaver not only allows it to transport food and evade predators, it also provides it with somewhere to live. Hidden benefits cut both ways, and, therefore, the appeal to them as an objection to the arguments of this chapter is just as methodologically unsound as the appeal to hidden costs.

Secondly, and even more seriously, the hidden benefits objection misunderstands the nature of evolution. In particular, evolution does not act *in the long run*. That is, evolutionary pressures do not select for long-term advantage over short-term disadvantage. Quite the contrary. Evolution crosses each bridge as it comes to it, and has no conception of the possibility of further bridges. Now, while it might be an extremely good thing for an organism to develop internal structures to perform a given task since these structures might give it the capacity to perform other important tasks also, the fact that it is a good thing cannot possibly be recognized by evolution. There may be good reasons to develop internal structures in this context, but these are not, and cannot be, good *evolutionary* reasons. Evolution does not act *in the long run*. Therefore, in assessing the relative costs and benefits of each strategy we must focus on the individual tasks themselves, and on the strategies adopted to meet them. We are not allowed to focus on possible extensions of these strategies to other, as yet unknown, tasks, since evolution is blind to the possibility of such tasks.

Environmentalism and evolution

4.6 BD, NOC, AND COGNITIVE PROCESSES

If the argument developed so far is correct, we have prima-facie reason to believe that manipulative strategies for the solution of a task T result in greater differential fitness, with respect to T, than do non-manipulative strategies. The reason is prima facie in the sense that it can be overridden. And it can be overridden because hidden costs or hidden benefits are always a possibility. None the less, the appeal to them as a general methodological worry is illegitimate. Therefore, we have prima-facie reason to suppose that manipulative strategies are, in this sense, and in this sense only, *better* solutions to problems set by evolution.

BD claims that when an organism O is faced with the 'option' of two adaptative strategies, (1) developing internal mechanisms m_1, m_2 ... m_n which are, by themselves, sufficient to give O the capacity to accomplish T, and (2) developing internal mechanisns $m_1{}^\star$, $m_2{}^\star$ ... $m_n{}^\star$ which, when combined with suitable environmental manipulation on the part of O, are sufficient to give O the capacity to perform T, then the second sort of strategy – the manipulative strategy – is more differentially selectively advantageous than the first non-manipulative one. This is because the manipulative strategy can be pursued at less evolutionary cost than the non-manipulative one. The manipulative strategy involves less investment of resources, resources which are, therefore, available for employment elsewhere in the organism's economy.

NOC claims that when an organism O adopts a manipulative adaptative strategy in the performance of a given evolutionary task T, then the internal mechanisms that O evolves which allow it, in conjunction with suitable environmental manipulation, to accomplish T are not always obvious ones given the nature of T. Hence, we cannot understand the structure or the function of such mechanisms in isolation from the nature of the manipulative activities of O. The non-obvious character of evolved internal mechanisms derives from the fact that it is not the mechanisms alone that accomplish the relevant task but, rather, the mechanisms in conjunction with suitable environmental manipulation on the part of the organism. The more that environmental manipulation plays a role in the performance of T, the less perspicuous becomes the connection between the task and the internal mechanisms.

95

The principles BD and NOC are, I think, fairly straightforward consequences of evolutionary theory. Before considering their possible application to the case of cognitive structures, two points concerning the status of BD and NOC are in order.

Firstly, BD and NOC are not advanced here as necessary truths. Firstly, there is, of course, nothing in the above accounts which entails that non-manipulative strategies could not evolve. Clearly such strategies have evolved for a large number of tasks, and often they are quite successful. Secondly, there is no claim that it is not *possible* for an internalist, non-manipulative strategy to the solution of task T be adopted at less cost than an alternative manipulative one. As we have seen, it is possible that a manipulative strategy has hidden costs (just as it is possible that a non-manipulative strategy possesses such costs also). The claim, rather, is that generally this will not be the case. That is, manipulative strategies can *typically* be adopted at less evolutionary cost than internalist non-manipulative ones.

Secondly, even if the arguments developed above are correct and manipulative strategies typically do cost less than non-manipulative ones, this does not mean that an organism, when faced with a given adaptive task, will inevitably adopt a manipulative strategy. Evolution does not always choose the best strategy; natural selection does not always result in the most efficient design. Therefore, although I am going to argue that, in the development of the structures that subserve cognition, evolution has chosen a manipulative strategy, the argument emphatically does *not* rest on the claim that this is because it is the best strategy to choose. This argument, resting as it does on some pretty controversial Panglossian assumptions, would be a weak argument. The purpose of this chapter has been to show that, in the evolutionary development of the structures that subserve cognition, manipulative strategies would, at least generally, be the best ones because they can be pursued at less evolutionary cost than non-manipulative alternatives. Therefore, a *manipulate the environment* strategy towards the accomplishment of certain cognitive tasks would make good evolutionary sense. Strategies which eschew environmental manipulation would make less evolutionary sense. That is the principal message of this chapter.

All that is needed, in fact, in order to apply these principles to cognitive processes is the assumption that the internal structures and mechanisms which allow us to accomplish various cognitive tasks are structures which have evolved through natural selection. And they have evolved at all because in our evolutionary past we were faced with certain cognitive tasks whose solution was conducive to our survival. Given that this is so, then the principles BD and NOC *could* apply to us, and to the strategies we have adopted in order to accomplish these cognitive tasks. Not only *could* they apply to us, if they did then it means we would have adopted the best – that is, most efficient – type of evolutionary strategy. That is what this chapter has tried to show.

In other words, when faced with a cognitive task such as perception, thinking, remembering, reasoning, problem-solving, and so on, we have prima-facie reason to suppose that it is more selectively advantageous for an organism to accomplish this task through the development of a combination of internal mechanisms *plus* the ability to manipulate the environment in appropriate ways, rather than through the development of internal mechanisms that are alone sufficient to perform the task. If this is so, and if the organism has adopted the most selectively advantageous approach, then we should expect that a proper understanding of how various internal mechanisms allow the organism to cognize cannot be achieved independently of an understanding of how the organism is able to manipulate appropriate structures in its environment. That is, a proper understanding of the functioning of the internal mechanisms responsible for cognition cannot be achieved without a concomitant understanding of the relevant ways in which the cognizer can manipulate its environment. Focusing on the operation of the internal mechanisms alone need shed no more light on how they perform the relevant cognitive operations than focusing on the large, flat teeth of the beaver explains how the beaver is able to avoid predators.

4.7 THE IRRELEVANCE OF EXAPTATION

The claim that the structures and mechanisms that allow us to cognize are evolutionary products might be thought problematic. For example, Gould and Vrba write:

> The brain, though undoubtedly built by natural selection for some complex set of functions, can, as a result of its intricate structure, work in an unlimited number of ways quite unrelated to the selective pressure

that constructed it. . . . Current utility carries no automatic implication about historical origin. Most of what the brain does now to enhance our survival lies in the domain of exaptation – and does not allow us to make hypotheses about the selective paths of human history.   (1982:13)

An adaptation, according to Gould and Vrba, is 'any feature that promotes fitness and was built by selection for its current role' (6). Exaptations, on the other hand, are 'characters . . . evolved for other uses (or for no function at all), and later "coopted" for their current role'. It might be argued, then, that the structures and mechanisms responsible for human cognition are exaptations, rather than adaptations. And, if this were so, it might be thought that the arguments developed in the present chapter would be undermined.

Happily, however, the arguments of the present chapter do not presuppose that the structures and mechanisms presently responsible for cognition evolved for that purpose. The distinction between adaptations and exaptations is simply irrelevant to these arguments. The claim is that when a structure or mechanism takes on the role of underwriting a cognitive process – whether it originally evolved for this role or not – then it is best, from the point of view of evolutionary cost, for that mechanism to fulfil its role in conjunction with manipulation of the environment. One must never forget that evolution acts not just to produce structures and mechanisms, it also acts to maintain them in existence once they have been produced. A structure or mechanism that is maintained because of the role it plays in underwriting certain cognitive processes, even though it was not originally developed for this role, is an evolutionary product no more and no less than a structure which was originally evolved for the role. Both adaptations and exaptations are products of evolution, and considerations of evolutionary cost apply equally to both of them. Whether a feature has been adapted for a role in underwriting cognition, or co-opted for this role, it is better, from the point of view of evolutionary cost, for it to fulfil this role in conjunction with manipulation, on the part of the organism, of relevant structures in the environment.

If the arguments of this chapter are correct, then the most efficient strategies for the development of our various cognitive capacities would be *manipulate the environment* strategies. Such strategies could, we have prima-facie reason to believe, generally be pursued at less evolutionary cost than non-manipulative alternatives. Thus, if the arguments of this chapter are correct, this would have been the best way for evolution to endow us with our cognitive capacities. In the chapters to follow, I shall argue that this is the way evolution actually did endow us with such capacities. Cognitive processes, I shall argue, are hybrid processes made up of, on the one hand, the operations of internal mechanisms and, on the other hand, certain types of environmental manipulation performed by cognizers. The arguments of this chapter, if correct, provide us with very general biological reasons as to why this should be so. In this sense, then, the evolutionary arguments developed here underpin the arguments to follow. Other than that, however, these evolutionary arguments will play no further direct role in motivating this view of cognitive processes. The arguments to follow will be independently motivated and independently defensible.

5

Perception

In the preceding chapter, two principles, BD and NOC, were defended. It was argued that if an organism has adopted the most efficient type of evolutionary strategy then this strategy would be one which (i) obeys BD, and (ii) exemplifies NOC. Chapter 3 put forward two claims, the ontological claim and the epistemological claim, which were said to be constitutive of the position to be developed in this book. There is, in fact a close connection between BD and NOC, on the one hand, and the ontological and epistemological claims on the other.

Firstly, when BD is applied to the strategies that organisms adopt to accomplish cognitive tasks, then it becomes basically an expression of the ontological claim. That is, according to BD, if, with respect to a given cognitive task T, an organism O has adopted the most efficient evolutionary strategy, then the strategy adopted will consist in the development of a combination of internal structures and their operations *plus* manipulation of environmental structures. Therefore, the processes by which O, adopting the most efficient evolutionary strategy, accomplishes a given cognitive task T will be hybrid, consisting of both internal and external operations. But if this is so, then these processes are not located purely inside the skin of the cognizing organism; they straddle both internal and external components. And this is precisely what the ontological claim asserts.

Secondly, NOC is basically an expression of the epistemological claim. According to NOC, when an organism O has adopted the most efficient evolutionary strategy (i.e., a *manipulate the environment* strategy) towards the accomplishment of a cognitive task T, then the internal structures that O will have evolved toward this end will not be obvious ones, given the nature of T. But this means that we cannot possibly understand how these internal structures function relative to the task without also understanding how O is able to manipulate relevant structures in its environment. But this entails that it is not possible to understand cognitive processes by focusing purely on what is occurring inside the skin of cognizing organisms. And this is precisely what the epistemological claim asserts.

Therefore, if the arguments of the previous chapter are correct, then the ontological and epistemological claims outlined in chapter 3 can be derived from some fairly general principles of evolutionary biology. That is, *if* an organism O has adopted the most efficient evolutionary strategy towards the accomplishment of a given cognitive task T, then the processes by which O accomplishes T are not located purely inside the skin of O (the ontological claim) and we cannot, therefore, understand the processes which allow O to accomplish T by focusing purely on what is occurring inside the skin of O (the epistemological claim).

Notice that this claim takes the form of a conditional: *if* an organism adopts the most efficient evolutionary strategy. . . . To base the ontological and epistemological claims on the evolutionary argument alone would be to presuppose the fairly controversial Panglossian thesis that organisms always adopt the most efficient evolutionary strategy. Now, within certain constraints, I happen to think that this principle is true, or very nearly true (for the relevant constraints, see Dawkins 1982:30–54). However, I will not suppose that it is true here, since it is, to say the least, controversial. So, I will assume that the conclusion of the evolutionary arguments of the previous chapter should be restricted to the conditional form described above. *If* an organism has adopted the most efficient evolutionary strategy with respect to the accomplishment of cognitive tasks, then we should expect both the ontological and epistemological claims to be true of the processes whereby that organism accomplishes those tasks.

In this and the remaining chapters of Part I, I want to extend the above claim beyond the conditional form. That is, I shall try to show not only that if we had adopted the most efficient evolutionary strategy towards the accomplishment of cognitive tasks then the ontological and epistemological claims would be true of our cognitive processes, but also that the ontological and epistemological claims are, in fact, true of our cognitive processes. To this end, I shall focus on specific cognitive tasks and examine the strategies we have adopted for accomplishing them. Since the view defended in these chapters is no doubt controversial, I want, at this point, to go out of my way to emphasize that I am not presupposing any controversial definition of cognition. Firstly, I shall assume, as a purely preliminary measure, that the notion of a cognitive task can be defined by *enumeration*. In this vein, the major cognitive tasks will include such things as perceiving, remembering, reasoning, and language use (i.e., understanding and production). These will be discussed in the chapters to follow. There is no assumption that these are the only major cognitive tasks, just that, on anyone's list, they would appear as fairly central ones. To perceive the environment is, thus, a task faced by many organisms at some point during their evolutionary history. To remember, and, on the basis of this, to be able to redeploy, perceived information, is another task. Each of these categories of tasks can be broken down into more restricted tasks. For example, the category of perception can be broken down into the categories of visual perception, auditory perception, tactile perception, and so on. And each of these categories can be broken down further. The category of visual perception, for example, can be broken down into such things as perception of objects, perception of events, perception of faces etc. At each of these levels we have a task that an organism, or an evolutionary lineage, may need to accomplish if it is to survive. By this method of enumeration or listing, then, we can arrive at a preliminary characterization of the notion of a cognitive task.

Evolution, of course, sets organisms many tasks, most of which are not cognitive. What is characteristic of cognitive tasks, and what justifies regarding them as forming a distinct class, is that their solution seems to involve the acquisition and employment of *information*. The concept of information will be explored in a later chapter (chapter 10). There, I shall argue for the (standard) view that information is best understood in terms of the idea of *nomological dependence*. On this view, then, a given state of a structure or mechanism will carry information about a source in virtue of there being a nomological connection between this state and the source. And information, we can say, is relevant to a task simply if it is required for the task to be solved or accomplished. Using this idea, we can then define the notion of a cognitive process as follows:

A process P is a cognitive process if and only if (i) P is essential to the accomplishing of a cognitive task T, and (ii) P involves operations

on information-bearing structures, where the information carried
by such structures is relevant to task T.

Thus, we arrive at the fairly standard view that a cognitive task is one
which involves the acquisition and employment of information, and
define a cognitive process as one which is essential to the accomplishing of a cognitive task *and* which involves operations on information-
bearing structures.

In this chapter I want to look at one particularly basic cognitive task:
perceiving. More specifically, I propose to focus on visual perception. I
shall argue that the cognitive processes that allow us to visually perceive the world – that is, to accomplish the task of visual perception –
are made up of both internal operations *and* manipulation of structures
in the perceiver's environment. If the arguments of chapter 4 are
correct, this is just what we would expect on evolutionary grounds.

5.1 CARTESIAN APPROACHES TO VISUAL PERCEPTION

The sort of view that I wish to oppose in this chapter is, still, very
much the orthodoxy. Indeed, this view constitutes what we might call
the *standard* approach to visual perception. The sort of view in question stems back at least as far as Descartes' theory of perception, and
receives current expression in theories such as that of David Marr.

The starting-point for what I shall call *Cartesian approaches to visual
perception*, or the standard approach, is provided by the *retinal image*.
This is a direct derivation from Descartes. During the emergence of a
separate science of psychology in the seventeenth and eighteenth
centuries, an understanding of image formation by lenses and the
observation by Descartes of a retinal image on the back of a bull's eye,
led to the belief that the eye functions much like a camera. The starting-point for visual perception was, therefore, conceived to be a
retinal image. However, it was also obvious that the images produced
by cameras and eyes are lacking in many of the qualities that we perceive in the world. Images are flat, static, and open to a variety of
interpretations. Visual perception, on the other hand, yields a three-
dimensional, mobile, and interpreted world. It seemed that perception must therefore involve processes that go beyond the information
present in the image. The image, in order to yield a perception, must
be *processed* in some way.

As J. J. Gibson (1966, 1979) has pointed out, almost all approaches to visual perception in contemporary cognitive psychology adhere firmly to this Cartesian paradigm. Although the retinal image is now recognized not to be an image in any literal sense, standard approaches to vision, none the less, continue to theorize *as if* the retinal image were such a thing. The retinal image is formed by light rays striking the retina, and is conceived of as a mosaic of point light intensities, where each point is characterized by wavelength and intensity. The retinal image, thus conceived, contains relatively little information and is, by itself, insufficient for visual perception. As a result, in order for perception to occur, the retinal image has to be processed by a large number of internal operations. Consider, for example, what is still probably the most influential representative of the standard account – the theory of vision developed by David Marr (Marr & Nishihara 1978; Marr & Hildreth 1980; Marr & Poggio 1981; Marr 1982). The discussion of Marr's theory to follow is arguably a little procrustean and, here, the remarks of chapter 1 must be kept in mind. My primary concern is a pre-theoretical picture of the mind, and the precise nature of its theoretical articulation comes a distant second. The theories of Marr and Gibson, I think, are best understood not as diametrically opposed but as occupying positions on a spectrum. And Gibson's position is, I think it is fair to say, considerably more over towards the environmentalist end of this spectrum than that of Marr. However, while this is so, it is also true that Marr's theory contains elements that are, at least arguably, environmentalist in character – for example, the role he gives to *assumptions* about the environment in visual processing. In the following discussion, I have chosen to ignore any of these possible environmental affiliations because my primary concern is not with Marr's theory as such, but with the pre-theoretical picture that it articulates. And this picture, I think it must be accepted, is essentially internalist.

According to Marr, three distinct theoretical levels need to be recognized in order to understand a complex information processing task such as visual perception. For any process (and vision consists of very many processes), we must first formulate a *computational* theory. Such a theory will specify what is being processed or computed and why. The next level consists of *algorithms* for achieving the computation (and also specifies representations which form the input to and output from those algorithms). Finally, there is the level which describes the *implementation* of the algorithm, whether in neural tissue or a computer.

The input for visual processing consists of a retinal image, where this is characterized in terms of intensity distributed over a large array of different locations. The distribution of intensity values (measured in pixels) is created by the way in which light is reflected by the physical structures that the observer is viewing. The goal of early visual processing is to create from the image a description of the physical structures – the shapes of surfaces and their orientations and distances from the observer – which are being observed.

The first stage in early visual processing consists in the construction of what Marr calls the primal sketch. The primal sketch describes the intensity changes present in the image and makes some of the more global image structures explicit. Construction of the primal sketch consists of two stages. Firstly, there is the construction of the raw primal sketch. The raw primal sketch is a representation of the pattern of light distributed over the retina in which information about the edges and textures of objects is made explicit. This information is expressed in a set of statements about the edges and blobs present in the image, their locations, orientations, and so on. Secondly, the application of various grouping principles (e.g., proximity, similarity, common fate, good continuation, closure, and so on) to the raw primal sketch results in the identification of larger structures – boundaries, regions, etc. This more refined representation is known as the full primal sketch. Further processing – specifically analyses of depth, motion, shading, etc. – result in what Marr calls the 2½D sketch. This is the culmination of early visual processing, and describes the layout of structures in the world from the vantage-point of the observer. A further and equally essential aspect of vision is recognition of objects. In order to recognize the object to which a particular shape corresponds, a third representational level is needed; a level centred on the object rather than the observer. This level consists in what Marr calls 3D model representations. It is at this stage of visual processing that a stored set of object descriptions is utilized. 3D model representations are the culmination of visual processing.

For present purposes, the details of each processing operation are not important. What is important are two constitutive features of Marr's account, features that are paradigmatic of the Cartesian approach. Firstly, the starting-point for visual processing is the retinal image. On Marr's view, and on Cartesian views in general, visual perception begins with the retinal image. Secondly, since this image manifestly contains little information, it must then be processed to yield visual perception. This processing is conceived of as *information processing*, processing of the information contained in the retinal image. And, since the retinal image occurs inside the skin of the perceiving organism, the information processing relevant to perception is also claimed to occur inside that organism's skin. Visual perception, then, is a purely internal process, constituted by the information processing operations performed by the brain on retinal images.

The pivotal claim in the construction of the Cartesian approach, therefore, lies in the claim that the starting-point for visual perception is the retinal image. Once this is accepted, it automatically follows that visual information processing is a purely internal process. However, the claim is not supported by any empirical evidence; it has the status of an assumption or axiom. In the sections to follow, I want to try to undermine this assumption.

5.2 VISUAL PERCEPTION AND THE EPISTEMOLOGICAL CLAIM

The most complete and comprehensive alternative to the Cartesian approach to visual perception is to be found in the work of J. J. Gibson (Gibson 1950, 1966, 1977, 1979, 1982; Reed 1988). Gibson's approach is generally regarded as, at best controversial, and, at worst, misguided. I, however, think his central claims are obviously true, and this fact is not generally recognized only because of mistaken interpretations of his claims. Once these are cleared up, I think, Gibson's work clearly shows why the Cartesian approach must be rejected. Therefore, I think the arguments put forward in the following pages are simply rehearsals of arguments already put forward by Gibson, and I shall present them as such. You, on the other hand, may think my interpretation of Gibson is clearly wrong. If so, you are free to regard the arguments of the following pages in their own right. That is, the principles defended in the remainder of this chapter can stand or fall on their own, irrespective of whether they are correctly attributable to Gibson.

In order to understand Gibson's approach to visual perception, it is necessary to understand the concept of an *optic array*. Light from the sun fills the air – the terrestrial medium – so that it is in a 'steady state' of reverberation. The environment is, in this way, filled with rays of light travelling between the surfaces of objects. At any point, light will converge from all directions. Therefore, at each physical point in the environment, there is what can be regarded as a densely nested set of solid visual angles which are composed of inhomogeneities in the intensity of light. Thus, we can imagine an observer, at least for the present, as a point surrounded by a sphere which is divided into tiny solid angles. The intensity of light and the mixture of wavelengths will vary from one solid angle to another. This spatial pattern of light is the optic array. Light carries information because the structure of the optic array is determined by the nature and position of the surfaces from which it has been reflected.

The optic array is divided into many segments or angles. Each of these contains light reflected from different surfaces, and the light contained in each segment will differ from that in other segments in terms of its average intensity and distribution of wavelengths. The boundaries between these segments of the optic array, since they mark a change in intensity and distribution of wavelength, provide information about the 3D structure of objects in the world. At a finer level of detail, each segment will, in turn, be sub-divided in a way determined by the texture of the surface from which the light is reflected. Therefore, at this level also, the optic array can carry information about further properties of objects and terrain. Once the possibility of describing the input for visual perception in terms of a structured optic array is accepted, it becomes possible to ask what relationships hold between a perceiver's environment and the structure of the optic array. Gibson advocated the development of an ecological optics to explore these relationships (Gibson 1966, 1979).

The realization of the importance of the optic array is, in many ways, Gibson's central insight. The rest of his ecological approach really stems from placing the concept of the optic array in its proper position of conceptual priority. The optic array is an *external information-bearing structure*. It is external in the quite obvious sense that it exists outside the skins of perceiving organisms, and is in no way dependent upon such organisms for its existence. It also carries information about the environment. Indeed, according to Gibson, there is enough information contained in the optic array to specify the nature of the environment which causes it. Information for Gibson consists in optical structure together with the deformation in this structure generated in a nomothetic way from the environmental layout and events. This optical structure is not similar in any way to the environment, but it is *specific* to it. That is, optical structure is nomically dependent upon environmental structure. The structure in the optic array is, thus, specific to its environmental sources in the sense that it is nomically covariant with such sources, and, because of this, an organism whose perceptual system detects optical structure in the array is thereby aware of what this structure specifies. Thus, the perceiving organism is aware of the environment not the array, and, more importantly, is in a position to utilize the information about the environment embodied in the array.

Once we allow that the optic array is an external structure which embodies information about the environment, then we are inevitably led to the following important methodological conclusion. Suppose we are faced with a particular perceptual task. If we accept the concept of the optic array, we have to allow that at least some of the information relevant to this task will be located in the array. Perhaps this information is not sufficient, in which case we would presumably wish to postulate some sort of internal processing operations which somehow supplement or embellish the information contained in the array. Even if this is so, however, one thing is clear. We cannot begin to estimate what internal processing an observer needs to accomplish unless we already understand how much information is available to that observer in its optic array. The more information available to the observer in its optic array, the less internal processing the observer needs to perform. Let us represent these claims as follows:

P1. The amount of internal information processing which an organism needs to perform in order to accomplish visual perception task T is inversely proportional to the amount of relevant information that is available to that organism in the optic array.

P2. In performing visual perception task T, we cannot begin to understand the internal information processing task facing an organism unless we understand what relevant information is contained in the optic array.

It is P1 and P2, I think, which most accurately capture Gibson's methodological attitude towards the postulation of internal processing operations. This is important and needs emphasizing. Many have interpreted Gibson's theory to entail that there is no need to postulate any sort of internal processing in order to account for visual perception (e.g., Bruce & Green 1985). And, in the same vein, it is common to see Gibson's account characterized as an anti-cognitive theory of perception; 'anti-cognitive' here indicating that perception can be achieved without the result of such cognitive processing operations as inference (e.g., Ullman 1980; Michaels & Carello 1981). However, this construal of Gibson, widespread and tenacious though it may be, seems largely unsupported by what Gibson actually says. Gibson does attack the notions of cognition and information processing embodied in standard Cartesian approaches. He regards the traditional view of these processes as based on an anachronistic and ultimately unworkable model of mental representations operating on stimulus inputs. But it is one thing to abandon a certain model of cognition or information processing, and quite another thing to abandon cognition or information processing altogether. Nothing that Gibson ever wrote suggests that he was engaged in the latter sort of project. That is, he was not engaged in the wholesale *rejection* of the concepts of cognition and information processing but, rather, with offering a *reinterpretation*, an alternative model, of these processes (Rowlands 1995c).

Nowhere in Gibson's work, then, is there any absolute prohibition on the postulation of internal information processing operations. What Gibson does object to most strenuously, however, is the *unnecessary* postulation of internal processing operations. That is, he objects to the fetish of playing fast and loose with the apparatus of internal processes, mental representations, and their ilk, when (a) because we have failed to examine what information is available to the observer in its optic array we have no idea what sorts of internal processes we need postulate anyway, and (b) proper examination of the information available in the optic array shows that the internal processes we have, in fact, postulated turn out to be completely unnecessary. Type (b) situations occur time and time again in cognitive theorizing. And it is this tendency which principally draws Gibson's fire. The idea that Gibson, on purely methodological grounds, has advocated some sort of blanket ban on the postulation of internal processing operations is a myth, and it stems from confusing an attack on specific instances of the postulation of internal processing with a more general ban on such postulation *per se*.

As an example of Gibson's attack on a specific instance of the postulation of internal processing, consider his account of our judgments of the size and distance of objects. Standard cognitivist approaches to explaining these judgments are variations on a theme which goes something like this. Firstly, the retinal image, conceived of as the raw material for internal processing, is informationally impoverished and, therefore, is essentially ambiguous with respect to the size and distance of the object perceived. Because of this ambiguity, a relatively large amount of internal processing would have to be postulated in order to account for the reliability of our judgments of size. However, on Gibson's view, such apparent ambiguity is simply the result of illicitly abstracting the perceived object from the environment in which that object would ordinarily be embedded. Consider, for example, our perception of a tree. We would not, ordinarily, experience the tree in isolation. Rather, it would be situated on the ground, and with, perhaps, other objects in its vicinity. Consider the ground. The ground recedes away from us into the distance. Associated with such recession will be a change in what is known as *texture density*. The ground on which the tree is situated recedes from us into the distance and will, therefore, give rise to a texture density gradient in the optic array. Thus, the optic array would contain information about a continuous ground receding from the observer in the form of a texture density gradient. The size of the particular tree would be specified by the amount of texture it conceals. Since a tree itself has texture, the fact that the tree is vertical, rather than inclined away from or towards the observer, would also be specified by the lack of change of texture density in the relevant part of the optic array. Thus, the optic array itself contains enough information to specify unambiguously the size and distance of the tree (Gibson 1950). However, if we did not appreciate this fact, if we did not pay sufficient attention to the information contained in the structure of the optic array, we would inevitably end up postulating an unnecessary amount of internal information processing, And, furthermore, we cannot begin to understand the sort of internal information processing we do need to postulate if we do not understand the amount of information available to the organism in the optic array.

A related phenomenon is our judgment of size constancy. An object 2x metres from an observer casts an image on the retina which is half the size of the image cast by that object at distance x metres from the observer. However, if you watch an object moving away from you, it does not appear to shrink to half size each time its distance from you doubles. Our perception of the sizes of objects is relatively constant, provided that the distances are not too great. On the standard account, the brain must take account of the perceived distances of objects, as given by various cues, and scale up perceptual size accordingly. The difficulty of this task is abetted by the fact that image size is one of the major cues for object distance. Thus the cues will also have to be weighted, and the complexity of internal processing operations increases accordingly. Armed with the concept of the optic array as an external, information-bearing, structure, we can view the problem differently. Texture gradients embodied in the optic array provide a continuous and constant scale for the perception of the world. Hence there is no problem of size constancy scaling. The size of the object is given – specified – by the scale of the background at the point where the object is attached. Therefore, there is no need for internal operations specifically designed to process this information (Gibson 1950). Once again, in this case, even if we assume that some internal information processing is necessary for judgments of size constancy, it is impossible to assess the internal information processing task if we do not understand the amount of information available to the organism in the optic array.

The crucial distinction implicated in the above examples is that between the *detection* or appropriation of information and the *processing* of information. If the information relevant to the perception of the size or distance of an object is available to the organism in the light around it, then this means that the optic array carries this information. And, if this is so, then the perceiving organism will, of course, require mechanisms which allow it to *detect* this information. But detecting information, at least on the standard account, is very different from processing it. Processing information is a matter of constructing it – usually by way of some sort of process of inference – from sources which only partially specify this information. That is, the perceptual sources are conceived of as being, by themselves, insufficient to yield the information necessary for the visual perception. The information given in the sources, then, has to be *processed* – supplemented and embellished by various inferential operations – in order to yield the information necessary for the visual perception.

The above examples show that it is not possible to judge what information needs to be processed internally unless one is aware of what information is available to the perceiving organism in its optic array.

That is, the more information that the perceiving organism is able to *detect* in its optic array, the less information that organism will have to *process* by means of internal quasi-inferential operations. This is the import of P1. Therefore, in order to understand what internal processing an organism must perform in order to accomplish a given visual task T, we must first understand what information, relevant to T, the organism is capable of detecting in its optic array. And, to do this, we must first understand what information is actually embodied in the optic array. This is the import of P2.

Neither P1 nor P2 deny that internal processing operations are needed in order to accomplish visual perception tasks. P1 and P2 are completely neutral on the issue of internal information processing operations. What P1 and P2 do claim is that, if internal processing operations do turn out to be necessary, we cannot begin to estimate their nature or extent until we understand what information is embodied in the optic array and, subsequently, what information the perceiving organism is capable of detecting.

If this is correct, it means that standard cognitivist criticisms of Gibson are simply misguided. Indeed, the import of the principles P1 and P2 is easily represented in Marrian terms. According to Marr, the first stage in a theory of visual perception should be a computational theory: a specification of what is being processed or computed and why. In these terms, the point of P1 and P2 is that any computational theory must involve an account of what information is available to the organism in the optic array. Without an understanding of this, the task of specifying what gets computed or processed cannot get off the ground. In other words, if a computational theory is the first step in a theory of vision, an understanding of the information available in the optic array is the first step in a computational theory.

Whether or not you think P1 and P2 provide an adequate account of Gibson's methodological position, it is clear that they can stand or fall as principles in their own right. And, given a very few uncontroversial assumptions, P1 and P2 are virtually inescapable. In fact the only assumption really necessary is that there is such a thing as an optic array, and this is surely undeniable. The optic array, as we have seen, is a structure which is (i) external to the perceiving organism, and (ii) information bearing. It is information bearing because the structure of the optic array is nomically covariant with the structure of the environment. Once this is accepted, then it follows that there is, external to the perceiving organism, information that is relevant to visual perception. And if this is so, then there are two further possibilities. With respect to a visual perception task T, either the organism will be able to detect the relevant information in the array or it will not. If the former, then there will be no reason to postulate internal information processing operations to explain the organism's capacity to accomplish T (though there will, of course, be reason to postulate internal information detection operations). If the latter, there will be reason to postulate internal information processing operations. However, one cannot begin to estimate what these operations are unless one knows what information, relevant to T, the organism can detect. And one cannot know this unless one knows what information is embodied in the optic array. Therefore, once we allow that information is embodied in the structure of the light surrounding the organism, P1 and P2 are inescapable.

Therefore, P1 and P2 can be established on the basis of one, very conservative, assumption: that information relevant to visual perception exists in the light external to perceiving organisms. And it is unclear, to say the least, who would want to deny this. P1 and P2, however, are simply expressions of what, in chapter 1, I called the *epistemological claim*: that it is not possible to understand the nature of cognitive processes by focusing exclusively on what is occurring inside the skin of cognizing organisms. Thus, the epistemological claim is clearly confirmed by reflections on the nature of visual perception.

5.3 VISUAL PERCEPTION AND THE ONTOLOGICAL CLAIM

In the above discussion, I have tended to view the observer as located at a single point in space. To remain with this conception, however, would be to ignore another crucial aspect of perception. This aspect is, again, emphasized by Gibson. As Gibson points out, perception is inextricably bound up with action. Perceiving organisms are not, typically, static creatures, but, rather, actively explore their environment. And, as Gibson has shown, movement is essential to seeing. The fact that perceiving organisms actively explore their environments allows crucial information from motion perspective to tell them not only about structures in the world, but also about their own position and movements relative to such structures. When an observer moves, the entire optic array is transformed, and such transformations contain information about the layout, shapes, and orientations of objects in the world. The fundamental importance of observer movement in Gibson's theory is reinforced by his notion of *perceptual systems* to contrast with the traditional *senses*: 'the eye is part of a dual organ, one of a pair of eyes, and they are set in a head that can turn, attached to a body that can move from place to place' (Gibson 1979:53). Thus, these organs make up a hierarchy and, together, constitute a perceptual system. One can correctly attribute the predicate 'sees' only to the entire perceptual system, not to the eye considered in isolation.

The importance of this point cannot be overemphasized. The optic array is a source of information for any organism equipped to take advantage of it. But, the optic array does not impinge on passive observers. Rather, the living organism will *actively sample* the optic array. The organism obtains information from the optic array by actively exploring it and, thus, actively appropriating the contained information. One way of doing this is by moving and thus transforming the ambient optic array. By effecting such transformations, perceiving organisms can identify and appropriate what Gibson called the *invariant* information contained in the optic array. This invariant information takes the form of higher-order variables. Consider, for example, what is known as the *horizon ratio relation* (Sedgwick 1973). The horizon intersects an object at a particular height. All objects of the same height, whatever their distance, are cut by the horizon in the same ratio. The horizon ratio relation provides an example of the invariant information contained in the optic array. Invariant information, by definition, is information that can be made available only through the transformation of one optic array into another. Thus, an organism can detect such invariant information only by moving and, hence, effecting transformations in the ambient array. Information, in this sense, is not something inside the organism. Rather, it is a function, a nomic consequence, of changes in the organism–environment relation or, equivalently, a function of the persistences and changes in the organism–environment system.

What is crucial here is that (i) the optic array, a structure external to the perceiving organism, is a *locus* of information for suitably equipped creatures and (ii) a creature can appropriate or make this information available to itself through acting upon the array, and thus effecting transformations in it. What the perceiving organism does, in effect, is *manipulate* a structure external to it – the optic array – in order

114

to make available to itself information which it can then use to navigate its way around the environment. And the notion of an organism *making information available* to itself, here, can be understood in terms of the organism rendering information susceptible to detection by itself.

If information relevant to perception is contained in the array, then manipulating the array to make this information available is, in effect, a form of information processing. If we want to think of visual perception in terms of the concept of information processing, then this is where information processing is primarily located. Or, more precisely, if we do want to think of visual perception in terms of the concept of information processing – and there is no objection to that in this book – then there is no good reason for insisting that information processing occurs only inside the skin of the perceiving organism. When an organism manipulates the optic array, it appropriates and makes available to itself the information contained therein. There seems to be no sound theoretical reason for denying that this process is one of information processing. Of course, one could always *stipulate* that the concept of information processing is to be restricted to processes occurring inside the skin of organisms. One can stipulate anything one wants. One can, moreover, cut the theoretical pie any way one likes. However, given that information is embodied in structures external to organisms, and given that an organism can manipulate these structures in order to appropriate the contained information, it is difficult to see the point of this restriction. In other words, there seems to be no great theoretical divide between manipulating *internal* information-bearing structures and manipulating *external* information-bearing structures in order to make available to oneself the results of such manipulation. In manipulating the optic array, the perceiving organism is manipulating an external information-bearing structure. I shall refer to this as a form of information processing, since I can see no good reason not to. Indeed, as far as I can see, it is only a prior commitment to an internalist view of the mind that could possibly motivate the decision to withhold the information processing appellation in this case. However, nothing much turns on this choice of terminology. And if, for some reason, you wish to restrict the concept of information processing to the manipulation of internal information-bearing structures, that is fine by me. What is important is not what we call the process, but that, by the manipulation of external information-bearing structures, a perceiving organism is able to make available to itself information that can allow it, or at least help it, to accomplish perceptual tasks.

Therefore, information processing, or at least something very like it, occurs when a perceiving organism acts upon an optic array and, by effecting transformations in it, appropriates, or makes available to itself, the contained information. To effect transformations in an array through acting upon it, or manipulating it, is, in effect, to process the information contained in that array. We can represent this conclusion as follows:

P3. An organism can process information relevant to visual perception task T through acting upon, and thus effecting transformations in, the optic array.

And, we can generalize P3 into something like the following principle:

P4. In certain circumstances, acting upon, or manipulating, external structures is a form of information processing.

And a corollary of P4, of course, is that not all the information processing effected by an organism occurs inside the skin of that organism. Again, let me reiterate, whether or not you wish to regard this manipulation of external structures as a form of information processing is of no great importance. What is crucial is that manipulation of these external structures is a *cognitive* process. The manipulation of external structures is a process which is essential to accomplishment of a cognitive task, namely perception of the external world. Moreover, it involves operations on information-bearing structures; structures which carry information that is relevant to the task at hand. Therefore, it counts as a cognitive process.

As an example of P3 and P4 at work, consider the phenomenon of *stereopsis*. If two eyes are focused on an object A, the images of A in each eye are said to lie on corresponding points on the two retinas. The images cast by a nearer or more distant object B will fall on disparate points on the two retinas and the amount of disparity will depend upon the distance between B and A. Thus, if the brain can compute this disparity, this will give information about the relative distance of objects in the world. On the standard model, stereopsis is understood as the matching of two disparate images into a single 3D percept. And such global matching of images is commonly thought to require large numbers of computations and comparisons at a local level. In many ways, this image-matching account of stereopsis is counterintuitive. No one has ever suggested that tactile perception, for example, involves such a synthetic step – yet, when one feels an object under a cloth, for example, each hand must obtain a quite different tactile impression, and, logically, the problem of the *singleness* of tactile perception is the same. Therefore, if tactile impressions need not be compared and integrated, why consider binocular vision to involve the comparison and fusion of two retinal images?

The concept of the optic array as an external information-bearing structure, and the idea that organisms can process information through the manipulation of this structure, gives us an alternative account (Barrand 1978). Binocular vision, and the stereopsis made possible by this, involves a constant and rapid shifting from one eye's view to the other. Such shifting effects transformations in the ambient array, and through such transformations it is possible to identify invariants in the array. These invariants can be shown, among other things, to specify the relative distances of objects. What this approach achieves here, again, is the replacement of a large amount of internal processing operations by the organism's capacity to act on, and effect transformations in, the external, information-bearing, optic array. Internal processes are replaced by external action.

P3 and P4 can, like P1 and P2, be established on the basis of very conservative assumptions. The assumptions are these. Firstly, the optic array is an external information-bearing structure. Secondly, a perceiving organism is able to make available to itself information contained in the optic array through manipulation, i.e., effecting transformations in, that optic array. The first assumption has already been dealt with in the earlier discussion of the epistemological claim. The second assumption has been conclusively demonstrated by Gibson. Again, note that, in order to endorse this aspect of his view, you do not have to buy into any of the more controversial of Gibson's claims, or alleged claims (e.g., the directness of perception, no internal information processing operations, etc.). The important point is that, once it is allowed that information is contained in the structure of light and is, hence, external to perceiving organisms, and once it is allowed that a perceiving organism can appropriate this information through manipulation of this external structure, P3 and P4 are inescapable.

The conclusion, then, is that manipulation of the external optic array is itself a *cognitive* process. That is, it is a process that (i) involves the manipulation of information-bearing structures, and (ii) is essential to the accomplishment of a cognitive task, namely visual perception. Whether perception involves internal information processing operations is something on which this chapter has remained neutral. What this chapter has tried to show is that at least some of the cognitive processes essentially involved in visual perception are *external* processes. They consist in the manipulation of information-bearing structures in the perceiving organism's environment. And this is precisely the message of what I have called the ontological claim.

6

Memory

In this chapter, the focus switches from perception to memory. I shall argue that the sort of principles which emerged in the discussion of perception also apply to the case of memory. More precisely, I shall argue that precise analogues of the principles P1–P4 occur for at least some memory processes. Consequently, at least some memory processes can be understood not as purely internal processes, but as a series of interactions between a remembering organism and its environment. For at least some memory processes, that is, there is no respectable theoretical reason for regarding them as purely internal processes. On the contrary, although not all forms of remembering necessarily involve interactions between organisms and environments, none the less the type of memory peculiar to modern human beings is typically made up of both internal and external processes, and, hence, the cognitive structures responsible for this type of memory are essentially environment-involving.

6.1 THE MODEL

The model of memory defended in this chapter closely parallels the model of visual perception defended in the previous one. Crucial to this model are (i) the existence of an external or environmental structure which carries information, and (ii) the ability of the cognizing organism to appropriate and make use of this information by way of suitable manipulation of this structure. In the case of visual perception, the environmental structure in question was the optic array, and this array was manipulated by means of various types of action on the part of the perceiving organism. These types of action, it was argued, are as constitutive of visual perception as any internal process: perception is constituted not only by the manipulation of *internal* information-bearing structures, but also by the manipulation of *external* information-bearing structures. The model of memory to be defended in this chapter closely follows this account of visual perception. In this section, I will simply outline the model.

Cole, Hood, and McDermott (1982) describe a case where a child is seeking an ingredient for baking a cake. The child does not need to remember exactly where the ingredient is located. Instead, the child simply goes to the shelf and works her way along it until this ingredient is found. In this case, part of the external world (specifically, the shelf) stands in, or goes proxy, for a detailed internal memory store.

The idea of using external cues to aid memory is, of course, well known. Tying a knot in one's handkerchief, writing down a shopping list, making calendars, asking someone else to give you a reminder, leaving something in a special place where it will be encountered at the time it needs to be remembered, and so on, all constitute a small sub-set of the total number of external memory aids people employ. These are typically viewed precisely as *external aids* to memory; as extrinsic devices which might help trigger the real process of remembering, itself regarded as a purely internal operation. It is the dichotomy between the internal process of remembering and external aids to remembering that this chapter seeks to break down.

Examples of the Cole, Hood, and McDermott variety can be extended indefinitely (Rowlands 1995c). Suppose I want to find a book at the library. I have seen the book before, but cannot remember what it is called or who the author is. Moreover, I do not remember exactly where it is in the library, but I do remember the floor, and I also remember that it is on a shelf with a peculiar distinguishing feature, say a red tray at the end. Therefore, I go to the correct floor, look for the shelf with the distinguishing feature, and then work my way along the shelf until I find the book. In this case, the library floor and the shelf together seem to go proxy for a complex internal memory store. Similar remarks would apply to the process of navigating one's way around the environment by way of remembered landmarks (I cannot remember exactly where X lives, but I know that if I turn right by the lake, go on as far as the pub and then take a left . . .). In this case, the landmarks also seem to stand in for a detailed internal memory store.

Suppose I am reading a book and come across an interesting argument which may prove relevant to my own work at some point. Having a propensity to forget arguments, I make no serious attempt to commit the argument to memory. Since I have no facility for remembering page numbers either, I instead remember something much simpler – I remember approximately where on the page the argument occurred. Then, when I want to consider the argument again, I flip through the book, scanning the relevant part of each page, until I come across the argument. In this case, the book itself seems to stand in for a detailed memory store. My remembering where the argument is seems to be a process formed from a combination of an internal representation of the location of the argument on a page together with actual physical manipulation of the book itself.

The orthodox, internalist, view of memory would, of course, regard the library shelf and the book merely as external aids to memory. As such, manipulation of such objects would not be part of the process of remembering *per se*, but simply an external heuristic accompaniment to this process. This claim might be backed up by a distinction between *remembering* and *finding* the book or argument. All the above examples show, it could be argued, is that the process of finding the book (or the argument) is not a purely internal process. But this is compatible with the process of remembering being an internal process. There are, of course, many ways of slicing up the theoretical pie. And there is nothing obviously *incoherent* with the decision to regard mental processes as purely internal in character. What I shall try to do in this chapter is challenge not the coherence of such a view, but its theoretical utility. I shall argue that, at least with regard to the memory systems possessed by modern human beings, there is no sound theoretical reason for setting up a dichotomy between internal memory processes and external aids to those processes. Indeed, there are sound theoretical reasons for viewing this distinction with extreme suspicion.

This, then, is the model of remembering to be defended in this chapter. In each of the cases described above, the process of remembering is *hybrid*, made up of internal representations and operations defined over those representations together with physical manipulation of structures in the environment. This seems to follow, very closely, the pattern identified for perception in the previous chapter. More precisely, I shall argue that, in the case of memory, we should adopt principles which precisely parallel P1–P4. That is:

M1. The amount of internal information processing that an organism needs to perform in order to accomplish memory task T is inversely proportional to the amount of relevant information that is available to the organism in the physical structures around it.

And, as in the case of visual perception, this will have an important methodological corollary:

M2. In performing memory task T, we cannot begin to understand the internal information processing task facing an organism unless we understand what relevant information is available to the organism in the physical structures around it.

Thus, the library shelf is an environmental structure that carries information about the location of the book. By working her way along the shelf, a person can, in effect, *process* some of the information embodied in it. And, if the person were not able to manipulate the shelf in this way, then the amount of internal processing – in the form of the laying down and accessing of an extremely detailed memory store – would be vastly greater. The external information-bearing structure stands in for the internal information-bearing structure. And we cannot begin to estimate what internal information-bearing structures are necessary for the achievement of a given memory task until we understand what relevant external information-bearing structures are available to the remembering organism.

In the above cases, the cognizing organism appropriates information relevant to its task through manipulation of physical structures that are external to it. Therefore, as in the discussion of visual perception in the previous chapter, if we want to understand cognitive operations in terms of the concept of information processing, then we should also understand that information processing can occur not just inside the organism but also in the interaction between the organism and structures instantiated in its environment. That is, information processing relevant to a given memory task can occur when a cognizing organism manipulates a physical structure in its environment and, in so doing, appropriates, or makes available to itself, information relevant to that task. Therefore, I shall argue, we should also adopt the following principles:

M3. An organism can process information relevant to memory task T through the manipulation of physical structures in its environment.

And, as in the case of visual perception, we can generalize this principle to the following:

M4. In certain circumstances, acting upon, or manipulating, external structures is a form of information processing.

Principles M1–M4, which parallel P1–P4, form the basis of the model of memory to be defended in this chapter.

6.2 VARIETIES OF REMEMBERING

I shall not argue that *all* processes of remembering necessarily involve manipulation of environmental structures. On the contrary, I shall assume that some types of memory do not involve such manipulation, at least not necessarily, and that, therefore, these types of memory may well turn out to be purely internal in character. What I shall argue, however, is that a certain type of memory process essentially involves manipulation of environmental structures. Moreover, this type of memory process is of central importance, since it is the type of memory characteristic of, and peculiar to, modern human beings. Thus, while certain types of memory process might be amenable to purely internal descriptions and explanations, if we want to understand specifically human memory processes then we shall also have to understand the ways in which humans can manipulate information-bearing structures in their environment.

A useful place to begin is with the well-known distinction between *procedural* and *episodic* memory (Tulving 1983). Procedural memory, in effect, is the mnemonic component of learned action patterns. Thus, procedural memory is possessed by any organism that is capable of learning new patterns of action. This class would certainly include mammals, birds, and reptiles and almost certainly at least some fish and amphibians. To have procedural memory in this sense is to remember how to do something, where the something in question is the result of learned, and not fixed, action patterns. Procedural memory presumably involves the storage of algorithms that underwrite patterns of action. And such storage can be achieved without detailed episodic recall of how the algorithms or schemas were acquired in the first place. It should be noted that I do not assume that these algorithms are linguistic in character. The notion of procedural memory is often strongly associated with the idea that underlying action patterns are sets of rules detailing what actions to take in any given situation. I shall regard such a set-up as merely one form of procedural memory; one way in which procedural memory may be realized. But, there is no assumption that this is the only possible way of realizing procedural memory in a system.

Episodic memory, on the other hand, is memory of specific episodes in life. These episodes, or events, are *concrete* in that they have a specific location in time and space. Episodically, we remember the specifics of an experience: the place, the time, the weather, the smells, sounds, colours, the emotions aroused, and so on. One's memory of first love, for those that have it, is likely to be episodic in this sense. A memory such as this is likely to be rich in specific experiential content. The essential feature of episodic memory, then, is its concrete experiential nature and its retention of specific episodic details.

Procedural memory systems are, by definition, present in all creatures capable of learning new behaviour patterns. Episodic memory systems also seem to be present in a variety of creatures, including all mammals and birds. There is good evidence that these systems evolved separately. This evidence stems both from considerations concerning the functional architecture of the systems and from considerations of neuroanatomical realization. Firstly, the two systems' storage strategies seem to be mutually incompatible. Procedural memory systems generalize across situations and events and, hence, abstract away from the specific details of these situations or events. Episodic memory, on the other hand, stores the specific details of experiences and events and ignores the general principles underlying them. In a nutshell, the procedural system stores the generalities and ignores the specifics, and the episodic system stores the specifics and ignores the generalities. Not only does each system store different sorts of information, they have to do things this way. No procedural system could possibly work unless it discarded the specifics of situations. One learns to ride a bicycle, for example, through practice. But the procedural system which underwrites one's memory of how to do this would be quickly overloaded if it tried to take in all the details of one's early cycling experiences. Thus, the storage strategies of procedural and episodic memory systems are incompatible, and necessarily so. Obviously, the same neural structure would have difficulty implementing both strategies. Therefore, it seems likely, two separate mechanisms evolved for two types of storage.

Secondly, the separate evolution of the two memory systems is strongly supported by neurological evidence. For example, birds will lose their songs (a procedural problem) if lesioned in one nucleus. If lesioned in the other nucleus, however, they will lose their ability to hide and relocate food (an episodic problem). Moreover, the distinctness of the systems is also evident in humans, as can be seen from certain cases of amnesia. In a well-known case, the patient, H.M., developed serious anterograde amnesia following neurosurgery (Milner 1966, 1975). H.M. retained a capacity for acquiring new procedural memories – he could, for example, still learn new motor skills. His capacity for new episodic memories was, however, lost. He could not remember any new events in his life. For example, he had to be repeatedly reintroduced to the doctors who were treating him. And, if he acquired a new motor skill, he was completely unable to remember doing so. Thus, although H.M. could acquire new procedural memories, he could not remember the specific episodes during which they were acquired.

The characteristic form of memory in modern human beings, however, is neither procedural nor episodic memory, but what Tulving (1983) has referred to as *semantic* memory. Roughly speaking, semantic memory is memory of facts.

It is common to find in psychological literature the claim that semantic memory is present only in humans (e.g., Donald 1991:152). However, there seems little empirical basis for this claim. The central problem in deciding who or what possesses semantic memory is that the distinction between episodic and semantic memory is most plausibly construed as one of degree. Does the dog's memory of the location of a territorial competitor qualify as a semantic or episodic memory. That is, does he remember *that* his adversary lives in a particular place, or does he simply have an episodic flashback to their previous encounter. It is difficult to see what empirical evidence could be used to adjudicate these claims, But, more importantly, it is difficult to see the conceptual basis for drawing any distinction of kind here. At some point, presumably, virtual flashback becomes sufficiently abstract, sufficiently attenuated from the point of view of concrete episodic detail, that it qualifies as semantic memory. But it is not clear that there is any firm distinction here. Similarly, it has been argued that the signing behaviour of apes does not qualify as a form of semantic memory because it is strongly episodic in character. Some have argued that the use of signing by apes is restricted to situations in which the eliciting stimulus, and the reward, are clearly specified and present, or at least very close to the ape at the time of signing (Terrace & Bever 1980). This, it might be thought, is evidence that they are using episodic memory to remember how to use the sign; they are employing a virtual 'flashback' of previous performances. Thus, their understanding of the sign is largely perceptual and situation specific, and situational specificity is not typical of semantic memory. But, once again, to claim that these findings simply preclude the attribution of semantic memory to apes is to attribute a false substantiality to the episodic/semantic distinction. However, for our purposes, all that is required is that there be a distinction of degree between episodic and semantic memory. Episodic memory is gradually transformed into semantic memory when its specific episodic or concrete experiential content becomes sufficiently abstract and attenuated that its situational specificity is lost.

Most animals possess procedural memory, and therefore the concept is not particularly useful in characterizing the dominant cognitive feature of mammalian memory. It is possible (though unlikely) that episodic memory is restricted to birds and mammals. Humans possess both procedural and episodic systems, but these have been superseded in us by semantic memory which, for humans, is by far the dominant form of memory. And semantic memory, although undoubtedly deriving from episodic memory, is governed by very different principles of operation than its epistemic substratum. Semantic memory, when developed to the extent evident in modern human beings is environment-involving in a way that episodic memory is not. Understanding this difference will allow us to see why semantic memory processes are governed by the principles M1–M4 listed earlier. That is, I shall argue, at least for semantic memory processes, memory must be understood as a combination of internal processes plus the manipulation of information-bearing structures in the environment of the remembering organism.

6.3 THE DEVELOPMENT OF SEMANTIC MEMORY

The development of the semantic memory characteristic of humans, I shall argue, does not lie primarily in biological innovation. There are two main sources of evidence to back up this claim.

The first source of evidence stems from consideration of the memory storage strategies of so called *primitive peoples*. This term is commonly used, admittedly as a conventional label, to designate certain peoples of the 'uncivilized' world, situated at the lower levels of cultural development. There are several things wrong with this expression. Firstly, it is politically incorrect (although replacement with more-or-less equivalent terms like 'savage' and 'uncivilized' does not seem to help). Secondly, and more seriously, it has no clear application. A greater or lesser degree of civilization can be observed in all extant peoples. All of them have already emerged from the pre-historic phase of human existence. Some of them have very ancient traditions. Some of them have been influenced by remote and powerful cultures, while the cultural development of others has become degraded. Primitive man, in the true sense of the term, does not exist anywhere at the present time, and the cultures in question can only be regarded as relatively primitive. Thirdly, and most seriously, it is not clear that the expression has any stable meaning or that it picks out any definite anthropological kind: the meaning of the primitive/modern distinction can vary from one context to another (Goody 1977). Nevertheless, consideration of the memory storage strategies of relatively primitive peoples can, I think, tell us something important about the origins of semantic memory.

It is widely believed that episodic methods of memory storage play a much more significant role in relatively primitive peoples. A glance at any introductory book on comparative anthropology will confirm this. Many observers and travellers have highlighted the outstanding *natural* memory of relatively primitive peoples. And, while this claim will receive serious qualification shortly, there is none the less some truth in it. The relatively primitive memory is, it is commonly thought, at once very accurate, very detailed, but also very specific. It retains representations with a great abundance of detail, and always in the same order in which the events represented are connected. Luria and Vygotsky, for example (in a work that is seriously flawed and outdated but still classic), claim that the natives of Queensland are reportedly able to repeat the whole of a song cycle lasting more than five nights with amazing accuracy. They are able to remember the form of the tracks for each animal and bird they come across, and can also remember the shape of footprints for each person they know (Luria & Vygotsky 1992). Livingstone remarked on the outstanding memory of the natives of

East Africa. Examples of such memory are to be found in the envoys of chiefs, who carried often very lengthy messages over great distances and then repeated them word for word (Luria & Vygotsky 1992).

We shall see shortly that these observations need to be seriously qualified. However, these qualifications will not make any essential difference to the argument to be developed in the following pages. Qualifications aside, what these well-known observations seem to indicate is that relatively primitive peoples make far more use of episodic memory systems than do peoples of the more developed world. Episodic memory in the latter group has become more vestigial. People of the more developed world clearly still possess episodic memory systems, but they do not perform with anything like the efficiency or accuracy of those of more primitive peoples. Despite this, however, there are no biological differences between us and these more primitive peoples. Therefore, if we want to explain the difference in importance of episodic memory storage in primitive peoples relative to us, we will have to look to other than biological differences for this explanation.

It would be a mistake to conclude that the memory of more primitive peoples is simply superior to that of the peoples of the more developed world. The issue here is not one of relative superiority of memory, but of difference in memory storage strategy. Lacking the written word, primitive man has to rely much more on episodic memory. And we find a similar reliance on episodic memory in illiterate people. The important point is that there is a clear difference in memory storage strategy exhibited by primitive peoples relative to more culturally developed peoples. Primitive peoples rely much more heavily on episodic storage strategies. More culturally developed peoples rely, in a sense to be made clear, on *semantic* storage strategies, and their episodic capacity has, compared to primitive peoples, become vestigial. Nevertheless, there are no significant biological differences between us and primitive peoples. Therefore, the differences in memory storage strategy cannot be given a simple biological explanation. Such an explanation will have to look to other than biological facts.

The second source of evidence for the claim that the origin of semantic memory does not lie in biological development derives from certain developmental facts, specifically facts concerning the transition from episodic to semantic methods of memory storage in children (Luria & Vygotsky 1992). The pattern exhibited here, in fact, closely parallels the pattern exhibited in the transition from primitive to more culturally developed peoples. Until they reach a certain stage of development, children seem to rely a lot more heavily on episodic strategies of memory storage. Their episodic memories are, consequently, generally much more powerful than those of literate adults. Photographic memory is, among the more developed peoples, found mainly in children; in adults it is a very rare exception. Adults seem to rely more on semantic strategies of memory storage; children rely more on episodic strategies. But, again, there are no significant biological differences between adults and children, at least none that could explain this change in storage strategy. So, again, we shall have to look to extra-biological considerations to explain the change.

The thesis I want to defend in this chapter is that the functional architecture of modern memory is fundamentally different from its procedural and episodic precursors. This difference in functional architecture is, moreover, reflected in a difference in the structure of the modern memory system. That is, in the development of the modern semantic memory system, there has been a fundamental change in the *hardware* involved in memory storage and retrieval. However, if the arguments of this section are correct, then we shall look in vain for biological developments in the modern brain to explain this hardware change. The fundamental development was not in the brain, but in the environment in which the modern brain is situated. The development of the modern semantic memory system derives, not from biological evolution, but from the development of *external means of representation*.

6.4 EXTERNAL REPRESENTATION AND SEMANTIC MEMORY

The great schism in the development of the modern mind was the incorporation of external means of representation. The significant development was not representation *per se*. This can be found in many non-human animals. All episodic experience is representational, at least in the minimal sense that it is *about* other things. What is distinctive about the modern human mind is not representation as such, but the development of *external* means of representation.

These external means of representation originally took the form of behaviour, almost certainly non-verbal behaviour. The concept of central importance here is that of *mimesis* (Donald 1991:168). Mimetic skill, or mimesis, rests on the ability to produce representational acts that are conscious, intentional, but non-linguistic. The relevant category of events here thus excludes actions that are produced by reflex mechanisms or the result of fixed or instinctive action patterns. The threefold distinction between *mimicry, imitation,* and *mimesis* helps clarify the concept.

Mimicry is literal, an attempt to render as exact a duplicate as possible. The exact reproduction of a facial expression, for example, is an act of mimicry. So, too, is the exact duplication of the call of another bird by, say, a parrot. Imitation is somewhat different. Imitation involves the attempt to perform actions of the same sort as those being imitated, but not, however, to the point of literal copying. The offspring copying its parents' behaviour imitates, but does not mimic, its parents. Mimesis adds to imitation a representational element. With mimesis, there is no attempt at literal or exact duplication of behaviour. Just as with imitation, mimesis involves the attempt to produce behaviour of the same type as that imitated. However, mimesis is also representational. Its purpose is to re-enact, or re-present, an event, action, or situation. Holding the heart, or covering the face to indicate grief, can be mimetic acts – when their purpose is to re-present grief on the part of their performer. Mimesis can incorporate a wide variety of actions and modalities: tones of voice, facial expressions, eye movements, manual signs and gestures, postural attitudes, patterned whole-body movements can all, in appropriate circumstances, constitute mimetic acts.

The origin of mimetic representation presumably lies, in part, in *expression*. Patterns of behaviour which developed into mimetic forms of representation developed out of patterns of behaviour which were typical *expressions* of internal states. The origin of mimetic forms of representation lies in the *iterability* of these forms of expressive behaviour, that is, their capacity to be repeated, or iterated, in the absence of their typical stimuli (Derrida 1976, 1977). Thus, a pattern of behaviour – for example, holding one's hands over one's face – typically provoked by grief can be iterated in the absence of grief. In this way, it then no longer *expresses* grief, but *represents* it. This transition from a form of expression to an external form of representation is crucial in the development of the modern mind in general, and modern methods of memory storage in particular.

It is not just the transformation of expressive forms of behaviour into representational forms that is important however. Representation can also be the result of the iterability of behaviour used towards some sort of cultural or instrumental end (Donald 1991:168). The actions involved in making a stone implement such as an axe or arrowhead, for example, are also iterable. Hence the actions can be transformed into representations in the same sort of way as expressions of grief can be transformed into representations of grief.

Mimetic representations of this sort have several important features. Firstly, they are, of course, *intentional* – directed towards objects, events, etc. This is what makes them representations. Secondly, they are *generative*. It is possible to parse one's own motor actions into components and then recombine these components in various ways to represent the relevant features of an event. This generativity allows for a large number of events to be represented by way of a relatively small 'lexicon' of motor actions. Thirdly, mimetic representations are *public*. And this is because they are *external*. Mimetic representation is the first external form of representation.

The beneficial social consequences of the development of mimetic representation are fairly easy to predict (Donald 1991). Mimetic representation results in the sharing of knowledge, without every member of the group having to rediscover or reinvent that knowledge. Group skills such as hunting and tool-making can now be passed on more efficiently. Social expectations can now be more readily taught and enforced. Mimetic representations might thus be of great importance in building a stable social structure.

For our purposes, however, what is of primary importance is the externality of mimetic representations. This transformation from the internal representations characteristic of episodic experience to external mimetic representations is the fundamental turning-point in the development of the modern mind. With the development of external means of representation, I shall argue, the mind, and strategies of memory storage in particular, took on a fundamentally different type of development. Until the development of external means of representation, any development undergone by the mind was biologically based, the result of evolutionary changes in the structure of the brain. Following the development of external means of representation, however, the mind began to develop in a very different way.

One of the crucial contrasts between internal representations – episodic experiences, episodic memories, and so on – and external representations is that the former, but not the latter, are medium-dependent. That is, internal representations are heavily dependent on properties of the brain. External representations are not similarly constrained by media. It is likely that the earliest forms of external representation took the form of patterns of action. But the same external representations can be realized in many different ways. One type of behaviour which could be employed, and eventually did come to be employed for the purpose of mimetic representation is vocal behaviour. The rapid development of the vocal tract (attendant upon changes in the flexure of the basicranium) evident with the advent of *Homo sapiens* about 200,000 years ago resulted in a rapid expansion of vocal repertoire (Donald 1991:102). Thus, vocal behaviour became a suitable new medium for external representations.

Eventually, the media of representation became more externalized and, at the same time, more permanent. The crucial development here, of course, was the development of writing. Approximately 40,000 years ago came the advent of *visuographic* methods of external representation. At about this time, a proliferation of engraved bones, carved ivory, and so on becomes evident. These objects were primarily two- and three-dimensional representations of contemporary animals. By 25,000 years ago, advanced cave paintings were beginning to appear, the most famous ones being at Altamira and Lascaux. By 15,000 years ago, clay sculptures and figurines started appearing. Early forms of writing started to appear around 6,000 years ago. And it was not until about 4,000 years ago that we find the beginnings of a phonetic alphabet.

The precise details and chronology of each form of visuographic representation are not important for our purposes. What are important are (i) the increasing externality, hence increasing independence, of visuographic over behavioural forms of representation, and (ii) the relative permanence of visuographic over behavioural forms of representation.

Visuographic forms of representation are, as we might say, more external than their behavioural predecessors. Each token behavioural representation, whether vocal or non-vocal, depends on a particular individual for its existence, and it continues to exist only as long as that individual keeps it in existence. When the individual no longer behaves in the appropriate way, then that token behavioural representation no longer exists. Thus, at any given time t, a token behavioural representation can exist only if there is some individual who is behaving appropriately. This is not true of visuographic representations. A visuographic representation token may be dependent upon a given individual for its original production, but, once produced, can exist independently of the behaviour of that individual.

Visuographic representations are also more permanent than their behavioural precursors. Since representations, by their nature, carry information, the relative permanence of visuographic representations yields, for the first time, the possibility of a *store* of information external to the individual. That is, it opens up the possibility of a relatively permanent depository of information external to the individual. Suitably equipped organisms are then able to 'tap in' to this depository; to appropriate and employ the information contained therein.

Just as in the case of visual perception, we have arrived at the idea of an external store of information. For perception, the information was contained in the structure of light – the optic array – which was external to the perceiver. In the case of memory, relevant information is contained in an external and relatively permanent system of representations. Just as with perception, I shall argue, the suitably equipped organism is able to plug in to this external information-bearing structure.

Consider the consequences that the existence of an external information store will have for the development of memory. Given the availability of a relatively permanent information store such as this, in what sort of direction will memory develop? In the remainder of this section, I want to outline, in fairly broad strokes, the nature of the changes brought about by external information stories. As will soon become clear, the account given in the following paragraphs is somewhat oversimplified. I shall, nevertheless, proceed with the account for expository reasons; it provides a very clear illustration of the principal thesis of this chapter. In the section to follow this one, I shall add some important theoretical qualifications and clarifications to the following account. None of these qualifications and clarifications, however, will impugn the general thrust of the following argument. In fact, as will become clear, they strengthen it.

Let us consider a very simple case of visuographic representation. The following account is, historically speaking, roughly accurate.

However, the fact of its historical accuracy is not really necessary to the argument I shall derive from it. The primary purpose of the following example, then, is expository.

One of the more ancient forms of visuographic representation is known as *kvinus* ('knots' in Peruvian). These are a system of knots, and were used in ancient Peru, China, Japan, and other parts of the world. They are conventional external representations which require precise knowledge on the part of those tying the knots. These *kvinus* were used in ancient Peru for recording chronicles, for the transmission of instructions to remote provinces, and detailed information about the state of the army. The *Chudi* tribe of Peru had a special officer assigned to the task of tying and interpreting *kvinus*. In the early stages of *kvinu* development, such officers were rarely able to read other people's *kvinus*, unless they were accompanied by oral comment. However, with time, the system was improved and standardized to such an extent that they could be used to record all the major matters of state, and depict laws and events.

Kvinus are obviously a fairly basic form of visuographic representation. Nevertheless, invention of *kvinus* will have had a profound effect on the development of strategies of remembering employed by those who were familiar with them. To see this effect, compare the memory of an African envoy, transmitting word for word the lengthy message of his tribal chief, with the memory of a Peruvian *kvinu* officer. The African envoy has to remember not simply the content of the message, but, much more difficult, the precise sequence of words uttered by his chief. The Peruvian *kvinu* officer, on the other hand, does not have to remember the information contained in the knot he has tied. What he has to remember is simply the 'code' which will allow him to extract this information. The African envoy relies on outstanding episodic memory to remember the information he has to transmit. The Peruvian officer's reliance is much less, amounting to, at most, the remembering of the code. Once he has remembered the code, he is able to 'tap in' to the information contained in the knot. Moreover, whereas the African envoy must employ his episodic memory resources each time he learns a message, the Peruvian *kvinu* officer need employ his episodic memory only once, in the learning of the code. Then, a potentially unlimited quantity of information becomes available to him without any further employment of episodic memory.

Once an external information store becomes available, it is easy to see how memory is going to develop. Episodic memory becomes a lot less important, restricted to the learning of the code necessary for the appropriation of information in the external information store. This is why, during the process of cultural development, the outstanding episodic memory of primitive man tends to wither away. The evolution of memory is, in this sense, also *involution*; constituted not only by an improvement in certain areas, but also retrograde processes whereby old forms shrink and wither away. This is an absolutely pivotal point in the development of modern memory. Internal development has now become external (Luria & Vygotsky 1992).

The Peruvian *kvinu* officer, having learned the appropriate code, has access to more information than the African envoy could absorb in a lifetime. And this is not bought by way of internal development. The internal demands on the Peruvian officer – the amount of information he must process internally – are, if anything, far less than those placed on the African envoy. The Peruvian is in a position to appropriate more information at less internal cost.

The external representation system constituted by the *kvinus* is relatively simple. The amount and kinds of information it can embody are strictly limited. However, with the development of more sophisticated forms of external representation, which embody greater quantities of information, the benefits of learning the code necessary to appropriate this information increase accordingly.

The parallels with the case of visual perception discussed in the previous chapter now become very clear. What is essential to both cases is the existence of a structure which is (i) external, and (ii) information-bearing. In the case of perception, this structure is the optic array. In the case of (semantic) memory the relevant structure is composed of external representations. In the case of perception, the perceiving organism is able to appropriate and use the information contained in the optic array through acting upon, and thus effecting transformations in, that array. In the case of memory, the remembering organism does not have to retain and process all the information necessary to solve a given memory task. Instead, the remembering organism is able to retain internally a relatively small amount of information – the information that will give it access to the information contained in the external representational structure. In this case, the remembering organism is human, since, on this planet at least, only *homo sapiens* has been able to develop external representational structures. But, in both cases, what is crucial is that the cognizing organism is able to manipulate, to make use of, an external information-bearing structure in order to solve cognitive tasks.

Therefore, if a modern human is faced with a cognitive task that requires a certain amount of information to be remembered, then the amount of internal information processing and/or storage which must occur in order for the information to be remembered, hence for the task to be successfully performed, is inversely proportional to the amount of relevant information that is contained in external representational form, providing that this external information can be accessed by the human. Thus, if an African envoy and a Peruvian *kvinu* officer were both entrusted with conveying the same message, the African's remembering of the message would require far more internal processing and storage than the corresponding memory processes on the part of the Peruvian. The Peruvian allows the external structure to do much of the information processing work for him. The more information that is carried and processed externally, the less needs to be carried and processed internally. And this is precisely the message of M1.

Similarly, when a modern human being performs a given memory task T, we cannot begin to understand what information needs to be processed internally unless we also understand the information that is contained in the form of external representations and the ways in which modern human beings can appropriate and employ such information. Understanding what information is available to us in the representational structures that exist in our environment is a necessary precondition of understanding what information we need to process internally in the accomplishment of the memory task. If we did not understand that the Peruvian officer could exploit information contained in *kvinus*, then we would end up giving a very different account of how he was able to remember information about taxes, wars, etc. This is what principle M2 tells us.

M1 and M2 together express what, in chapter 2, I referred to as the epistemological claim: the thesis that it is not possible to understand the nature of cognitive processes by focusing exclusively on what is occurring inside the skin of cognizing organisms. Therefore, in addition to perception, the case of memory also seems to confirm the epistemological claim.

The Peruvian officer, of course, must, to some extent, engage in internal processing. However, the internal processing that it is *necessary* for him to perform in order to solve a particular memory task is, in this case, restricted to remembering the 'code' which allows him to access the information contained in the knots. The rest of the necessary information is carried by the knots themselves. Through use, or manipulation, of these knots, the officer is able to process whatever information is necessary for him to perform the memory task. And this is true for external information stores in general. For a given memory task T, an organism can process the information necessary for accomplishing that task through the use, or manipulation, or exploitation, of physical representational structures in the environment. So, in certain circumstances, acting upon, or manipulating, external information-bearing representational structures is a form of information processing. And this is what principles M3 and M4 tell us.

Once again, what is crucial here is not the legitimacy or otherwise of applying the label 'information processing' to the manipulation of external information-bearing structures, though it seems to me that only a prior commitment to an internalist view of cognition – that is, an internalist bias – could warrant refusal. The crucial point is that manipulation of external information-bearing structures is a process that (i) involves the manipulation of information-bearing structures, and (ii) is often essential to the accomplishment of a cognitive task, namely remembering. Therefore, it is a cognitive process. And, if this is correct, not all cognitive processes are located exclusively inside the skin of cognizing organisms. And this claim is an expression of what, in chapter 1, I referred to as the ontological claim. Therefore, the case of memory also seems to confirm the ontological claim.

6.5 EXTERNAL INFORMATION STORES IN ORAL TRADITIONS

The account described above is correct in overall direction but, none the less, contains a misleading oversimplification. It was suggested that the African envoy, in learning the message of his chieftain, would rely purely on his episodic memory. This claim is, in fact, almost certainly false. The Peruvian *kvinu* officer is not alone in relying on external information-bearing structures; the African envoy will rely on them also. In fact, the position described in the previous section is a gross oversimplification of the memory strategies involved in non-literate cultures. The reason for this is that the above account is based on two dichotomies, neither of which ultimately prove to be tenable.

The first of these is that between primitive and modern man, hence between primitive and modern memory. As Goody (1977) has pointed out, the distinction between primitive and modern does not record some single rigid dichotomy, but means different things in different contexts. That is, there is not one distinction at work, but a set of distinctions. To the extent, therefore, that the account of the previous section sets up primitive and modern memory strategies as ideal types, the account needs to be modified.

The dichotomy drawn between primitive and modern memory strategies, however, is merely symptomatic of another, deeper, dichotomy. This second, and for our purposes more important, dichotomy is that typically drawn between speech and writing. While writing is immediately recognized as an external symbolic structure, this status is often, sometimes implicitly, not accorded speech. The idea that there is a fundamental difference between speech and writing has had a long history, stemming back at least as far as Plato. However, this dichotomizing of speech and writing is untenable (Derrida 1976, 1977). Speech is no less an external symbolic structure than writing. That is, the difference between speech and writing, viewed as external symbolic structures, is one of degree not kind. The difference is not that writing is, whereas speech is not, an external symbolic structure, but that speech is essentially evanescent; it is a much less permanent external symbolic structure than is writing.

The realization that speech is, after all, an external symbolic structure entails substantial revision of the account of the previous section. According to that account, the difference between the African envoy and the Peruvian *kvinu* officer consists in the fact that the officer, but not the envoy, is able to make use of external symbolic structures. The former remembers the code which allows him to tap into the external information store, but the latter, having no such store into which to tap, must rely on his outstanding episodic memory. The realization that speech, no less than writing, is an external symbolic structure, should make us wary of this whole general idea. If speech is an external symbolic structure, then the oral memory of the envoy might also depend on his ability to manipulate or exploit this structure also. And examination of memory strategies in oral traditions confirms this idea.

In an excellent study, David Rubin (1995) has demonstrated the importance of *sound* in the memory strategies employed by members of non-literate, or oral, traditions. Remembering in oral traditions depends on various constraints which cue memories and restrict choices. Two of these – meaning and imagery – are well known. The idea is that remembering lines from, for example, an epic poem is aided by identification of a semantic theme, or a salient associated image. These often help cue memory of a particular word, and, at the very least, function to restrict word choice so that the correct word is more likely to be remembered. One of the most important features of Rubin's account, however, is its emphasis on *sound* as cuing memories and restricting word choice in a similar sort of way. And sound patterns, of course, are external or environmental structures.

The two most important types of sound pattern relevant to remembering in oral traditions are *rhyme* and *rhythm*. Consider, first, rhyme.

Rhyme, on Rubin's use, covers three distinct types of sound pattern. *Rhyme*, as it is ordinarily used, occurs when the last stressed vowel of a word repeats all sounds that follow it. When the initial consonant cluster of a word repeats, the device is called *alliteration*. When a stressed vowel of a word repeats, the device is called *assonance*. (Definitions of these can, in fact, vary.) All of these Rubin collectively refers to as rhyme.

It is fairly clear how the repetition of a sound can be an aid to memory. When a sound repeats, the first occurrence of the sound restricts the choices for the second occurrence and also supplies a strong cue for it. This function of sound was clarified in a classic series of experiments by Bower & Bolton (1969). Subjects learned a list of 36 paired associate words. For each pair of three letter consonant–vowel–consonant (CVC) words, the subjects were presented with the first and required to remember the second member of the pair. This procedure was repeated, for all 36 pairs, for a total of nine learning trials. Eighteen of the pairs rhymed, the other half were unrelated. Words from the rhyming pairs were always in red, whereas the unrelated words were in black in order to let the subjects know whether to give a rhyming response to the first word. The response members of the rhyming pairs were better remembered on all nine trials, by a margin of 66 per cent to 46 per cent.

The same sorts of results also obtained for alliteration and assonance. Different undergraduates performed the same task of providing response members for pairs of words. However, instead of half the words being rhyming pairs – that is, pairs in which only the first letter of the word differed – in this case 18 pairs consisted of words differing only in the last letter, and the remaining 18 pairs consisted of unrelated words. Thus, pairs that shared both alliteration and assonance were compared with unrelated pairs. Once again, on all nine trials the related words were remembered better than the unrelated ones, by a margin, this time, of 60 per cent to 40 per cent. Thus, with regard to the cuing of memories and restriction of choices, alliteration and assonance together function almost as well as rhyme.

The next task consisted in a multiple-choice test. Instead of having to respond with the correct response member when shown the stimulus member of the pair, the undergraduates had to choose from among a set of five possible responses. In the case of rhyming pairs, both the correct choice and the four incorrect ones all rhymed. For the unrelated pairs, none rhymed. And this removed the ability of rhyme to restrict choice. Thus, there should have been no choice-restricting advantage of rhyming, and, thus, there should have been no difference in the recall of paired associates of each type. And this, in fact, turned out to be the case.

Rubin's account builds on Bower and Bolton's results, and adds another important point. The existence of rhyming words in a song, or speech, will aid recall, but only after the first member of the rhyming set has been uttered and is available to cue recall of the later members. If a song, for example, has many rhyming words in its closing lines, this will not aid recall of the words until the closing lines are reached (Rubin 1995:76). Thus, rhyme, in order to fulfil its proper function of restricting memory choices, must be *externalized*. That is, it must be turned into a sound pattern in the air around the speaker or hearer. A rhyme internalized in the speaker's mind, so to speak, plays no significant role in recall. This observation, in fact, is central to the theory of serial recall developed by Rubin.

Rhythm functions in much the same way as rhyme. That is, the major function of rhythm is that of a constraint, cuing memories and restricting choices. With rhythm, both word choice and choice of larger units is restricted to those with the correct rhythmic pattern, that is, with the correct number of syllables and stress pattern. For example, in a Homeric epic, where the rhythmic constraints are relatively pronounced, words of three or more syllables in length can appear in only one or two places in a line (Foley 1990; Rubin

1995:85). Such placement, in this case, depends only on the pattern of syllables in the word, not on other considerations such as meaning (O'Neill 1942). Memory for units larger than words also benefits from rhythmic constraints, especially units approximately the length of intonation units (Rubin 1995).

Rubin's theory of remembering for oral traditions is partly based on such findings. According to Rubin, recall in oral traditions is *serial*. That is, it starts at the first word and proceeds sequentially. At the beginning of a song, poem, or rhyme, for example, fairly general cues are provided by the constraints of the genre. Then, each word, as it is uttered, provides additional cues that are specific to the particular piece in question. To take a very simple example, consider the rhyme *Eenie Meenie*. On Rubin's view, as the recall begins, the entire sound pattern of the word *Eenie* will cue the word *meenie*, in which it is embedded. *Meenie* will cue *miney* through rhyme, and *miney* cues *mo* through alliteration. Once *mo* is recited, the first line is complete; the meter of the piece has been set, and also, significantly, the *mo*, *toe*, *go*, *mo* end-rhyme pattern. For a short piece like this, the serial nature of the unfolding of the cuing may not be necessary, but for longer pieces, as Rubin points out, it almost certainly is.

Whether or not Rubin's general theory of serial recall proves to be correct is really beyond the concerns of this book. What is important for our purposes is the role played by rhyme (in Rubin's sense) and rhythm in cuing memories and restricting choices in recall. And their importance in this context has been conclusively demonstrated by Rubin, even if his general theory turns out to be incorrect. What is crucial, of course, is that rhyme and rhythm are environmental structures. They consist of patterns of sound that exist outside the skins of remembering organisms. And it is, in part, through exploitation of these patterns in the structure of ambient sound that the rememberer is able to accomplish given recall tasks. Exploitation of these external structures is, thus, partly constitutive of certain types of remembering.

Nor is exploitation of these structures restricted to the remembering of things like epic poems in oral traditions. As Rubin shows, the same sorts of factors are essential to serial recall outside oral traditions. They are, for example, clearly present in the attempts of students to recall items such as the Preamble to the Constitution of the United States (Rubin 1995:177–83). Thus, the considerations apply even to pieces that do not have conspicuous rhyming features, or a striking rhythmic cadence. This can be seen from the fact that in the recall of the Preamble, points where memory failed in the subjects under test correspond very closely with natural stopping points in a recitation - i.e., points to take a breath. Also, when a subject omits part of the Preamble, the part omitted almost invariably corresponds to an intonation unit; partial intonation units are almost never omitted.

Given that this is so, it was an oversimplification to present the African envoy as relying only on episodic memory in order to remember the message of his chief. In such a memory task, the envoy also exploits external structures – specifically the structure in the pattern of ambient sound. But this, of course, does not undermine the principal thesis of this chapter; on the contrary, it reinforces it all the more strongly. Even cases of apparently purely internal memory – episodic memory as that is classically understood – appear to be made up, in part, of exploitation of external structures. In this sense, then, the points made in this section are far from incompatible with the general picture presented in the previous one. In fact, they strengthen that picture quite considerably.

6.6 AN ANALOGY

An external representational system is a store of information which can be relevant to the performance of a given memory task. Invention of such a system is inherently a method of external memory storage. As long as a person possesses the 'code' (and such possession presumably is constituted by an internal store of some sort) for a given set of representational symbols, the information stored in the symbols is available to that person. The development of external representational systems constitutes a radical change in human strategies of memory storage. Indeed, it constitutes a *hardware* change, albeit a non-biological one. External representational systems can be regarded as the exact external analogue of internal memory, namely a storage and retrieval system that allows humans to solve various memory tasks. So, we can make a distinction between two types of storage and retrieval strategies for memory. There is the internal, biological, strategy where information is stored in the brain and retrieved by way of suitable operations occurring there. And there is the external, non-biological, storage and retrieval strategy. Here information can be stored in a variety of different external stores, visual, auditory, etc., and also in culturally transmitted memories that reside in other individuals.

Merlin Donald has introduced a useful analogy here, one I truly wish I had thought of first (Donald 1991:308–25). The analogy is based on the notion of *networking*. For any computer, it is possible to identify both hardware and software properties of that computer. The processing capacities of a given computer can be described in terms of its hardware features (such as memory size, central processing, and speed) and its software features (such as its operating system and available programming support). The distinction is also commonly applied to humans: a hardware description would commonly be thought of as a description at the level of neurophysiology; a software description might describe the skills, language, and knowledge carried by the individual (though, in fact, there are numerous, non-equivalent, ways of drawing the hardware/software distinction as applied to human beings, and possibly also in the case of computers).

However, as Donald points out, both the software *and* the hardware features of an individual computer will change if it is embedded in a network of computers. In any specification of what a computer can do, the features of the network in which it is embedded must be taken into account. Networking, that is, essentially involves a structural change. Once it is part of a network, the computer can delegate to other parts of the system computations that exceed its own internal capacity. It can also assign priorities within the larger system of which it has become part. Its outputs can be stored anywhere in the network, that is, in external information stores. In a true network, the resources of the system are distributed across the whole system, and that system functions as a unit larger than any of its individual components.

Another relevant analogy (also due to Donald) might be the addition of magnetic tape or disc storage to a computer. The random-access-memory (RAM) of a computer is somewhat analogous to biological memory in that it depends for its existence on the intrinsic properties of the machine. One way of expanding the memory capacity of a computer is to bolster its RAM. This, however, could not go on indefinitely, and would be extremely costly. Similarly, an expansion of biological memory capacities would eventually be stymied by considerations of evolutionary cost, energy requirements, etc. (see chapter 4). The other way of increasing the memory capacity of a computer is by way of hard external storage, and this is far more economical and, indeed, flexible, than the strategy of bolstering its RAM. In essentially the same way, human memory capacity can be increased, in a similarly economic and flexible manner, by the development of external representational systems.

The invention of external representational systems should be regarded as, in the first instance, a hardware rather than a software change. Such systems constitute a collective memory hardware, and this is as real as any external memory device for a computer. Individuals in possession of reading, writing, and other relevant skills have access to the 'code' that allows them to plug into this external network. They thus become somewhat like computers with networking capabilities; they are equipped to interface, to plug into whatever network becomes available. And, once plugged in, their memory capacities are determined both by the network and by their own biological endowments. Those who possess the 'code', the means of access to the external system, share a common memory system. And, as the content of this system expands far beyond the scope of any single individual, the system becomes by far the most significant factor in the memory of individuals.

In a network, where is the program that runs a computer located? Does it reside in the computer? Is it located there in whole? Or in part? Even if these questions make any sense, they do not matter. The crucial thing is that the information required for the performance of a given task, such as an information retrieval (i.e., memory) task is located 'out there', that is, in the network. For humans engaged in an information retrieval task, the major *locus* of stored information is 'out there' in the external representational system. It is not stored biologically, but environmentally. Biological retrieval strategies are largely limited to storage and retrieval of the relevant code that yields access to this external information store, and not with the storage and retrieval of a great deal of specific information.

6.7 THE ENVIRONMENTALIST CONCEPT OF WORKING MEMORY

The defender of the traditional internalist view of memory might adopt the following line. We can distinguish between the external bearers of information, and the methods of gaining access to them, and the process of remembering proper. The former are simply *aids* to memory. The process of remembering proper occurs inside the brain, specifically within that functionally specified part of the brain that is often referred to as *working memory*.

Working memory is typically conceived of as a system whose function is to temporarily hold information required for various cognitive operations. There is, in fact, little agreement on the structure of working memory, but the expression is generally used to refer to an exclusively biological memory system, which functions something like a short-term store, and which supports problem-solving, learning, and thought. If a given cognitive task requires deployment of information contained in long-term memory, then this information supposedly has to be brought into working memory in order to be available for this task. Again, it is not clear what is involved in bringing material from long-term memory into the working memory system, although this is typically conceived as a matter of certain files being 'open' or 'active' while others remain closed. Whatever its algorithmic basis, the core idea is that information contained in working memory is more accessible to conscious sequential thought than information contained in long-term memory stores. Working memory is a biologically realized, but functionally individuated, short-term store into which information can be brought and then manipulated and transformed.

There are, however, serious problems with this idea. In particular, experimental evidence indicates that there are enormous limitations on biological working memory. Human beings can take only five to seven items into their temporary store at the same time (Miller 1956), and such assimilation is extremely vulnerable to interference, therefore extremely unreliable (Broadbent 1958). Short glimpses of scenes often yield highly unreliable accounts of what transpired, to the point where eyewitness testimony, even when tested immediately after the event, is demonstrably inaccurate (Buckout 1982). It is, therefore, difficult to see how such a limited, delicate, and manifestly fallible instrument could be the functional location where complex, and often very lengthy, cognitive tasks are accomplished.

These problems can be avoided by revising the concept of working memory along the lines of the environmentalist model developed in this chapter. On this model, humans do not perform complex cognitive operations exclusively in working memory, at least not if this is understood exclusively as a biologically realized system. As a purely biological system, working memory would be far too unstable and unreliable. In modern human culture, people engaged in all but the simplest memory tasks virtually always employ external information-bearing structures. It is the information contained in these external structures which is the true *locus* of working memory. This is not, of course, to deny that the biological memory system plays any role in memory tasks. It clearly does. Rather, the point is that the biological system is, in modern humans, employed in such a way that it functions in conjunction with external information-bearing structures. The biological system, in many cases at least, is employed as a loop in the cognitive processes that perform transformations on the information contained in external structures. It is these structures themselves that become the temporary holding store. It is these structures that play the role traditionally attributed to working memory.

The external information-bearing structure can, here, be regarded as a temporary cognitive structure, where the cognizer uses this structure for a limited time, both to hold certain items and to process the relevant information in appropriate ways. Advanced memory tasks virtually always depend on this sort of arrangement. The cognizer selects appropriate external information-bearing structures and uses its perceptual systems to examine, process, and rearrange these structures; and uses its motor capacities to transform and add to those structures already present. Each purely biological operation is necessarily a short one, whose function is to work off the external information-bearing structures in the way described.

How can the notion of working memory be redefined to incorporate the environmental nature of complex thought? Consider the processes involved in comprehension of the information contained on this page. Such comprehension might, it seems, be effected by way of the following procedure: (1) The page is scanned and some of the external items (i.e., words) entered into biological working memory; (2) these items are decoded; (3) the semantic content of the items is reduced to a few essentials; (4) the process continues until some criterion of completion is reached. This process undoubtedly involves biological working memory systems, but not, crucially, in an independent role. They do not perform the actual scanning; they do not decode; and they do not effect the semantic reduction (the brain's language systems presumably do that. See chapter 8). Biological working memory is no doubt involved, and involved quite centrally, but it is not functioning in an independent role. In complex memory tasks, biological working memory is employed in such a way that it functions, for all practical purposes essentially, only in conjunction with external information-bearing structures.

Thus, upon examination, the concept of working memory seems to fragment into two components. There is what we can call biological working memory. And there is what we might call external working memory. Traditionally, working memory has been conceived of as exclusively biological in character; that is, as a sub-system of the brain. However, upon examination, the functions of a truly biological working memory are seen to be extremely attenuated, and amount to nothing like the functions and capacities usually ascribed to working memory systems. In order to successfully account for these functions and capacities we must view working memory as not purely biological in character. Instead, it must be viewed as essentially *hybrid*, made up of two distinct components. In particular, the processes involved in working memory must be viewed as made up of both biological processes *and* processes of external manipulation of relevant information-bearing structures in the environment.

One final point is worthy of note. If we view working memory in this way, then this will seem to entail a re-emergence in the importance of procedural memory systems. That is, what is vital in the accomplishment of a given memory task will be a certain type of procedural knowledge, specifically, knowledge of how to work with, how to employ, how to manipulate, how to exploit, relevant environmental structures in appropriate ways. Thus, the employment of external information-bearing structures in the performance of cognitive tasks points to a new, and perhaps hitherto unsuspected, role for procedural memory. This is a suggestion that will be explored in the next chapter.

7

Thought

In this chapter and the next, the focus of discussion switches to thought and language. It is in psychological theorizing about the processes responsible for thinking and language use that the internalist picture of the mind has exerted, I think, a particularly powerful influence. This influence has manifested itself in a variety of ways and along a variety of axes. Consequently, in this chapter and the next, the task of unseating the internalist picture takes a variety of forms.

I shall argue, roughly, that the internalist pre-theoretical picture of the mind has influenced theorizing in the following sorts of ways. Firstly, by conceiving of the processes responsible for thought and language use as ones occurring purely inside the head of cognizing, language-using organisms, the picture tempts us into inserting all the constitutive features of thought and language use inside the head. If thought or language use is generative, then the internalist picture tempts us into thinking that the relevant processes occurring inside the head must be generative. If thought or language use is systematic, then the picture tempts us to think that the relevant processes occurring inside the head must be systematic. That is, if thought or language use has a certain structure, a structure judged to be essential to it as such, then the internalist picture tempts us into believing that the relevant processes occurring inside the head, processes which allow us to think or use language, must have that same structure. This is because, according to the internalist picture, it is these processes, and these processes alone, that are essential (in a psychotectonic sense, at any rate) to thought or language use. One of the tasks of this chapter, then, is to subvert this effect of the internalist picture.

Secondly, in virtue of conceiving of the processes relevant to thought or language use as purely internal processes, the internalist picture encourages us to conceive of the type of cognition involved in such processes in a particular way. The internal processes responsible

148

for thought or language use are, it will be argued, typically conceived of as *rules* which determine how, in any given situation, thinking or use of language is to proceed. Propositional knowledge, or *knowing that*, thus becomes the key concept in internalist attempts to account for thought and language use. Contrast this with the environmentalist picture whose beginnings can be discerned in the previous chapter. Suppose we emphasize, as will this chapter, the role of an external information store in explaining the ability of organisms to think or use language. Then, at least part of the explanation of how organisms can think or use language will rely on how the organism is capable of manipulating, exploiting, or in other ways using, this external store. Thus, the explanatory task will involve, at least in part, explaining how the organism is capable of making such use of the external store. Thus, with the environmentalist picture of thought and language, procedural knowledge, or *knowing how,* assumes an importance it did not possess with the internalist picture. And this, of course, will have significant consequences for our conception of the psychotectonic processes involved in thought and language use.

This chapter discusses thought. The discussion here will be rather programmatic, and concerned, in the main, simply with indicating the differences between accounts of thinking predicated on the internalist picture, and those predicated on the environmentalist one. The following chapter discusses language use, but, at the same time, attempts to fill in some of the details overlooked in this chapter's discussion of thought.

One point, however, is crucial to understanding both chapters. The purpose of this book, one should remember, is to unseat or subvert a particular pre-theoretical picture of the mind. The purpose is not to demonstrate the falsity or incoherence of this picture. The strategy of subversion proceeds by trying to show that, firstly, we do not have to think of things in the way this internalist picture requires us to, and, secondly, there are, in fact, really no good theoretical reasons for thinking of things in the way the internalist picture requires us to. Consequently, there is no attempt in these chapters to show that the various theoretical articulations of the internalist picture are false or incoherent. The aim of the chapter is to subvert these theoretical articulations by showing that they are not required. The aim, that is, is not to demonstrate their falsity but remove their motivation.

7.1 THE SYMBOLIC PARADIGM

According to the symbolic paradigm, cognition should be understood as a form of symbol manipulation. This view of cognitive processes has two principal roots.

The first of these is formal logic. What makes formal logic such a powerful tool is the possibility of adopting two, non-competing, perspectives towards it. According to the *model-theoretic* perspective, the symbols for propositions can be understood as representational devices. In particular, the symbol can be understood as representing a state of affairs that may or may not hold in the actual world. Thus, from this perspective, the proposition expressed by the symbol is true if the actual world contains the state of affairs – the model – represented by the proposition. It is false if it does not. A model, here, is a set of entities. From this perspective, then, it is possible to assess whether a pattern of inference is such that for any model in which the premises are true the conclusion will also be true. The model-theoretic perspective, then, allows us to capture the notion of *truth-preservation*, and, from this perspective, a valid argument is one which is truth-preserving.

The second perspective it is possible to adopt towards formal logic is known as the *proof-theoretic* perspective. The focus of this perspective consists in the relations among the symbols themselves, and not between the symbols and the states of affairs they represent. Rules of inference are, thus, proof-theoretically defined over symbols; and these are construed as formal entities, individuated by way of their syntactic and not their semantic properties.

The power of formal logic derives, in large part, from the possibility of integrating these two perspectives. Such integration will yield proof procedures that are both *complete* and *consistent*, where a proof procedure is complete if it allows us to derive *all* propositions that are true in all models in which the premises are true, and a procedure is consistent if it enables us to derive *only* propositions that are true in all models where the premises are true.

Therefore, if intelligence could be understood simply as reasoning in accordance with the principles of deductive logic, it should be possible to identify formal proof procedures that adequately describe intelligence, hence possible to develop systems capable of intelligent performance. However, intelligence clearly depends on more than being able to make truth-preserving inferences. In certain circumstances, for example, it requires the ability to make judgments about what is *likely* to be true. Such judgments are the concern of inductive logic. The goal of inductive logic is to identify formal rules, analogous to the proof-theoretic rules of deductive logic, that lead from propositions that are true to those that have a certain specified probability of being true. Modelling intelligence, therefore, requires, at the very least, the identification of formal inference procedures of two sorts: those that are truth-preserving and those that yield a certain probability of truth-preservation. The crucial assumption in the identification of both procedures is that we need focus only on the formal properties of symbols; their representational function can be disregarded.

Reflections of this sort on the nature of formal logic inform much of the theorizing in artificial intelligence. The digital computer is often conceived of simply as a device for implementing formal logical systems. Symbols are simply sequences of 1s and 0s, implemented by *on* and *off* settings of switches. The basic operations of the computer allow symbols to be recalled from memory and then transformed according to rules. These rules are typically carried by a stored program. And, like the formal rules of logic, the rules in the computer program are sensitive only to the formal properties of the symbols they transform.

The symbolic view of the mind, motivated as it is by these considerations, is thus characterized by the following principles. Firstly:

S1. Cognitive states are relations to representations.

A representation is a state or structure that represents the world; that is, in some sense, it carries information about the world. Positing representations, of course, is by itself fairly uncontroversial. What is distinctive of the symbolic view of the mind is not the positing of representations as such, but its view of the nature of representations:

S2. Representations are symbols; they have both formal and semantic properties.

Just like logical symbols, mental representations not only represent the world, they also have a certain form, structure, or *shape* (in some suitably abstract sense). Just as the symbolization 'P → Q' can represent a certain state of affairs in the world, so, too, can a mental representation.

And, just as 'P→Q' can interact with other symbols (e.g., P, ¬Q) in virtue of its form, so, too, can mental representations.

S3. Cognitive processes consist in the transformation of symbols.

Again, the parallel with logical processes is fairly exact. Just as a logical process might consist, for example, in the transformation of the symbols 'P→Q' into the symbols '¬Q→¬P', or the transformation of '¬P & ¬Q' into ¬(P v Q), so too, it is claimed, cognitive processes consist in the transformation of the symbols which constitute mental representations.

S4. Such transformations are effected by way of rules which are themselves symbolic.

In logic, a rule of inference such as 'P→Q ⊣ ⊢ ¬Q→¬P' is itself a symbol structure (i.e., a combination of symbols). And, in artificial intelligence, a stored program which tells the computer which operations to execute is simply a sequence of symbols that directly determines what operations the computer will perform on other symbols. Similarly, according to the symbolic view of the mind, transformation of mental representations is brought about by other symbols which are also instantiated in the brain, although, on the usual understanding of the symbolic model, these rules do not have to be explicitly represented there.

S5. These rules apply to symbols in virtue of the formal properties of those symbols.

Just as the logical rule of inference known as DeMorgan's theorem applies to any proposition of the form ¬(P & Q) (or ¬P & ¬Q) irrespective of the content, hence the representational properties, of that proposition, so, too, it is claimed, the rules which govern the transformation of symbolic mental representations apply to those representations in virtue of their formal, and not their semantic, properties. The brain is a syntactic, not a semantic, engine.

This, in broad outline, is the symbolic view of the mind. This paradigm has been developed in a variety of ways by symbolic theorists such as Dennett (1978a), Fodor (1981), and Pylyshyn (1984).

There are several variations on this general model, none of which, however, take us outside the general symbolic paradigm. An alternative way of understanding the semantic properties of symbolic systems has been put forward by Newell and Simon (1981). According to Newell and Simon, a computer is a *physical symbol system*, where this consists of three distinguishable elements. There are symbols, understood, roughly speaking, as higher-order physical patterns. There are expressions, understood as complex symbols constructed out of the combination of physical patterns. And there are processes that operate on expressions. Newell and Simon argue that the semantics associated with such a system exists within the system itself. For example, expressions in stored programs can designate locations in computer memory, and these expressions can, therefore, be semantically interpreted by accessing those locations. This internal semantics, Newell and Simon claim, clearly distinguishes computer symbol systems from formal symbol systems such as those of logic. Moreover, they argue that this sort of internal semantics is essential to intelligence (this is the famous *physical symbol system hypothesis*). Newell and Simon's claim, however, is still of a piece with the symbolic view of the mind as sketched above. Their claim concerns the question of the autonomy of semantics from syntax, and they argue that there is nowhere near the degree of autonomy here that would be expected if the mind were a formal symbol system exactly like logic. This claim, however, even if true, in no way undermines the view that cognitive states are relations to symbols, and that cognitive operations act on these symbols in virtue of their formal properties. Newell and Simon's position, that is, should be seen as a variation upon, rather than a departure from, the symbolic view of the mind.

A similar position, I think, should be taken with regard to another important claim made by Simon (1967). Computers can be viewed as devices for implementing logical operations: programs implement algorithms that function in the same way as rules of inference in a logical system. An algorithm, here, is a procedure that is guaranteed to produce a certain solution in a certain number of steps. An algorithm's guarantee of success, however, is bought at the cost of efficiency. For real time processing operations, Simon argued, *heuristics* – i.e., procedures that *might* obtain the desired result, often by means of an intelligent shortcut such as ignoring unpromising search paths – are often more important than algorithms. Again, this claim should be viewed as a supplementation of, rather than a departure from, the symbolic model. If Simon is correct, then heuristic rules of thumb would have to be introduced as, in part, governing transformations between mental representations. But, just as with logical rules of inference, heuristic rules of thumb can be viewed as being themselves symbolic – i.e., symbol structures. Hence, the claim that heuristic rules of thumb play an important role in cognition in no way undermines the symbolic view of the mind.

The other main root of the symbolic paradigm is found in Noam Chomsky's programme in linguistics. In his famous (1959) review of B. F. Skinner's *Verbal Behaviour*, Chomsky argued that a behaviouristic model was inadequate to account for the ability of humans to learn and use language. The central focus of his argument was provided by the creativity or *generativity* of language. Any natural language has an infinite number of well-formed, i.e., grammatical, sentences, and its speakers can understand and produce an indefinitely large number of sentences that they have not previously encountered (Chomsky 1957, 1959, 1968). This ability, Chomsky argued, is not behaviouristically explicable, even when supplemented by processes such as analogy and generalization.

Chomsky's approach to explaining linguistic competence centres around the notion of *generative grammar*. Writing a grammar amounts to specifying an automaton that can generate infinite sets of sentences (this is assured by including at least one recursive rule). Whether or not such a grammar is adequate depends on whether it generates *all* of the well-formed sentences of the target language, and *only* those sentences. Chomsky argued that finite-state grammars – those implicated in a behaviourist account – are inadequate. They do not generate the correct set of sentences. In particular, finite-state grammars cannot account for dependencies across indefinitely long strings of symbols. These dependencies require at least a phrase-structure grammar, and preferably a transformational grammar. A phrase-structure grammar consists in rules which expand one symbol into a string of subordinate symbols. They thus allow indefinitely long strings to be embedded within a phrase-structure tree, and thus isolated from the surrounding dependencies. The power of phrase-structure rules can be enhanced by combining them with transformational rules, rules which modify one phrase-structure tree to obtain a related tree.

Chomsky regarded generative grammars as providing a model of linguistic *competence*, not *performance*. Because of this, his implementation of the symbolic approach is more abstract than that typically employed by computational psychologists. Nevertheless, Chomsky proved extremely influential in facilitating the transition from behaviourism to cognitivism. And this, to a great extent, was due to the fact that his grammars suggested ways to model human cognition using formally specified operations on strings of symbols.

Chomsky's notion of a generative grammar provides another way of developing the symbolic view of the mind. Whereas the view described in the previous pages assimilates the mind to a formal logical system, of the sort which might be provided by deductive, inductive, abductive, epistemic, etc. logic, the view of the mind implicated in Chomsky's work, or which develops out of Chomsky's work, sees the mind less as a logical system and more of a linguistic system. On this view, cognition requires the internal instantiation of linguistic, or quasi-linguistic, symbols together with the phrase-structure and transformational principles which allow these symbols to be combined in grammatical ways. It is this sort of interpretation of the symbolic view which receives expression in the *language of thought* hypothesis (Fodor 1975, 1981). However, this model is simply another version of the symbolic view of the mind, and not a departure from that view. Principles S1–S5 apply equally to this development of the symbolic view. It is just that in its Chomskyan development, the formal properties possessed by mental representations will be, at least in part, what we might call *syntactic* properties, where this is to be understood on analogy with the syntactic properties possessed by properly linguistic items. And the rules which govern the transformation of mental representations will now, at least in part, be made up of grammatical (phrase-structure, transformational) rules.

Thus, both the logical and the linguistic developments of the symbolic view can be correctly seen as versions of the same underlying view. According to this view, cognitive processes consist in the manipulation of internal, logically or syntactically structured, representations. The arguments developed in the earlier chapters of this book do not sit easily with such a view. However, this is not just because of the externality or environmental character of cognition. According to the position developed in this book, cognition is made up of both internal and external components; it involves manipulation of *both* external *and* internal structures. This prompts the following suggestion. The symbolic approach can be made compatible with the environmentalist position developed in this book by restricting its scope to the internal component of cognition. That is, the symbolic approach should be understood as concerned with supplying an account of the nature of internal structures whose manipulation is, in part, constitutive of cognition. In this chapter I shall try to show that, while there is no logical incompatibility involved in conjoining the form of environmentalism developed in this book with a symbolic understanding of the nature of the internal component, nevertheless, environmentalism does make it less likely that a symbolic understanding of the nature of the internal component will turn out to be correct. More precisely, I shall argue that (i) *if* we accept the environmentalist position developed in the earlier chapters, then the sort of role or function that the internal component has to accomplish is ill-suited to being modelled in terms of the apparatus of internal syntactically structured representations, and (ii) *given* the form of externalism developed above, the sorts of considerations that typically motivate the symbolic approach are no longer as compelling.

7.2 PATTERN MAPPING AND PROCEDURAL KNOWLEDGE

In the previous chapter, I suggested that at least part of the function of the internal component of memory should be conceptualized as a form of *procedural* knowledge; or as a form of *knowing how*, specifically, knowing how to manipulate the relevant external information-bearing structures. It is this suggestion that will be explored and developed in the following sections. In this section, I want to explore the connection between this sort of procedural knowledge and the concept of *pattern mapping*.

Once we allow that cognition involves manipulation of environmental structures, then it becomes quite plausible that the internal processes which, together with external manipulation, constitute cognition consist of pattern-mapping operations. Pattern mapping, in this sense, is made up of four different types of process. *Pattern recognition* is the mapping of a given pattern on to a more general one. *Pattern completion* is the mapping of an incomplete pattern on to a completed version of the same pattern. *Pattern transformation* is the mapping of one pattern on to a different but related pattern. And *pattern association* is the arbitrary mapping of one pattern on to another, unrelated, pattern (Bechtel & Abrahamsen 1991:106).

The view that cognitive processes consist in pattern-mapping operations has been defended in several quarters. J. R. Anderson's

ACT* model is a rule-based production system that functions by recognizing patterns (Anderson 1983). And a number of other cognitive theories can be viewed as emphasizing pattern mapping also (see Margolis 1987). However, pattern-mapping devices *par excellence* are to be found in *connectionist* systems, also known as *parallel distributed processing* systems, or *neural network* models (Rumelhart et al. 1986). To see how these systems are able to effect one type of pattern–mapping operation, specifically pattern recognition, consider an early version of such a system: Rumelhart and McClelland's *interactive activation model* (McClelland & Rumelhart 1981). This model illustrates how a multi-layered network can recognize visual patterns, specifically four-letter words, presented in a particular font. The network possesses an input layer of *features* (e.g., bottom left vertical bar); a middle layer of *letters* (e.g., E); and an output layer of four-letter *words* (e.g., EACH). Unlike more recent multi-layered networks, its middle layer of units is not actually a hidden layer. Specifically, the connection weights of this layer are specified by the designers rather than extracted by the network itself, and the activation patterns of this layer are visible in the sense that when the network recognizes a word (top layer), it also recognizes letters (middle layer) and can repeat either level depending on the task. Since the system is designed to deal with words of four letters, there are four copies of the feature and letter sets, one copy for each letter of the word. Each feature unit is positively connected to units for letters that possess the feature and negatively connected to those that do not. Similarly, the letter units are positively connected to units for words that contain the letter in the appropriate position, and negatively connected to those that do not. There are also connections in the converse direction: the word units are positively connected to units for the letters they contain. Finally, word units and letter units are each negatively connected to all competitors in the same layer.

An input is provided to this network by activating the appropriate features in each of the four letter positions. For a word with an E in position two, five of the units in the second ensemble of feature units will be activated. These are, bottom horizontal bar, bottom left vertical bar, middle horizontal bar, top left vertical bar, top horizontal bar. Activation is then propagated from each of the excited feature units to all those letter units of the middle layer that possess these features. For example, the bottom horizontal bar sends activation to such letter units as E, Z, and B. While virtually all letter units will be activated to some extent, activation will be highest for the E unit, since this possesses all of the activated features. As the letter units become active, they send this activation on to the word units with which they are consistent. These word units will then reverse excitation back to those same latter units.

This is a primitive type of connectionist system, developed before the back propagation learning technique was available. Nevertheless, it produces responses similar to those of human beings under a variety of non-ideal conditions, including missing features and low contrast. It is able to successfully negotiate these sorts of non-ideal conditions because, like any connectionist network, it operates to satisfy multiple soft constraints. It also exhibits more subtle phenomena of human word recognition such as the word superiority effect: the effect that very briefly displayed letters are better recognized when they are presented in the context of a word.

The McClelland and Rumelhart model is one fairly basic attempt to show how visual processing involves a process of pattern recognition. Pattern recognition, of course, together with the other three kinds of pattern-mapping operation, is what connectionist systems do best. Indeed, it is no exaggeration to say that, in essence, connectionist systems *are* pattern-mapping devices. Therefore, if connectionism is to be regarded as capable of providing an account of cognition in general, it must be shown that, and how, other types of cognitive process – in particular, the so called *higher* cognitive processes – can be reduced to pattern-mapping operations.

Now, it is well beyond the scope of this book to show that (and certainly not how) all cognitive processes can be reduced to pattern-mapping operations. Firstly, I am not at all sure (to say the least) that this can be done; and, secondly, it is, anyway, essentially an empirical issue. My concern here, in common with the wider concerns of this book, is how the internalist pre-theoretical picture of the mental closes down a certain legitimate and important line of theoretical inquiry. For, even if it is not true that all cognitive processes can be reduced to pattern-mapping operations, it is true, I shall argue, that the internalist picture has played a significant role in minimizing the possible importance of pattern-mapping operations to cognition. Therefore, in the remainder of this chapter, I shall try to show how the environmentalist position can provide a boost to the connectionist attempt to model cognitive processes. And, I shall argue, the environmentalist position supports the connectionist one by showing how pattern-mapping operations can play a much more significant role in cognition than can be allowed for by the internalist picture.

Another crucial feature of the connectionist, as opposed to a more traditional symbolic, view of pattern mapping is that it is inherently *non-propositional* in character. If the connectionist approach is correct, then recognizing patterns (i.e., matching current patterns to the cognitive residue of previous patterns) is not only widely applicable, but is also carried out without the use of symbols as such. A well-known distinction developed by Gilbert Ryle is useful here: the connectionist approach assimilates pattern mapping to the category of *knowing how* rather than *knowing that* (Ryle 1949).

This distinction is, of course, manifest in our language. We speak not just of knowing certain facts, but also of knowing how to do things. The *knowing that* construction invites completion with a *proposition*; the *knowing how* construction invites completion with an *infinitive*. The linguistic distinction also seems manifest at a deeper psychological level. A person who knows that Cardiff is the capital of Wales will be able to retrieve the proposition that expresses this fact from memory, or to retrieve other propositions that entail this one. But the same sort of thing does not seem to be true for a person who knows how to drive a car. In this latter case, what is required is an ability; specifically the ability to do appropriate things in appropriate circumstances. It would be a mistake, however, to regard knowing how as purely non-cognitive in character. Many types of knowing how have a cognitive dimension. One might know how to make or appreciate jokes, to talk grammatically, to play chess, to argue, etc.

Ryle's thesis with regard to the relation between these two types of knowledge is well known: knowing that is not primary but is derivative upon knowing how to perform certain activities. 'Intelligent practice is not a step-child of theory. On the contrary, theorizing is one practice amongst others and is itself intelligently or stupidly conducted' (Ryle 1949:26). Propositional knowledge is not *sui generis*, but subsequent to and derivative upon possession of certain abilities. And Ryle, of course, gave this idea a behaviouristic gloss. Knowing how is not to be understood in terms of something hidden and internal, but as a disposition to perform a given action in appropriate circumstances. However, this behaviouristic gloss is not essential to the distinction.

A more cognitivist approach, for example, can accept the distinction but seek an explanation of the internal mechanisms which underwrite the capacity.

Until the advent of connectionist modelling, the only available cognitivist accounts of such mechanisms involved rules. Such knowledge was referred to as *procedural knowledge*. This is knowledge of procedures that can be adopted in order to accomplish a specified goal. This knowledge was typically conceived as being encoded in rules that are proposition-like in their basic structure, but are imperative rather than indicative in character. Phrase structure and transformational grammars provide examples of procedural rule-based structures (although these rules are abstract representations of competence rather than performance). The most obvious examples of procedural systems, however, are undoubtedly production systems. Each rule in a production system is of the form 'If A then B', where A is some condition that must be met, and B is an action that is carried out if A is indeed met.

Procedural systems, however, based as they are on procedural knowledge of this sort, effectively invert Ryle's account of the relation between knowing how and knowing that. If procedural knowledge is conceptualized in terms of essentially proposition-like rules, then production systems and their ilk constitute nothing more than an attempt to ground knowing how in terms of knowing that. And this, of course, is the reverse of the relation envisaged by Ryle. However, there is nothing in the concept of procedural knowledge itself which mandates that it be understood as proposition-like and rule based in this sense. And, henceforth, when I use the expression *procedural knowledge*, I shall not assume that it should be thus conceptualized. That is, procedural knowledge, I shall assume, can be either proposition-like or nonproposition-like in character.

What might a non-propositional procedural system look like? The answer is: like a connectionist system. Unlike rule-based systems, connectionist networks bear little relation to propositional formats. They are composed of units that are interconnected rather than ordered in strings, and often these units are not even symbols in the ordinary sense. However, when some of these units are activated, the system, in effect, *knows how* to respond. That is, when some units are excited, this activation will be propagated along weighted connections until a steady state, or *solution,* is reached. In this way, *knowing how* can consist in processing in a network rather than the sequential application of proposition-like rules.

Indeed, one of the problems faced by connectionist approaches to cognitive modelling is giving an account not of knowing how, but of knowing that. If connectionism abandons symbol strings as a modelling medium, can it still account for the human ability to assert propositions and argue for their truth. One possibility, here, is for the connectionist to adopt the Rylean approach and try to conceptualize knowing that as derived from, or as a special case of, knowing how. This, however, is (to say the least) a controversial claim, and one to which I shall *not* commit myself. The purpose of this chapter and the next is not to show that knowing that can be reduced to knowing how but, rather, to show both how and that the internalist pre-theoretical picture of the mind has systematically minimized the possible relevance of knowing how to cognition. Thus, it will be argued, the environmentalist position greatly enhances the significance of knowing how with respect to the processes involved in thinking and language use.

It will be argued that the internalist pre-theoretical picture of cognition has greatly prejudiced the case against connectionism. It has done this by systematically minimizing the importance of both pattern-mapping operations, and the associated idea of knowing how, to cognition. Instead, the picture has tempted us into conceiving of cognition as proposition-like and rule-based in character. Therefore, the internalist picture has shut off legitimate and potentially important avenues of inquiry. And, therefore, environmentalism is, to this extent, a good friend of connectionism; perhaps its best friend. One can make this point without being committed to the claim that connectionism is a correct account of all cognitive processes. One can make this point without being committed to the claim that all cognitive processes are a form of pattern mapping. And one can make this point without being committed to the claim that knowing that reduces to knowing how.

7.3 PATTERN MAPPING, PROCEDURES, AND THE 'MANIPULATE THE ENVIRONMENT' STRATEGY

Connectionist systems are very good at certain tasks, and very bad at others. Part of the allure of connectionism, in fact, is that the tasks connectionist systems are good at are the sort of tasks that can be easily, or relatively easily, performed by human beings. Conversely, the sort of tasks that connectionist systems are not very good at are those tasks that human beings also seem to find difficult. The tasks that human beings and connectionist systems seem to be very good at number, broadly speaking, the tasks that can easily be reduced to pattern-mapping – recognizing, completing, transforming, and associating – operations. These include visual perception/recognition tasks, categorization, recalling information from memory, and finding adequate solutions to problems with multiple partial and inconsistent constraints. The tasks that humans and connectionist systems are relatively bad at include, most notably, logical and mathematical calculations and formal reasoning in general.

The object of comparison in this talk of the relative proficiency of human or connectionist systems in the performance of certain tasks is, of course, the traditional symbolic system. The tasks that human and connectionist systems are good at are precisely those tasks that have been most difficult to implement in traditional symbolic systems. And the tasks that connectionist systems and human beings are not very good at are precisely those tasks that are most easily implemented in traditional symbolic systems. In short, connectionist models are good at the sort of things at which humans are good, and bad at the sorts of things at which humans are bad, while for traditional symbolic systems the reverse is true. And this is a good prima facie reason for supposing that connectionist systems are more promising models of human cognition than are symbolic systems.

Connectionist systems are good at modelling any type of cognitive process that can be reduced to some sort of pattern-mapping operation, or a series of such operations. From the connectionist point of view, the problem with a process such as formal reasoning is that it does not, prima facie, seem reducible to operations of this sort. Connectionist and symbolic approaches seem to face converse problems here. According to the symbolic approach, the capacity of humans to engage in formal reasoning processes is to be explained in terms of there being formal structures, together with rules governing transformation of these structures, instantiated in human heads. One of the problems with this sort of approach is that it makes it difficult to explain why humans are so *bad* at formal reasoning processes such as those involved in mathematics and deductive logic. More precisely, the symbolic approach makes it difficult to explain characteristic patterns of errors exhibited by humans engaged in formal reasoning processes. If formal reasoning is a matter of manipulating structures in a rule-governed way, and if the relevant structures and rules are instantiated in the head, then it seems that we human beings should be, if not infallible, then at least a lot better than we are at formal reasoning procedures.

The connectionist approach faces the opposite problem, namely explaining how human beings can be so *good* at formal reasoning. Connectionist systems specialize in pattern-mapping operations and this leaves no room for there being, instantiated in human heads, formal structures and rules governing their transformation. Thus, since formal reasoning does not, prima facie, seem reducible to pattern mapping, it seems as if connectionism is going to have difficulty explaining how human beings have achieved the level of competence in formal reasoning they have in fact achieved. It is precisely here that the *manipulate the environment* strategy described and defended in this book can be of help to the connectionist.

Rumelhart, Smolensky, McClelland, and Hinton's modelling of our ability to engage in mathematical reasoning shows that connectionists have already, in effect, adopted the manipulate the environment strategy (Rumelhart et al. 1986, chapter 14). In a fairly simple case of multiplication, say $2 \times 2 = 4$, most of us can learn to just see the answer. This, suggest Rumelhart et al., is evidence of a pattern-completing mechanism of the sort that can easily be modelled by a connectionist network. But, for most of us, the answer to more complex multiplications will not be so easily discernible. For example, 343×822 is not easy to do in the head. Instead, we avail ourselves of an external formalism that reduces the larger task to an iterated series of smaller steps. Thus we write the numbers down on paper and go through a series of simple pattern-completing operations (2×3, 2×4, etc.), storing the intermediate results on paper according to a well-defined algorithm. Rumelhart et al.'s point is that if we have a connectionist system that is *embodied* in the sense that it is incorporated into a further system that is capable of manipulating mathematical structures external to it, then a process such as long multiplication, which ostensibly requires postulation of internally instantiated mathematical symbols, can be reduced to other processes which require no such thing. The main features of this embodied network are:

(1) A pattern-*recognition* device necessary for recognizing external structures such as '2', '×', '3' etc.

This sort of device would be easily implementable by a connectionist network. Rumelhart and McClelland's interactive activation model, or a suitable modification thereof, provides one illustration of the sort of model the connectionist might adopt.

(2) A pattern-*completion* device necessary for completing already recognized patterns such as '2 × 3 = '.

Again, pattern-completion devices of this sort can be easily implemented by connectionist networks. Finally:

(3) A capacity to manipulate mathematical structures (or physical instantiations of mathematical structures) in the environment.

Thus, for example, upon recognition of the pattern '2 × 3 = ', the embodied system is able to complete that pattern and then, crucially, write or record the numeral '6'. This then forms a new pattern for the system to recognize, and its completion and recording, in turn, direct the system to a further pattern to be recognized and completed, and so on.

In this way a process – long multiplication – which seems prima facie to require the postulation of internally instantiated mathematical symbols can be reduced to an *internal* process of pattern recognition and completion together with a process of manipulation of *external* mathematical structures. The entire process can be regarded as a combination of internal pattern-mapping operations and manipulation of external information-bearing structures. The internal pattern-mapping operations, in part, constitute a sort of procedural knowledge, a type of knowing how; specifically, knowing how to manipulate, in relevant ways, certain appropriate external information-bearing structures. And, as we have seen, neither of these processes, external or internal, require the postulation of internally instantiated mathematical symbols; nor do they require postulation of rules governing the transformation of such symbols. The role that was thought to be played by *internal* symbols and rules has largely been usurped by *external* symbols and rules, and the internal residue consists of non-symbolic pattern-recognition and completion mechanisms. These mechanisms, in part, realize the procedural knowledge necessary to manipulate the external symbols in the relevant (i.e., rule governed) ways.

This is a very clear analogue of the *principle of the non-obvious character of (evolved) internal mechanisms*, even if the mechanisms in question here are not evolved ones. The most obvious character or structure to be possessed by the internal structures necessary for performing a mathematical-reasoning task would, of course, be mathematical. And if there existed an organism or system that could accomplish mathematical-reasoning tasks and yet was not able to manipulate mathematical structures in its environment, then, it seems very likely that the organism or system would have to possess an internally instantiated system of mathematical structures and rules. However, once we allow the organism the ability to manipulate mathematical structures (or the physical instantiations thereof) in its environment, all this changes. Now, the only internal mechanisms required are procedural and pattern mapping in character. And these sorts of internal processes are not at all obvious ones given that the task in hand is that of solving a mathematical problem. If the nature of the task is mathematical, then non-mathematically structured internal processes are not obvious candidates for underwriting the ability to accomplish this task. None the less, when combined with the appropriate type of environmental manipulation, they can, in fact, underwrite this ability.

Rumelhart et al.'s strategy also, in fact, provides a very clear analogue of the *barking dog principle*. Manipulation of mathematical structures in its environment reduces what an organism must accomplish internally in order to perform a given mathematical task. How is this so? It seems that all that has gone on internally is that one sort of process – a process involving mathematical symbols and rules governing their transformation – has been replaced by another sort of internal process – a process that is pattern recognizing/completing in character. How exactly does such a replacement constitute a *reduction* in the demands on the internal processing that the mathematically competent organism must perform?

The answer is that pattern recognition and completion operations seem to impose less cognitive demands on human beings than do symbolic operations of similar computational power. Pattern-mapping operations seem to place relatively low demands on the human cognitive system in the sense that they seem to be operations that are implementable fairly easily in such a system. And, once we allow the system the capacity of manipulating external mathematical structures, then there is no need to postulate any sort of cognitive processing that places higher demands on the cognizer; of the sort, for example, that might be involved in the manipulation of *internal* mathematical symbols. If this is not immediately obvious, then consider the following. In performing a mathematical calculation of the above sort, the symbolic approach construes the process involved as one of manipulating internal mathematical symbols and comparing the results of such manipulation. The environmentalist position developed in this book construes the process involved as one of manipulating external mathematical symbols and comparing the results of this manipulation. But it seems fairly clear that the cognitive burden of comparing suitably manipulated external symbols is a good deal less than the burden of performing the manipulation internally and comparing the results of this internal manipulation. Think of the extraordinary difficulty completing jigsaw puzzles would have if we were not allowed to physically manipulate the pieces but could only form internal representations of the pieces and manipulate these representations; that is, if we had to complete the jigsaw *in our head*.

So, the general pattern that emerges from these reflections on Rumelhart et al.'s connectionist approach to mathematical reasoning looks something like this. Suppose we are presented with a specific kind of cognitive process, P, such as mathematical reasoning. This process, we can suppose, does not obviously consist in pattern matching or completing operations and, hence, does not seem to be amenable to connectionist modelling. However, if we take into account the ways in which an organism can, in the performance of P, manipulate relevant structures in its environment, then P can, upon further analysis, be broken down into a composite process of (i) manipulation of relevant environmental structures, and (ii) internal pattern-mapping processes. That is, a cognitive process that does *not* ostensibly *appear* to be pattern mapping in nature can be factored into two components, one of which is essentially pattern mapping in nature, and the other of which is essentially environmental. In other words, processes that might appear to require the postulation of internal symbolic structures and rules for their transformation can be reduced to pattern-mapping operations that require no such rules and structures plus manipulation of relevant environmental structures. Since the structure of the environment mirrors the structure of the cognitive task at hand, there is no need for this structure to also be possessed by the internal milieu. It is the environmental component, the manipulation of external structures, that obviates the need for internal symbolic structures and rules.

Two conclusions emerge from these reflections, and they are clearly expressions of the environmentalist position defended in previous chapters. Firstly, at least in the case of mathematical reasoning, we cannot begin to understand what internal processing a cognizer must perform in order to accomplish a given mathematical task unless we understand the extent to which, and the ways in which, that cognizer is able to manipulate relevant structures in its environment. These external structures are bearers of information relevant to the performance of given mathematical tasks, and an organism that is suitably equipped – that is, possessing appropriate manipulative capacities plus the ability to recognize and complete patterns in collections of external symbol structures – is able to appropriate this information. Secondly, to manipulate these external symbols in relevant ways is, in effect, to process the information contained in them. Not all the information processing necessary for the performance of mathematical tasks takes place inside the skin of organisms. The first of the above conclusions is an expression of what was earlier referred to as the *epistemological claim*. The second is an expression of the *ontological claim*.

The same sorts of considerations apply, I think, to other sorts of formal reasoning process. According to the symbolic approach, the ability to make logical inferences should be understood as a primitive cognitive ability. Consider, again, a production system. A production system works because it has encoded in it the inference rule *modus ponens*, $P \rightarrow Q$, $P \vdash Q$. In such a system, when the antecedent P is satisfied, this, in conjunction with firing of the production $P \rightarrow Q$, produces the specified action Q. If our minds are symbolic systems, then, like a production system, such rules of inference are already encoded in it. Learning an inference rule such as *modus ponens*, then, is essentially akin to Plato's idea of anamnesis. We are learning to express a principle already encoded in our minds (although presumably in a different format). And, when we learn a rule our mind has not already encoded, DeMorgan's theorem for example, this rule then becomes encoded into our symbolic reasoning system as new productions that may fire when their antecedents are satisfied.

The environmentalist position defended in this book is not logically incompatible with such a view. What it does do, however, is undermine this sort of symbolic approach by robbing it of its primary motivation. Bechtel and Abrahamsen have shown how the connectionist approach to mathematical reasoning exemplified by Rumelhart et al. can be extended to formal logic (Bechtel & Abrahamsen 1991). They discuss the problems of teaching students to use the argument forms of formal logic and conclude that what students must learn to recognize is patterns in *external* symbols. This is slightly more complicated than the above mathematical case, since the patterns have place fillers for variables, and what is required to instantiate the pattern is that the symbols occupy the place fillers and stand in the right relations to each other. Once a student is capable of recognizing such patterns, then she is able to both evaluate arguments and construct new ones. Constructing proofs, Bechtel and Abrahamsen argue, is an extension of this ability.

Bechtel and Abrahamsen's point is this. If we *embody* a connectionist network in a system that is capable of manipulating external formal structures, then the processing demands on the connectionist network can be substantially reduced. In this case, we again find the following sort of pattern. A process – formal/logical reasoning – which prima facie requires the postulation of internal symbols and operations defined over them is reduced to a combination of (i) a connectionist pattern recognition and completion system, and (ii) an ability to manipulate logical structures (or physical instantiations of such structures) in the environment. Once again, a process that is very difficult to implement in a connectionist system is made very much easier once we allow that system to be embodied in another system that is capable of manipulating its environment. And, once again, the reason why this reduction entails a diminution of the internal processing demands is that the cognitive costs of physically manipulating external symbols and comparing the results of such manipulation are less than the cognitive costs of performing the manipulation internally and comparing the results of this internal manipulation.

Therefore, and in exactly the same way as the case of mathematical reasoning, the need for internal processes of a certain type P – in this case processes involving logically structured symbols together with rules governing their transformation – is eliminated in favour of (i) internal processes of a distinct type Q (in this case, pattern mapping), plus (ii) the ability to manipulate relevant portions of the environment. Process Q can be implemented at less cognitive cost than process P since part of the burden of processing the information necessary for achieving the cognitive task in question is achieved through the manipulation of the environment. That is, the logical structures in the cognizer's environment are bearers of information relevant to the performance of certain types of cognitive task, namely formal/logical reasoning. When an organism manipulates these structures, it is, in effect, processing the information contained therein. Therefore, some of the burden of information processing is carried by the manipulation of external structures, and the need for internal information processing is correspondingly reduced. Of course, if we did not adequately attend to the ways in which an organism, in the performance of a given cognitive task, is able to process information through manipulation of the environment, then we could not begin to understand the nature of the internal information processing task facing that organism. In fact, we would almost certainly end up overestimating the extent of the internal information processing task, probably to the extent of postulating processes of an entirely different order than those that are, in fact, instantiated.

If the arguments of this chapter are correct, then processes of reasoning – at least of the formal/mathematical variety – seem to follow the framework identified in earlier chapters. Our capacity to engage in processes of formal reasoning depends essentially on our ability to manipulate formal structures in the environment. And, therefore we cannot understand the capacity to engage in formal reasoning independently of our ability to manipulate environmental structures. Thus, once again, the ontological and epistemological claims, identified at the beginning of the book, are confirmed. These claims can come to the aid of connectionist attempts at cognitive modelling. Mathematical and logical reasoning processes constitute *hard cases* for connectionism because they do not, prima facie, seem reducible to pattern-mapping operations. If we embody a connectionist network in a system that is capable of manipulating environmental structures in an appropriate way, then the demands on the internal processing the network must accomplish are correspondingly reduced. In particular, by embodying the network in this way, we no longer place it under the burden of modelling or implementing internal logically or mathe-matically structured symbols. The environmentalist position devel-oped here allows that rule–governed manipulation of mathematically or logically structured entities is essential to mathematical and logical reasoning. However, what is crucial is that these structures do not have to be internal structures, and their manipulation does not have to take place internally. Instead, the mathematical or logical structures can be environmental items, and their manipulation can take bodily or behavioural form. In other words, the role envisaged by the sym-bolic tradition for internal rules and representations is externalized, it is moved outwards. It is precisely because we are able to manipulate externally located mathematical and logical structures that we *might* have no need to manipulate internally located ones.

Within the environmentalist framework, what a connectionist net has to accomplish is not the modelling of internal, syntactically struc-tured, symbols plus rules which act on those symbols in ways sensitive to their structure. Instead, what the net must be able to satisfactorily model is the ability to *use* an appropriately structured external symbol system in appropriate ways. That is, what the net must be able to model, and account for, is a certain type of *procedural knowledge* (in the non–propositional sense identified earlier). In order to give the embodied system the ability to engage in processes of formal reason-ing, that is, the net must give the system the ability to *know how* to use an external symbol system. And, this, as earlier discussion hopefully makes clear, seems to be a much easier task for a neural net.

In this chapter, I have not argued that connectionism is correct as an account of all cognitive processes. Nor have I argued that the sym-bolic approach is incorrect or misguided. My primary concern has been to show how a tacit commitment to the internalist pre-theoreti-cal picture of the mind has prejudiced the case against connectionism. Pattern-mapping operations and the associated notion of knowing how have a difficult time finding a home in the internalist picture and in theoretical articulations of that picture. Within this picture, they find themselves essentially marginalized, of little or no relevance to understanding the notion of cognition in general and that of reason-ing in particular. If, on the other hand, we adopt the environmentalist picture, cognition in general and reasoning in particular come to be understood, at least in part, as processes of manipulating or exploiting environmental structures. And, in this context, the importance both of pattern-mapping operations and of knowing how, are significantly enhanced.

In the next chapter, I want to explore the possibility of extending this general approach to attempts to model language. In the next chapter, also, some of the oversimplifications and lacunas perhaps evident in the above discussion will be addressed.

8

Language

In this chapter, the focus switches from thought to language, specifically to the higher-order cognitive processes involved in allowing us to successfully use language. Once again, the primary concern of this chapter is not to demonstrate that a particular theoretical account of these processes is wrong (or right). This, as probably will be clear by now, would not cohere with the overall strategy of this book. This has been not to demonstrate the falsity of the internalist pre-theoretical picture of the mind but to unseat or subvert it by showing that we are not required to think about the mind in the way this picture requires. In this way, the motivation for the internalist picture is, at least to some extent, removed. Consequently, the strategy in these chapters has been not to show that particular theoretical articulations of this internalist picture are false; the strategy has, rather, been to remove their motivation and thus loosen the grip their underlying picture has on us. Part of this strategy, moreover, has been to show the deleterious, or potentially deleterious, effect a tacit commitment to the internalist picture can have on our thinking and theorizing about the mind; how the picture can close off various legitimate and potentially important avenues of inquiry. In the case of our theorizing about language use, I shall argue, this is precisely what has happened.

One central question in recent discussions of the processes responsible for language use has been this: in virtue of what can a system or organism be capable of obeying principles of linguistic composition? If we are in the grip of the internalist picture, we will think that only internal processes can be essentially relevant to the answering of this question. But, then, we will be tempted to suppose, it is necessary that the principles of composition be, in some way, built into the organism or system. If we build in processes which obey principles of linguistic composition, then we can explain how the system as a whole can obey these principles. The environmentalist picture, however, gives us another way of thinking about the problem. Instead of building the principles of linguistic composition into the internal processes themselves, we make the internal processes such that they imbue the organism or system in which they are embodied with the capacity to discern patterns in an external system that obeys such principles. And we place these internal processes in a system that is capable of manipulating and exploiting or in other ways utilizing the external structures which make up this system. As we shall see, it is very likely that a system which is capable of discerning patterns of composition in external structures does *not* thereby require these principles to be built directly into it.

Once again, I will not be arguing directly that the environmentalist approach is necessarily superior to the internalist one. My point is that, firstly, we do not have to think about the problem in the way the internalist picture seems to require, and, secondly, tacit commitment to the internalist picture automatically closes off legitimate and important avenues of inquiry. As in the last chapter, the debate between symbolic and connectionist approaches provides a useful organizing principle.

8.1 FODOR AND PYLYSHYN'S CASE AGAINST CONNECTIONISM

A typical symbolic approach to understanding the cognitive processes involved in language production and understanding is reflected in work that developed out of early Chomskyan linguistics (Chomsky 1957, 1968). Chomsky's generative grammar, as we have seen, details procedures for manipulating strings of symbols that are composed in particular ways. These procedures include both phrase structure and transformational rules. The symbolic approach to understanding how the mind is capable of understanding and producing language involves a fairly simple extension of this idea to the view that the mind might process language by performing these sorts of operations. Thus, on this view, understanding and speaking a language requires the internal instantiation of linguistically structured symbols together with the phrase structure and transformational rules that allow these symbols to be concatenated in grammatical ways. Note that the symbols must be linguistically structured in order for the phrase structure and transformational rules to be applicable to them. This sort of model, involving rules and linguistically structured representations, can be taken as representative of the symbolic approach towards understanding the cognitive skills involved in language use.

Many have gone further than this, noticeably further, in fact, than Chomsky has been prepared to go. It has been argued that not only are the cognitive processes involved in understanding and speaking a language linguistic in character, but so, too, are all higher-order cognitive processes. This is the *language of thought hypothesis* made famous by Fodor (1975, 1981). According to this hypothesis, all higher-order cognitive activities require information to be stored or represented in the mind in the form of symbol strings. This information is then processed by way of transformations of these symbols, where these transformations are rule governed. These symbol strings are conceived as constituting a language in that they are composed according to syntactic rules. Cognition consists in a process of transforming these symbols in appropriate ways, and the transformation operations are performed on the symbols in virtue of their syntax.

It has been widely pointed out, of course, that it is very difficult to see how this sort of internal linguistic system could be implemented in a connectionist network. And, if such a system is essential not only to our ability to understand and process language, but also to our ability to engage in any sort of higher cognitive process, then connectionism would obviously be in very serious trouble. Fodor and Pylyshyn have attacked connectionism on precisely these grounds. Their arguments are of some importance and it is to them that we now turn.

Fodor and Pylyshyn argue that only a system with *linguistically structured* symbolic representations can adequately model cognitive processes (Fodor & Pylyshyn 1988). Any adequate model of these processes must exhibit three features:

(1) *Productivity* (generativity). This is the capacity to understand and produce a potential infinity of propositions (or, more precisely, an indefinite and arbitrarily selected number of propositions from an infinite set). This capacity must be achieved with the use of finite resources. Therefore, recursive operations are required.

(2) *Systematicity*. There is an essential connection between the ability to think one thought and the ability to think others. They argue, for example, that anyone who can think 'John loves the girl' can also,

necessarily, think 'The girl loves John.' For this to be so, the two mental representations, like the two sentences, must be composed of the same parts.

(3) *Inferential coherence*. This is the ability to make syntactically and semantically cogent inferences. One can infer, for example, from a true conjunction (A & B) that both conjuncts are true. And one can infer from the proposition 'It is raining in Spain' to the proposition 'It is raining somewhere.'

These features are all possessed by natural languages. And the reason this is so, according to Fodor and Pylyshyn, is that natural languages possess a combinatorial syntax and semantics. Fodor and Pylyshyn infer from this that the only viable way of modelling these features is to build into one's model a combinatorial syntax and semantics. And this, they claim, involves linguistically or syntactically structured representations together with recursive rules which apply to those representations in virtue of their syntax.

Fodor and Pylyshyn argue that connectionist systems have no way of combining simple representations into (the correct sort of) more complex ones. Therefore, connectionist systems, they argue, cannot exhibit the above three features. The reasons for this differ depending on whether the connectionist system in question is given a *localist* or *distributed* semantic interpretation. Consider, first, a connectionist system under a localist interpretation. In this case, each representational unit is atomic, and units relate to each other exclusively by way of pairwise causal connections. Thus, if A&B and A are two units in a network, it is possible to set the weight of the connection from A&B to A in such a way that activating A&B results in the activation of A. This could be viewed as a kind of inference. The problem is, however, that the representation of A is not a syntactic part of the representation A&B. And this means that the connection between A&B and A is not compositional in nature. Thus, any two nodes could be wired to have the same pattern of influence; for example, A&B might excite unit Z. But this means, crucially, that the inference must be built in separately for each instance of conjunction rather than by means of a rule that utilizes variables to specify the syntactic relation of inclusion. The A&B unit must be specifically linked to the A unit; the B&C unit must be specifically linked to the B unit, etc. Therefore, Fodor and Pylyshyn argue, connectionist networks under a localist interpretation cannot exhibit a feature such as systematicity.

The inadequacy of connectionist systems under a distributed interpretation derives from somewhat different reasons. In such networks, the units that are active in a particular representation encode not objects but features or microfeatures of represented objects. Smolensky, for example, suggests, by way of example, a set of *ad hoc* features for the representation *cup of coffee*, a set divisible into three sub-sets with respect to combinatorial structure: (i) the set of features that applies to *cup* alone (e.g., porcelain curved surface), (ii) the set that applies to *coffee* alone (e.g., brown liquid), and (iii) the set that applies only to *cup* and *coffee* as they interact (e.g., brown liquid contacting porcelain). On Smolensky's view, compositional structure can be achieved by the incorporation of the sub-sets for *cup* and *coffee* in the set for *cup of coffee* (Smolensky 1987, 1988).

This sort of response, however, really misses the point (as, alas, does Rowlands 1994 also). As Fodor and Pylyshyn point out, the sort of compositionality secured by the distributed representation approach is not the correct sort of compositionality. Specifically, a microfeature is part of a representation of an object in a quite different way than that in which one syntactic unit is part of another. The notion of syntactic inclusion cannot be captured in terms of the notion of set membership. Thus, in a symbolic representation of the proposition 'John loves the girl', it is because the representation of 'John' stands in a particular syntactic relationship to the rest of the proposition that the proposition is distinct from 'The girl loves John.' The same, however, does not seem to be true of a distributed representation. For example, a (minimally) distributed representation of the proposition 'John loves the girl' could be achieved in a network whose units corresponded to various microfeatures of John and the girl. Activating the units for these microfeatures would provide a distributed representation of the proposition. However, Fodor and Pylyshyn argue, this representation would be indistinguishable from the representation of 'The girl loves John.' The problem, at root, is that the units are not ordered syntactically, but merely bundled together in a relation of co-occurrence, without the sort of hierarchical structure that syntax would provide. Fodor and Pylyshyn conclude that connectionist networks, whether localist or distributed, are unable to model a properly combinatorial syntax and semantics.

Fodor and Pylyshyn do allow that the nervous system in which our symbolic representations are instantiated may be a connectionist system. But, even if this were true, they claim, this would only show that connectionism provides an account of the *implementation* of the symbolic representational system. According to Fodor and Pylyshyn, only an analysis at the level of symbolic processing is relevant to cognitive theorizing. And, if their argument is correct, this level must, it seems, be non-connectionist.

In this way, Fodor and Pylyshyn present connectionism with a potentially devastating dilemma. On the one hand, if connectionist systems are presented as models of cognitive processes, then they are incapable of capturing such features as productivity, systematicity, and inferential coherence which, argue Fodor and Pylyshyn, are constitutive of cognition. On the other hand, if connectionist systems are presented merely as models of the implementation of cognitive processes, then such systems are not relevant to the understanding of cognition as such. Either connectionism provides an inadequate account of cognition, or it doesn't provide an account of cognition at all.

8.2 CONNECTIONISM AND THE MANIPULATION OF EXTERNAL LINGUISTIC STRUCTURES

According to the symbolic approach, the human capacity for language use should be understood in terms of an internally instantiated system of symbols together with a set of rules governing the transformation of these symbols. The symbols have compositional or syntactic structure, and the rules apply to the symbols in virtue of this structure. The system of rules and representations provides a medium where such features as generativity, systematicity, and inferential coherence can be both *effected* and *enforced*. Productivity, systematicity, and inferential coherence can be effected in this internal medium because the symbols have compositional structure. And they can be enforced in this medium because the grammatical rules apply to the symbols in virtue of this structure. However, if the general position advanced and defended in this book is correct, connectionism *may* be able to explain the human capacity for language use without recourse to an internal system of symbols and rules. Just as in the case of logical and mathematical reasoning, it is possible to *relocate* the relevant symbolic system. That is, it is possible to shift the explanatory focus from an *internal* system of rules and representations to an *external* one. There are two types of relevant environmental structures.

The first of these consists in the physical instantiations of linguistic symbols used in language. These can take various forms – sound patterns, written characters, manual signs, and so on. The symbols however, in all these forms, have compositional or syntactic structure. These physically instantiated symbols allow certain sorts of use – for example, referring to objects, issuing orders, expressing feelings, etc. They also, crucially, afford certain sorts of composition. This compositionality is sensitive to the structure of the symbols, and allows composite structures to become available to language users. These external symbols, in whatever form they take, are the external analogues of the internal syntactically structured representations postulated by the symbolic approach.

The second environmental structure is, in effect, the external analogue of the internally instantiated linguistic rules postulated by the symbolic approach, and is provided by other users of the language. Language use, in the first instance, is embodied in a social context, and its private uses are derivative upon this. Learning to use a language depends on developing the capacity to interact in a social context in which the particular principles of language use embodied in the community are exhibited. This sort of point was made famous by Wittgenstein (1953), who argued that meaningfulness of a linguistic item depended upon the capacity of a user to adjust his or her use of that item to bring it into accordance with customary norms. The project of giving meaning to a sign is not something that has to, or indeed can, be achieved by the individual language user. The same sort of point applies equally at the level of syntax and grammaticality. The rules which govern the ways in which external symbols can be legitimately combined to form more complex symbol structures are best cashed out in terms of community-wide patterns of behaviour. Ultimately, what determines the grammatical correctness or otherwise of combining one symbol with another in a particular way is the pattern of grammatical usage exhibited by the linguistic community.

The external symbolic system which we call language is, of course, a system that is compositionally structured in just the same way as the internal symbolic system postulated by the symbolic paradigm. And, equally clearly, it, too, provides a medium where compositionality, and the attendant features of generativity, systematicity, and inferential coherence, can be *effected*. The community-wide practices or patterns of grammatical use, as the determinants of the grammatical rules which apply to this symbolic system, might then provide the means by which compositionality is *enforced* (Bechtel 1993).

The parallel with the cases of mathematical and logical reasoning discussed in the previous chapter proves illuminating. In the case of mathematical reasoning, a straightforward application of the symbolic approach would recommend the postulation of an internal system of mathematically structured symbols together with rules which apply to these symbols in virtue of their structure. The approach defended in this book, and which is, in fact, adopted by Rumelhart et al., is to recommend the postulation of a system that is capable of using the rule-governed, mathematically structured, system present in the environment. It is in this external medium that mathematical compositionality is both *effected* (in virtue of the structure of the external symbols) and *enforced* (in virtue of community-wide patterns of use of these symbols). And the capacity to use this external system in the appropriate way is achieved by way of a pattern recognition and completion device of the sort that can easily be modelled by a connectionist system.

In the case of logical reasoning, a straightforward application of the symbolic approach would recommend postulation of an internal system of logically structured representations together with rules which apply to them in virtue of their structure. The approach defended in this book, and which is in fact adopted by Bechtel and Abrahamsen, is to recommend postulation of a system that is capable of using the rule-governed, logically structured, system present in the environment. It is in this system that logical compositionality is both *effected* (in virtue of the logical structure of the external symbols) and *enforced* (in virtue of community-wide patterns of use of these symbols). And the capacity to use this external system is, again, achieved by way of a pattern recognition and completion device of the sort that is easily constructed along connectionist lines.

Given the correctness of the above approach to mathematical and logical reasoning, it seems reasonable to see how far a similar approach to language can be developed, since language is, at least prima facie, a symbol system no different in kind from logic or mathematics. In order to explain our capacity for language production or understanding we should not automatically assume that it is necessary to postulate an internal linguistic or quasi-linguistic system. In order to explain an organism's capacity for language use, there may be no need to, so to speak, *plug* language into that organism. Instead, we *plug* the organism into a linguistically structured environment, and we give it the capacity to use, to utilize, this environment.

Developing this account requires, at the very least, that we (i) build in to the language-using system the ability to recognize, complete, and perhaps transform and associate, patterns in its linguistic environment, and (ii) act on this environment so as to create new linguistic patterns.

The first step in this process is to view the linguistic community, and not the language user, as the primary enforcer of principles of grammatical compositionality in the language. This is very much in keeping with a Wittgensteinian approach to language. What the individual language user must have, on this account, is not internally instantiated principles of linguistic composition, but the capacity to adjust his or her use of linguistic items to customarily accepted norms. And this capacity, in turn, will involve a sensitivity to patterns of usage instantiated in the linguistic community. This sensitivity will, then, be explainable in terms of pattern recognition and completion operations of the sort that are amenable to connectionist modelling. Therefore, just as in the case of logical and mathematical reasoning, what the language user must possess is the ability to identify patterns that are instantiated in the environment. Thus, it is sensitivity to environmental patterns that, in part, enables the language user to obey principles of linguistic, syntactic or grammatical composition, and not the fact that these principles are somehow internally instantiated.

The second step in this process will then focus on the ability of the organism to manipulate and/or exploit linguistic structures in its environment. If it is the patterns of use embodied in the linguistic community which *enforce* principles of syntactic compositionality, then it is in the external linguistic structures that syntactic compositionality is *achieved*. In the cases of logical and mathematical reasoning described earlier, we envisaged a system that was capable of manipulating external symbols according to well-defined algorithms and then discerning the results of such manipulation. These results could then enable the system to engage in further manipulation of the symbols, discern further results, and so on. And, crudely speaking, it is the ability of the system to engage in manipulation of external symbols which eliminates the need for it to engage in manipulation of internal symbols. The same sort of point could be applied to language. If a system possesses the capacity to engage in appropriate (where the notion of appropriateness is enforced by the linguistic community) manipulation of external syntactically structured symbols then, to this extent, it might not have to engage in manipulation of internal syntactically structured symbols. We imagine a system that is capable of producing external linguistic structures, whether sound patterns, written characters, or manual signs. It is also, through a fairly straightforward connectionist pattern-recognition device, capable of recognizing patterns in these external structures, and modulating its production of structures on the basis of what gets recognized. If we suppose that the system's production of linguistic structures depends on (i) recognition of patterns in external linguistic structures (the *locus* of grammatical compositionality) and (ii) recognition of patterns of use embodied in the linguistic community (the enforcer of grammatical compositionality), then there seems to be no more (and also no less) reason for positing an internal linguistic system to explain language use than there is to introduce an internal mathematical system to explain mathematical reasoning, or an internal logical system to explain logical reasoning.

If the approach outlined above is correct, then it should apply not only to the case of language use, but also to Fodor and Pylyshyn's more general concerns about the nature of thought. Given the correctness of the above account, connectionist systems might be capable of exhibiting such features as generativity, systematicity, and inferential coherence, not because they themselves are structured in such a way as to exhibit these features, but, rather, because, in virtue of the structure they do have, they are capable of using or employing an external linguistic system which exhibits these features. And the structures by means of which a system is capable of using or manipulating an external linguistic system are not the same as the structures instantiated in that system itself.

The account of the environmentalist alternative presented in this and the previous chapter has been somewhat programmatic. It is time to fill in some of the details; and such filling in must occur on two fronts. Firstly, some account of the nature of the internal processes involved must be given. Giving such an account basically amounts to specifying the nature of the connectionist network that can realistically be thought to have a reasonable chance of explaining language acquisition. Secondly, a much more detailed account must be given of the various environmental features which allow the system to become linguistically competent. The account we can then give would explain how the system's interactions with these environmental structures allow that system to achieve the task of language acquisition.

To avert misunderstanding, the following points should be borne in mind. Firstly, in what follows there is no claim that it is definitely possible to explain language without recourse to internally instantiated, linguistically structured, representations and rules. There is, that is, no blanket ban on the postulation of such items. Methodologically, my position here parallels principles P1 and P2 for the case of perception and M1 and M2 for the case of memory. That is, we cannot begin to assess whether an internal linguistically structured system is required in order to explain language use until we appreciate the extent to which such use can be effected by the use of an external linguistically structured system. Secondly, and relatedly, the purpose of this chapter is not to demonstrate that the traditional internalist symbolic account of language use is incorrect. Rather, the purpose is to demonstrate the grip that the internalist picture has on our theorizing about the mind. The grip manifests itself by making us think that things *must* be the way the symbolic model tells us. The purpose of the arguments of this chapter is to show that things do not have to be that way at all. Finally, the following arguments have no direct bearing on the nature versus nurture dispute with regard to language acquisition. Innatist accounts of language acquisition are often contrasted with what are referred to as 'environmentalist' accounts. But, and this, perhaps, cannot be emphasized too much, this is a different sense of environmentalism from the position defended here. The environmentalist position defended here allows that there is significant internal dimension to language acquisition, and is completely neutral on the question of whether or not this internal dimension is innate.

8.3 THE INTERNAL COMPONENT: ELMAN'S NET

The main sticking points for connectionist accounts of language acquisition have, of course, centred around the notion of *grammar* in general, and grammatical or syntactic structure in particular. Connectionist networks are, ultimately, just associative networks. And associative networks, no matter how complex, are, it is thought, simply not capable of delivering grammatical structure. This claim is the basis of Fodor and Pylyshyn's case against connectionism. In fact, however, there exists a neural network which has had (admittedly limited) success in reconstructing grammatical categories.

The network in question has been developed by Elman (1991a, 1991b, 1991c; see also Clark 1993:139–42). The goal of this network is to model 'complex hierarchically organized information' of the sort embodied in the syntactic structure of language. Its success would constitute, in effect, a sort of *existence proof*: an example of a connectionist network that is able to do things – roughly the construction of grammatical categories and the sorting of lexical items into such categories – that it is not supposed to be able to do. To this end, Elman attempts to get a connectionist net to learn to model grammatical structures in a simple artificial language. This language exhibits various features, including subject–verb number agreement, multiple-clause embeddings, and long-distance dependencies, and the goal of the network is to construct these features and categorize lexical items according to their possession of them.

Elman's net, therefore, has two central goals. Firstly, it aims to classify words according to lexical category – noun, verb, proposition, etc. As such, the first goal of the net is to learn, by way of exposure to sequences of linguistic input, to what categories the words presented to it belong. Secondly, and equally importantly, the network aims to learn representations of grammatical structure. For example, it aims to identify such features as subject–verb number agreement and dependence of embedded clauses in various complex sentences.

The architecture employed by Elman consists of a standard three-layer feed forward network combined with an additional set of context units connected to the hidden unit layer. The context units are set up to copy the activation of the hidden units and, on the next time step, to feed that information back to the hidden units at the same time as they are receiving activation from the input layer. The context units, then, act, in effect, as a sort of short-term memory device, sending information to the hidden units about their own previous state.

In initial trials, the Elman network failed quite badly. The network failed to generalize to new cases. That is, it failed to adequately deal with input sentences not given in training. It also managed to get only an incomplete grip on the training sentences themselves. The network failed to model the deep organizing features – grammatical structures and rules – of the linguistic domain. The reasons for this failure are actually quite important, and can be gleaned from looking at the way in which the Elman net eventually became able to deal with these features.

The best way to model the grammatical target features of the artificial language involves adopting a *hierarchical* approach. The construction of the relevant grammatical categories requires, for its successful completion, that the network be able to decompose the overall process of construction into a carefully ordered series of subprocesses. In the construction of grammatical categories, the network must be able to construct the simplest types of category first. These simplest categories then become the building blocks, so to speak, for the construction of more complex categories. For example, the network must be able to construct the subject–verb number agreement category first, and only then go on to more complex ones – such as the category of relative clauses, of long-distance dependencies, and so on. The salient point is that, in a domain of linguistic/grammatical structures, solutions to certain problems act as essential *building blocks* for the solution to more complex problems. In such domains, connectionist modelling will be possible only if the overall problem domain can somehow be parsed into a hierarchically ordered sequence and presented to the net in this way. If such decomposition is not achieved, then the basic problem solutions, to be used as the conceptual building blocks for the solution of more complex problems, are obscured by the network's attempts to solve the more complex problems. And these more complex problem solutions cannot, for all practical purposes, be identified by the network.

This sort of problem will arise with respect to any recursively or hierarchically structured domain of inquiry. That is, the problem arises whenever the target domain is structured around basic rules and features which interact to yield complex rules and features. In such a case, the methodological problem is to avoid prematurely exposing the net to overly complex cases. There are, however, at least two distinct ways of avoiding such premature exposure.

Phasing the training

The first method is to employ a *phased-training* method. This involves dividing the set of training sentences into sub-sets graded according to their level of complexity. The network is then trained up by exposure to a sequence of such sub-sets, beginning with one containing only the simplest sentence structures and ending with one containing the most complex structures. For example, the net can first be trained on 10,000 sentences exhibiting, say, subject–verb number agreement, but not containing any relative or dependent clauses, long-distance embeddings, etc. Then it is gradually introduced, by way of graded intervals, to sentences with more and more complex structures. This is accomplished by grading the sentences into five levels of complexity and then exposing the network to sample batches from each level. Furthermore, at each training interval, the lessons of the previous training will be reinforced by re-exposing the network to some of the sentences to which it was exposed in the previous intervals. For example, a typical stage 1 in a phased-training method might consist in exposure to 10,000 very simple sentences. Stage 2, then, might consist in exposure to 2,500 slightly more complex sentences plus 7,500 simple sentences characteristic of stage 1.

This phased-training regime enables the network to solve the problem that plagued the original Elman net. That is, the regime enables the net to model the key grammatical features of the artificial language. The key difference this method makes lies in the sequential order of the training sentences. The reason this is so effective is that phasing the training allows the network to identify, in the early stages of training, the most primitive domain rules – for example, the idea of singular and plural and the idea of subject–verb number agreement. Once the network has successfully learned or modelled the most basic rules and features, it then has a much smaller logical space to traverse in order to identify the more complex ones. Because of this, it is much more effectively able to restrict its search to that portion of logical space where the solution lies. The original net, on the other hand, not being the beneficiary of phased training, was presented with some very complex cases at the outset. This gave it a very large area of logical space to search for a solution and, therefore, caused it to search wildly for solutions to problems where these solutions, in fact, depended upon solutions to more simple problems. As a result, in the attempt to handle the complex cases it generated a lot of very specific *ad hoc* hypotheses which effectively obscured the grammatical structure of the simple cases. The network, in effect, became *lost in (logical) space.*

185

The key to success, then, is to somehow manipulate the network's learning trajectory – to force it to identify the simplest rules first. And one solution here is to phase the training in the above way. In this case, manipulation of the net's learning trajectory is effected by way of a careful manipulation of the training data.

It might be objected that the phased-training procedure is psychologically unrealistic. The basis of this claim is that the language learner is unlikely to be presented with such a contrived structure of examples in the learning period. And here we are sailing close to the well-known *poverty of the stimulus* argument for existence of an internal symbolically structured linguistic system. This objection is partly true. However, the objection, at least in this form, also rests on an extremely attenuated conception of the linguistic input received by the language learner; a conception which is itself psychologically unrealistic. Later in the chapter, I shall argue that, when the nature of the information presented to the language learner is properly understood, there is a clear environmental analogue to phased training.

Phasing the memory

There is another way of sculpting the learning trajectory of the network in the desired way. This method Elman refers to as *phasing the memory*.

As was pointed out earlier, the functional analogue of short-term memory in the Elman net is provided by a set of context units whose task is to reproduce, alongside the next input to the net, a replica of the pattern of activation distributed across the hidden units in the previous cycle. The phased-memory strategy begins by depriving the network of much of the feedback from the context units. As training continues, however, feedback to the hidden units from the context units is gradually increased until, finally, the net has the full feedback information from the units.

The method employed for depriving the net of the feedback from the context units is achieved by setting the context units to 0.5, thus eliminating any useful feedback, as soon as a specified number of words have been presented as input. With this method also, there are five training phases. But this time, however, the corpus of training sentences is not sorted according to level of complexity. Instead, a fully mixed set is presented every time. In phase 1 of training, feedback is eliminated after every third or fourth word. In phase 2, feed-back is eliminated after every fourth or fifth word. The length of the word string presented prior to feedback is thus increased until, with phase 5, full feedback resources are allowed. This network is able to model the grammatical structures of the artificial language just as well as did the net which underwent phased training. And the reason for this is that the limitations on feedback from context units imposed in the phased-memory strategy perform essentially the same function as the limitations on complexity of sentences imposed in the phased-training strategy. The early feedback or memory limitations prevent the net having initial access to the full grammatical complexity of the training sentences. Hence the net cannot be tempted to flail about seeking to model the grammatical structures exhibited by the complex sentences. It is, therefore, far less likely to get lost in logical space. With the feedback limitations in effect, the early learning of the net must be based on only those sentences and sentence fragments whose grammatical structure can be presented in a three- or four-word window. And, quite unsurprisingly, this grammatical structure will be relatively simple.

The functional effects of the phased-memory and phased-training approaches are, therefore, identical: each automatically decomposes the network's task into a series of sub-tasks that are ordered along a scale of increasing complexity, thus allowing the net to successfully model certain grammatical categories. And they show that problems had by associative devices in modelling grammatical structures stem, not from the nature of those structures themselves, but from the fact that such modelling requires the sort of task decomposition that a connectionist network has difficulty in achieving in the absence of a phased-training or phased-memory strategy.

Therefore, the claim that an associative engine such as a connectionist network is *intrinsically* incapable of modelling symbolic structures – i.e., syntactically structured symbols plus rules of combination for such symbols – is simply a myth. A connectionist network *is* capable of modelling grammatical or syntactic structures as long as it decomposes the modelling task in the correct way. And the correct decomposition of the task involves arranging the structures to be modelled according to increasing order of complexity, and dealing with the structures in that order.

The phased-training and phased-memory approaches are what

allow a connectionist net to achieve the correct sort of task decomposition. This claim, I believe, connects up, in a very powerful way, with the arguments developed in earlier chapters. In the remainder of this chapter, I shall argue that in the environment of any language learner there are certain structures, where the concept of a structure is here broadly understood to include types of behaviour exhibited by other language users, and the language learner interacts with these structures in such a way that it is forced to adopt both a phased-memory and a phased-training approach to learning the language. Phased-training and phased-memory procedures are, when we learn a language for the first time, undergone by us quite naturally in virtue of our environment, and in virtue of the way in which we interact with certain relevant structures in our environment. Therefore, because of the way we interact with our environment, and with certain structures in that environment, our ability to obey principles of linguistic composition might be explainable in terms of our being essentially associative devices.

8.4 THE ENVIRONMENTAL COMPONENT I: PHASED MEMORY

Chapter 6 discussed the profound effect the development of external representational structures will have had on human episodic memory capacity. The African envoy, transmitting word for word the lengthy message of his tribal chief, has to remember not simply the content of the message, but also, the precise, or at least reasonably precise, sequence of words uttered by the chief. The Peruvian *kvinu* officer, on the other hand, does not have to remember the information contained in the knot he has tied. What he has to remember is simply the 'code' which will allow him to extract this information. The African envoy relies on outstanding episodic memory to remember the information he has to transmit (although, as we also saw in chapter 6, it would be incorrect to think that the envoy makes absolutely no use of external structures in accomplishing his memory task). The Peruvian officer's reliance on episodic memory is much less, amounting to only the remembering of the code. Whereas the African envoy must employ his episodic memory resources each time he learns a message, the Peruvian *kvinu* officer need employ his episodic memory only once, in the learning of the code.

Once an external information store becomes available, episodic memory is going to become a lot less important, restricted to what is required for learning the code necessary for appropriation of the information in the external information store. Thus, during the process of cultural development, the outstanding episodic memory of primitive man tends to vestigialize. Subsequent to the development of external information stores, the evolution of human memory has, at the same time, been *involution*: constituted not only by an improvement in certain areas, but also by retrograde processes whereby old forms shrink and wither away.

In chapter 6, this involution or vestigialization of episodic memory was portrayed simply as a consequence of the development of external information stores. That is, the involution of episodic memory was portrayed as a consequence of such development, a consequence which, in itself, serves no useful purpose. However, Elman's net now suggests a more positive role for this vestigialization.

Elman's employment of a phased-memory strategy seems to indicate that limitations on certain types of memory might, in fact, be a crucial and positive factor in determining the ability of statistical inference engines to penetrate theoretical domains that are hierarchically ordered in the sense of being formed by way of recursive combinatory rules. Correct use of external linguistically structured symbol systems requires correct modelling of the grammatical rules of combination for such systems. Such modelling can be achieved by a connectionist pattern associator only if a successful task decomposition is achieved; that is, the grammatical rules must be grasped in the correct order, namely in order of increasing complexity. And, as Elman's model makes clear, extensive episodic-memory capacities might constitute a significant hindrance to a network in this regard. Achieving the necessary task decomposition requires focusing on the simplest sentences first and, as Elman's analysis makes very clear, this would be very difficult to implement in a system with extensive episodic-memory capacity.

Therefore, not only is the involution of episodic memory a direct consequence of the use of external information stores, it may well also be a *facilitator* of such use. Episodic involution and environmental manipulation might, thus, co-evolve. Episodic limitations are a facilitator of such use to the extent that they allow us adequately to model the hierarchical and recursive rules governing the construction of such stores. Thus, the limitations on our episodic-memory capacity, occasioned by our use of external information stores, play essentially the same role as the phased-memory strategy in Elman's network. Our exploitation of environmental structures has given us, in effect, our own version of the phased-memory strategy.

8.5 THE ENVIRONMENTAL COMPONENT II: PHASED TRAINING

In this section, I shall argue that the environment in which the typical language learner finds herself provides what is essentially a phased-training programme for that learner. This claim may seem counter-intuitive. After all, it seems manifestly false that a first-time language learner will initially be presented with simple sentences of three to four words and then be gradually introduced to four- and five-word sentences, five- and six-word sentences, and so on in the gradual, even, and progressive manner required by Elman's phased-training procedure. Therefore, it might seem that the phased-training procedure is psychologically unrealistic, and so cannot be used to explain the capacity for language acquisition possessed by the first time learner.

It is true that a typical language learner is not presented with progressively more difficult sentences in the smooth and even way suggested by Elman's procedure. None the less, to infer that the environment of the learner provides no analogue of phased training, and that phased training is, therefore, psychologically unrealistic, would be wrong. The reason is that the 'input' being presented to the language learner consists of much more than just sentences. The relevant information contained in the learner's environment is constituted by many structures and features – both linguistic and non-linguistic. And a proper understanding of the nature of this information, and of the structures that underlie it, allows us to see that the environment of the first-time learner does, in fact, provide what is, in essence, a phased-training programme for the learner. Thus, the objection that phased training is psychologically unrealistic, I shall argue, is based on a hopelessly attenuated conception of the environment of the first-time language learner, and, hence, on a hopelessly attenuated conception of the linguistic 'input' presented to the learner. And it is this conception, and not the phased-training procedure, which is psychologically unrealistic.

Four phases of language acquisition

It is useful to distinguish four phases of language acquisition for the first-time learner (Reed 1995). These distinctions may be partly stipulative, since each stage shades by degrees into the other. However, this fourfold distinction is by no means idiosyncratic, and the phenomena associated with each phase are well known.

1. *Prelinguistic.* This phase is essentially constituted by interactions between child and caretaker made up of face-to-face and back-and-forth vocalizations. Such vocalizations are not linguistic as such and there is no expectation that they should meet the formal requirements of the language community (Snow 1977).
2. *Indicational.* To possess an indicational capacity, in the sense adopted here, is to possess the ability to draw the attention of another to some aspect of the environment. In this phase, the child is increasingly treated as a language user. The caretaker and other interlocutors begin to modify their phrasing and other aspects of speech in relation to the child, and the child, in turn, exhibits a developing skill of articulation (Reed 1995).
3. *Transitional.* This phase represents the child's entrance into the surrounding linguistic community. This entrance seems to be driven by two central factors, one environmental, one internal, both of which strongly reinforce each other. Firstly, during indicational language use, the child eventually acquires special lexemes that serve, in the linguistic community, as argument-structuring devices (Tomasello 1992). Secondly, the transitional language user undergoes considerable cognitive development which enables her to better understand environmental structures and relationships which are of fundamental importance in learning how to predicate (Pinker 1984; Gopnik & Meltzoff 1993).
4. *Predicational.* In this phase, the child is a fully-fledged member of the linguistic community, having mastered the practice of predication and, in virtue of this, being able to use language in a generative, systematic, and inferentially coherent way.

Each of these phases is driven, to a considerable extent, by various environmental factors which interact with, emphasize, and reinforce the internal development undergone by the learner. The reason the environment provides, in essence, a phased-training programme for the learner is the following. Each of the first three phases of linguistic development outlined above contains within it, so to speak, the seeds of its own transcendence. That is, not only is each phase a necessary precondition of the phase which succeeds it, but also, crucially, each phase pushes its successful negotiator into the next. When one has successfully negotiated the prelinguistic phase, one cannot help being pushed into the indicational phase. Roughly speaking, it is not possible to successfully negotiate one phase without being forced into beginning the next one. Or, to put the same point another way, being pushed into the next phase is a criterion of having successfully negotiated its predecessor.

On this view, then, the phased-training regime necessary for a language learner to successfully model the grammatical structures required for mature (i.e., predicational) language use does not take the form of being presented with progressively more and more complex sentence forms. This was, in any case, a naïve and oversimplified idea. Rather, it takes the form of a successive and phased acquisition of more and more complex skills. And not only is acquisition of each skill in the sequence a necessary condition of acquiring the one that follows it but, more importantly, acquisition of a given skill inevitably forces its acquirer to begin the process of acquiring its successor.

The prelinguistic phase

Reed (1993) draws an important distinction between what he calls the environmental *field of promoted action* and the environmental *field of free action*. Although Reed does not frame the distinction in precisely these terms, each concept, it seems, can be represented as follows:

Field of promoted action: An environmental feature F is, at time t, part of the field of promoted action for an organism O if and only if F is attended to or utilized by O at t in part or in whole because of the actions of an organism O_1, where O is distinct from O_1.

Field of free action: An environmental feature F is, at time t, part of the field of free action for an organism O if and only if O's attending to or utilizing F at t is not occasioned in part or in whole by the actions of an organism O_1, where O is distinct from O_1.

The fields of free and promoted action are essentially relational in character; they can be defined only in relation to particular organisms. What is part of the field of free action for one organism can be part of the field of promoted action for another, and vice versa. Moreover, the restriction to a given time t is essential because what can be part of the field of promoted action for a given organism can later become part of the field of free action for that same organism. An example may help make all this clearer.

A very common mammalian developmental pattern is the *transference* or *bridging* (Rogoff 1990) of a skill from the field of promoted action to the field of free action. For example, adult humans often make infants sit up as a first stage of learning how to sit for themselves. They similarly promote bipedal locomotion in infants by supporting their weight and even simulating movement across the ground, again as a first stage in the child learning to do this for herself (Reed 1995).

One pattern of such transference has particular significance for linguistic development. This is the pattern whereby infants learn to promote attention and action in their caretakers (Reed 1995). In fact, what is essential to the prelinguistic phase is that it transforms the child from an individual who is simply the recipient of fields of promoted action created by others to an individual who is the author or creator of fields of promoted action of its own. At the beginning of the prelinguistic phase, the child's action and attention are wholly dependent on fields of action promoted by others. By the end of the prelinguistic phase, the child has learned to promote attention and action in its caretakers; it has learned, that is, to create fields of promoted action for others. And the move from being a recipient of the field of action promoted by another to being the author of a field of promoted action (of which another is recipient) is one version of the transference of a skill from the field of promoted into the field of free action.

This transference is brought about by way of several environmental structures. These structures have a dual character. On the one hand, they promote action in a child. But, on the other, they act as a natural encouragement to the child to engage in his own promotion of action in others.

The first relevant structure is a universal feature of how adult humans promote child action – *infant-directed speech*. Adults routinely produce a special kind of speech to infants. Various features of this speech are prevalent across all linguistic groups, and include simplification of syntax, semantics, and lexical choice, also added repetitions and both simplification and exaggeration of phonological contours (Papoušek & Papoušek 1991). Infant-directed speech is not used towards very young infants, only becoming common midway through the infant's first year. As Pinker (1984) notes, infant-directed speech is not a good vehicle for the learning of complex syntactic structure. Nevertheless, it still has a crucially important purpose in the eventual learning of such structure. Specifically, it entrains the infant in a certain type of rhythmic dyadic activity, an activity essential to human conversation (Reed 1995). Not only is infant-directed speech a way of focusing the child's attention, it is also a vehicle for teaching the child that the gaining of another's attention can be facilitated by a rhythmic vocal activity which also involves head and hand movements, special postures of the body, head, hands, and face.

A second relevant environmental feature is known as *redundancy*. Caregivers often redundantly specify the object of the child's attention, using variational event structuring to achieve this end. Objects are loomed and zoomed, events are repeatedly demonstrated, such repeated demonstration often being accompanied by rhythm and intensity variations. And, importantly, gestures and vocalizations are typically produced in conjunction with these happenings. Redundancy is also a vehicle for achieving a transition from a capacity that requires a caretaker's promotion to one that can be achieved autonomously in the field of free action. The child is introduced to a set of variations that serve as organizers of what cognitive linguists call *image schemas* (Langacker 1987). These image schemas are patterns of repeated experiences illustrative of the beginnings and endings of events, the typical patterns of activity associated with the events, etc. These routines are structured events, often happening at specific times of day and in specific places (e.g., food, bathing, etc.). As a result, by the end of the first year of life, human infants have acquired an extensive list of expectations: certain events to occur at specific times and places, certain objects to have certain properties, particular events to have particular outcomes. The resulting increase in the child's powers of identification of objects, events, etc. is what allows the child to focus attention on a given item not simply as part of the field of action promoted by another but, for the first time, as part of the child's field of free action.

A third important environmental structure is to be found in *games*, in particular in the development of the nature of the games played with the child between the ages of 6 and 12 months. At 6 months of age, games in which the infant is largely the recipient of adult activity account for about two-thirds of all games. By 12 months of age, however, many of these games have been superseded by ones in which the child plays a much more prominent role in orchestrating activity. Once again, this facilitates the transference from being a recipient of a field of promoted action to being author of such a field.

Environmental structures such as infant-directed speech, redundancy, and games are the central components in the first phase of 'training up' a child for language. In essence, what the prelinguistic phase – characterized by these structures – does is teach the child a skill: the skill of moving certain environmental items from their field of promoted action to their field of free action. More specifically, it enables the child to move from being a mere recipient of a field of action promoted by another to being the author, creator, and promoter of fields of action of its own. That is, the environmental structures enable the child for the first time to move items from the field of promoted to the field of free action and to create for others fields in which their attentions and activities are promoted. And, crucially, through its interaction with these environmental structures, the child has learned that the best way of incorporating another into a field of action which he, the child, has promoted is by way of rhythmic actions of various sorts; actions which include vocalizations, head and hand movements, special postures of the body, and so on. This is the goal and culmination of the prelinguistic phase.

The indicational phase

The skill of indication is the ability of the child, through vocalization or gesture, to draw the attention of others to some feature of the environment. The child acts specifically to indicate a certain object, place, or event, and is not merely attracting the caregiver's attention in a non-specific manner. This skill of indication emerges only when a child adapts to her caregiver's fields of promoted action by producing her own first attempts at promoting her caregiver's activities. It is where these two fields of promoted action meet that indicational ability arises.

Indicational skill, in this sense, is a natural consequence of the skills developed during the prelinguistic phase. More precisely, any child who has successfully negotiated the prelinguistic phase will necessarily also possess the *rudiments* of indicational language use. That is not to say that the child is a competent user of indicational language. It is just to say that the beginnings, or foundation, of indicational language use are present in, or entailed by, the successful negotiation of the prelinguistic phase. The prelinguistic phase is concerned with developing in the child the ability to create a field of promoted action. However, certain structures put in place in the prelinguistic phase have also acquainted the child with the fact that a kind of rhythmic dyadic vocalization is a very effective means of creating a field of promoted action. Skill at indication, therefore, begins to emerge from the combination of environmental structures put in place during the prelinguistic phase.

The nascent indicational language user can perhaps indicate not only objects, events, places, and persons who are present, she can also even indicate, to an extent, items that are not present, including conditions of satisfaction of her own needs and desires. However, her skills are extremely limited. In particular, she will possess indicational capacities that are extremely *idiosyncratic*: one or only a small number of interlocutors can understand what the child is indicating – i.e., grasp what aspect of the environment it is to which the child is drawing attention. For example, young children often produce utterances that exhibit errors in sound shape and word choice. And, even when they are producing a lexeme correctly, they may use it in idiosyncratic ways, as in 'dog' to mean any pet animal. To transcend such idiosyncrasy is to become more skilled in indicational language use. And to do this, the child must adapt her skill at promoting others' attention to be suitable to many listeners. The frustration inevitably occasioned by her failure to adequate promote a field of action for the other will motivate the child to overcome it, perhaps by reshaping her speech patterns. Therefore, the central environmental structure responsible for turning the untutored indicational language user at the end of the prelinguistic phase to the more skilled user at the end of the indicational phase is *other people*, in particular *less common caregiver*; adults who interact with the child but who do not have the background knowledge necessary to interpret the child's idiosyncratic utterances.

Indicational language is also *inflexible*. Even if one has progressed sufficiently to make one's indicational use non-idiosyncratic enough to be understood by a relatively large number of adults, one still has the problem of inflexibility. Ordinary events, for example, often involve several objects and actions in different combinations. If one attempted to describe even a simple state of affairs merely by indicating all its components, this would be a complex and convoluted process, and would probably result in a description riddled with ambiguity. The inflexibility involved in communicating by way of successive indications must be overcome by learning how to structure one's indication to reflect the structure of the world (Reed 1995).

It is the idiosyncrasy and inflexibility of indicational language that provides the impetus for the development of generative language skills. Once the child has learned to create, for others, its own field of promoted action, the inherent inadequacy of indicational language for this purpose naturally leads to the development of generative language skills. Just as the acquisition of indicational language skills were, in effect, forced on one by the successful negotiation of the prelinguistic phase, so, too, the acquisition of generative or predicational language skills is, in effect, forced on one by the successful negotiation of the indicational phase. As we shall see in the next section, the rudiments of predicational language skills are, essentially, to be found at the culmination of the skills developed during the indicational phase.

The transitional phase

The inherent inadequacies, then, of indicational language use provide a natural impetus for the development of generative or predicational language skills. But the impetus for transition is one thing, the mechanisms of transition quite another. In this section, I shall argue that there are essentially two types of mechanism involved. Firstly, there are certain features of indicational language use itself. Secondly, there are certain features of the wider environment in which indicational language use occurs. Consider, first, the environmental mechanisms.

An environmental mechanism of central importance consists in certain forms of behaviour performed by less common caregivers. This behaviour functions not just to drive the child from being a rudimentary user of indicational language to being a more sophisticated one, but also to drive them over the boundary from indicational to predicational use. In the latter case, however, the less common caregiver achieves this in a slightly different way. The basic idea is as follows. The linguistic environment of indicational speakers is replete with situations of conflict which, at least in some instances, require the child to engage in controlled variation of segmental phonological structures. This is because, within the confines of indicational language, the only way to successfully indicate the increasingly complex situations the child inevitably encounters is by using multiple indicational items. As the number and variety of multiple word items increases, there is an increasing need for segmental control in order to be able to perform the utterance (Studdert-Kennedy 1991).

Now, prior to the development of syntax, some of the variations in the child's utterances will fit the pattern of use in the linguistic community, and some will not. To these unfit utterances, adults may respond with requests for clarification. Tomasello et al. (1983) have studied the responses to such requests made by 2-year-olds. When the child's most common caregiver asks for clarification, 2-year-olds mostly simply reiterate what they have just said. When a less common caregiver asks for clarification, 2-year-olds will often recast their statements, changing not only the sound pattern but also, in many instances, the words. Less common caregivers thus provide a bridge into the linguistic community, creating both the opportunity and, indeed, the necessity, for children to learn to vary their speech in controlled ways, according to the demands of the community (Tomasello et al. 1983; Reed 1995). Often, when the child's utterance has veered away from community accepted norms, adults, instead of asking for clarification, recast or rephrase the child's utterance and communicate, largely by intonation, that the form of the utterance was incorrect. These caregivers are thus promoting the same kind of variation in action, as a prelude to the child learning to do this on her own.

In addition to these environmental structures acting on the transitional child, there is also a central feature of indicational language which itself provides an essential mechanism for the development of predicational language. A number of recent studies in grammatical theory have all identified lexemes as crucially important carriers of syntactic structure. The most celebrated of these is Pinker's well-known concept of *semantic bootstrapping* as a basis for early generative language (Pinker 1984, 1989). According to Pinker, when a child learns a lexical item, she learns the concept that this item expresses. And this item, in virtue of the concept it expresses, conveys enough syntactic structure to bootstrap the child into a properly predicational use of language. This general idea can be developed in several different ways. One development points to the fact that, when a child understands a word, she will understand that it is used to refer to, say, a particular kind of object. However, she will then also know that this sort of object will have properties. And the relation between the object and its properties will also have to be captured in language. Thus, the child who has, in the indicational phase of language use, learned hundreds of words has also, at first implicitly, learned a complex network of local syntactic relationships (Maratsos & Chalkley 1980; Maratsos 1983).

Consider one example of how this theory might work. Croft (1991) has offered a useful overview of the semantic properties of various lexical items, one which is easily applicable to early language development. The results can be expressed in tabular form as follows:

	objects	properties	actions	prepositions
valency	0	1	≥ 1	≥ 2
stativity	state	state	process	process
persistence	persistent	persistent	transitory	transitory
gradedness	ungradable	graded	ungradable	ungradable

Valency refers to the number of other entities entailed by the existence of the item in question. An object is self-sufficient and so has a valence of 0. A property must attach to something else, and so has a valence of 1. An action must be something both done by an agent and done to something. However, in some cases these are identical – and therefore an action has a valence of ≥ 1. Prepositions entail the existence of at least two things and so have a valence of ≥ 2. Stativity denotes whether something is static or process-like. Persistence concerns whether the item is essentially transient or persists though time. Gradability pertains to whether the item varies along a dimension.

Croft argues that the above table illustrates the kind of knowledge needed for possession of the concepts expressed by words in the given classes. Thus, an indicational language user who is coming to understand the concepts expressed by the words she uses will, at the same time, acquire, at least implicitly, knowledge of this set of relations between concepts. And it is this knowledge, Croft argues, which bootstraps the indicational language user into genuine predicational language use.

If these arguments are correct, then, proper development of indicational language skills will inevitably force the language learner into acquiring the rudiments of predicational language use. Thus, we have the following situation: proper acquisition of the skills imparted during the prelinguistic phase will inevitably pitch the first-time language learner into rudimentary indicational language use. The rudimentary indicational language user is driven, by a combination of environmental factors, to become a more sophisticated user of indicational language. The sophisticated indicational language user, driven by the inherent inadequacy of indicational language is motivated to develop predicational skills. And a combination of environmental factors plus certain structures inherent to indicational language use provide the essential mechanisms whereby an indicational user is bootstrapped into genuine, if rudimentary, predicational use. This, I think, certainly looks like a description of a phased training regime for the first-time language learner.

The conclusions we can draw from this discussion of language acquisition closely parallel the conclusions reached in previous chapters.

Firstly, one can understand neither the quantity nor the nature of the internal information processing that a language learning system (natural or artificial) must undergo unless one understands the nature of the relevant information that is available to the learner in her (social and linguistic) environment. Thus, we have seen that an extremely attenuated conception of the nature of this information will lead us essentially down the garden path in our efforts to understand language acquisition. If we begin with the attenuated conception of the linguistic environment according to which the only relevant information presented to the learner consists in spoken or written sentences, of varying degrees of complexity, then we will inevitably reject a connectionist model, such as that of Elman, on the grounds that it requires a training regimen that is psychologically unrealistic. Then, in order to explain the ability of the first-time language learner, we might well end up postulating, along the lines of the symbolic paradigm, the existence of an internally instantiated system of linguistically structured representations, and a set of rules applying to those representations in virtue of their structure. However, this move might only be necessary because we have seriously underestimated the amount of relevant information available to the first-time learner in her environment. Once we adequately understand the nature and extent of this information, we will also come to see that Elman's net is, in fact, not all that psychologically unrealistic after all. It is not psychologically unrealistic because the social and linguistic environment of the language learner provides her with just what Elman's net requires in order to work effectively: a phased-training regime. Therefore, generalizing the above, it is not possible to understand the process of language acquisition by focusing exclusively on what is occurring inside the skin of the language acquirer. This is, essentially, a version of the epistemological claim.

Secondly, the first-time learning of a language is not something which occurs exclusively inside the head or skin of the language learner. Learning a language is as much something we do in our world as something we do in our head. That is, the process of learning a language is essentially constituted, at least in part, by processes of interaction with, and exploitation of, environmental structures. And this is an expression of the ontological claim.

The purpose of this chapter has not been to show that a particular theoretical view of the nature of the processes involved in language use is right, or that a particular view is wrong. Nowhere in the above discussion, for example, will one find the claim that, with respect to the processes involved in language acquisition, connectionism is right and the symbolic approach wrong (or vice versa). Nor will one find the claim that innatist accounts should be rejected. Rather, the purpose of this chapter has been to loosen the grip that the internalist picture of the mind has on us with respect to the higher-order cognitive processes involved in speaking and understanding language. This task was broken down into two parts. Firstly, it was argued that tacit commitment to the internalist picture, by tempting us into looking at the problem in a certain way, closed off certain legitimate and potentially important avenues of inquiry (avenues that, in this case, dovetailed very nicely with connectionist approaches to language). Secondly, that we do not have to think of the processes involved in language use in the way that the internalist picture requires us to. There is a fruitful theoretical alternative based on the environmentalist idea of a language-using organism exploiting certain relevant structures in its environment. And once again, it was argued, this lends support to connectionist models of language acquisition.

PART II

Psychosemantics

9

Introduction to Part II: the need for and the place of a theory of representation

Intentionality, the aboutness or directedness of certain mental states towards their objects, was identified by Brentano as one of the essential features of the mental. Indeed, Brentano thought that it was this feature of the mental, in particular, the ability of the mind to stand in relations to intentionally inexistent objects, that marked the mind off as an essentially non-physical thing. One of the principal tasks of recent philosophy of mind, *pace* Brentano, has been to naturalize intentionality, to find a place for it in the natural, physical, order. And to naturalize intentionality in this sense requires showing how it can arise out of non-intentional, or non-semantic, properties and relations. This is the principal task of this second part of the book. As I shall try to show, there is, in fact, an intrinsic connection between this project and the position developed in Part I. The position defended in Part I, I shall argue, both requires a theory of representation and puts in place a framework within which a theory of representation is best located.

9.1 THE NEED FOR A THEORY OF REPRESENTATION

The need for a theory of representation can best be seen in terms of Paul Grice's (1957) famous distinction between *natural* meaning and *non-natural* meaning. Smoke naturally means fire, whereas the word 'fire', and not the word 'smoke', non-naturally means fire. To say that X naturally means Y, in this sense, is to say, roughly, that X *indicates* Y, whereas to say that X non-naturally means Y is to say, again roughly, that X *denotes*, *designates*, or *refers* to Y. The central message of Part I was that the tokens of many types of cognitive process are, in part, constituted by manipulation of external information-bearing structures; structures that carry information relevant to the accomplishing of the cognitive task in question. However, it is also true that there is a crucial difference in the way such information-bearing structures can actually bear information. Some of these structures can be natural bearers of information, where, roughly, a structure is a natural bearer of information if it carries information independently of the propositional attitudes of organisms that detect it, or are capable of detecting it. If Gibson is right, for example, the optic array is a natural bearer of information in this sense. However, it is also true that, in many, and perhaps most, cases, the external information-bearing structures used by cognizers carry information that depends, at least in part, on the propositional attitudes of those users. When Rumelhart, McClelland et al. talk of an embodied connectionist system utilizing external representations of mathematical symbols, for example, it is fairly clear that the information these structures carry is not natural in the relevant sense. The representations are, in Grice's terminology, nonnatural bearers of information. Similarly, when we talk of differences in strategies of remembering occasioned by the development of language (both spoken and written), the external linguistic structures in question here are non-natural bearers of information.

It is characteristic of those external structures that are non-natural bearers of information that at least some of the information they carry is dependent on the representational capacities of their users. And if this is so, and if many of the external structures employed by cognizers are non-natural bearers of information in this way, then the environmentalist account of cognition developed in Part I needs to be supplemented with an account of representation. Without such supplementation, we are left with a seriously incomplete account of cognition. Thus, far from abolishing the need for mental representation, the environmentalist account of cognition developed in Part I of this book actually requires a theory of representation.

There is, of course, no incompatibility between the arguments of Part I and the present appeal to the notion of representation. To see this, we must distinguish two clearly different projects. The first is that of accounting for certain features of representations. For example, chapters 7 and 8 were concerned with one important feature – compositionality; the capacity of certain representations to obey principles of linguistic composition. The second project, however, is that of accounting for the relation of representation itself; that is, the project of explaining in virtue of what properties representations can represent. These projects are often lumped together under the rubric 'representation'; they are, however, distinct projects. The former is a psychotectonic project; the latter a (indeed, *the*) psychosemantic one. The arguments of Part I concerned features of representations, not the relation of representation itself. And, it was argued, certain features of representations – compositionality, for example – might best be explained by way of certain features of environmental structures and the capacity of cognitive systems to manipulate and exploit these structures. But this, even if correct, says nothing at all about the relation of representation itself. It says nothing, that is, of how it is that representations represent the world. It is with this question that Part II is concerned. And Part II is concerned with this question because, as was argued above, the arguments of Part I are seriously incomplete without a theory of representation as such.

The invocation of the relation of representation at this point, however, might prompt another, related, concern. Representations are typically conceived as involving a form of propositional knowledge. Representations are typically identified as carrying the information *that* such and such is the case. If so, then it seems the tendency of Part I (particularly chapters 7 and 8) to downplay the importance of propositional knowledge in favour of a (non-propositional) form of procedural knowledge cannot be sustained. If the position developed in Part I is incomplete without representation, and if representation is propositional in character, then we seem to have reintroduced propositional knowledge by, so to speak, the back door.

There are two points which should be made here. Firstly, it was, as was emphasized on many occasions, no part of the arguments of Part I to claim that propositional knowledge can be reduced to non-propositional knowledge, that knowing *that* can be reduced to knowing *how*. The arguments of Part I, in fact, left the question of the relation of knowing how to knowing that completely open. It *was* argued in Part I that commitment to the internalist picture might lead us to underestimate the extent to which non-propositional forms of knowledge could be involved in cognition. So, Part I *did* claim that non-propositional forms of knowledge might have a much larger role in cognitive processes than was hitherto recognized. But, clearly, this is a far cry from claiming that propositional knowledge can be reduced to, or derived from, non-propositional knowledge. This latter claim was neither made in Part I, nor was it required by the arguments of Part I.

Secondly, and even more importantly, it is not clear whether basic cases of representation should be understood as essentially propositional in character. The following chapters, particularly chapter 11, will explore the connection between representation and action. One consequence of this discussion is that it is doubtful at best whether basic cases of representation are best conceived of as propositional in character. It is far more likely, I shall argue, either that the propositionally encoded information carried by a representation is built upon a superstructure of non-propositionally encoded information, or that, slightly less dramatically, the information carried in propositional form by a representation is inextricably bound up with, and cannot be separated from, the information carried, by that representation, in non-propositional form. And, if this is correct, the introduction of the notion of representation at this point does not, at least not essentially, amount to reintroduction of propositional knowledge through the back door.

9.2 THE PLACE OF A THEORY OF REPRESENTATION

The environmentalist account of cognition in Part I, then, requires, for its completeness, an account of mental representation. However, and even more importantly, I think the environmentalist view also helps us properly to identify both the correct location of a theory of representation and the form such a theory should take. Part I emphasizes the role of *action* in cognition. And the best framework for understanding the nature of representation, I am going to argue, is as a phenomenon that emerges from a background or horizon of action. The capacity of an organism to represent, I shall argue, cannot be understood in isolation from its capacity to act. And precisely what an organism is capable of representing, and what on any occasion it does in fact represent, cannot be understood in isolation from its possibilities for action.

Historically, there are clear precedents for the view I propose to defend here. Both Gibson (1966; 1979) and Merleau-Ponty (1962) have emphasized the connection between representation and action. Gibson, for example, introduces the useful notion of an *affordance*. The affordances of the environment are, for a given creature, what it *offers* that creature, what it *furnishes* or *provides*, whether this benefits or harms that creature. A relatively flat, horizontal, rigid, and sufficiently

208

extended surface, for example, affords support for many animals, though not, obviously, for all. For many animals, such a surface is stand-on-able, permitting an upright posture. It also affords locomotion; it is walk-on-able and run-on-able. A non-rigid surface, like the surface of a lake, however, does not afford support or easy locomotion for medium-sized mammals. It is not stand-on-able, but sink-into-able.

Affordances are relational properties of things; they have to be specified relative to the creature in question. Crucially, affordances are relative to the capacities for action of individual creatures. The surface of a lake affords neither support nor easy locomotion for a horse, but if offers both of these things for a water-bug. Thus, to speak of an affordance is to speak elliptically; an affordance exists only in relation to particular organisms and particular modes of behaviour and capacities for action.

From the point of view of survival, what is of immediate importance to an organism is not so much the substances and objects *in* its environment but the affordances *of* its environment. That is, what is of immediate importance to an organism is not what an object is but what it affords. From the point of view of survival, the identity of an object is important only to the extent that this identity can be associated with certain types of affordance. Any organism that can recognize objects but not detect the affordances of those objects would not survive. However, any organism that can detect the affordances of objects even though it was incapable of identifying those objects could survive. From the point of view of survival, then, it is the affordances of the environment, and not the objects in the environment that are of primary importance.

If this is true, then it should not be assumed that an organism should be primarily sensitive to objects in its environment. On the contrary, it is far more likely that the sensitivities of an organism have evolved to track the affordances, for that organism, of its environment. And, if this is so, many cases of basic representation at least will be representation of affordances, not of objects or substances.

Theories of representation can be more or less ambitious in their scope and goals. A modest theory of representation might see itself as restricted in its scope to fairly basic representational mechanisms, probably innate, probably mechanisms of perceptual representation, and probably possessed by creatures whose representational capacities

209

are fairly fixed and limited. Thus, much of the argument both for and against particular accounts of representation has centred around such things as the frog's sight–strike–feed mechanism, bacterial magnetosomes, rattlesnake hunting mechanisms, and so on. More ambitious theories of representation will seek to extend this approach beyond these basic cases of representation to account for all mental content, or at least much of it. One of the most common objections to recent accounts of representation is that, while they may work for relatively basic cases, it is very difficult to extend this general approach to cover mechanisms that are not innate, not mechanisms of perceptual representation, and possessed by creatures whose representational capacities are fairly rich. I do not endorse this objection. However, it is true that more ambitious theories of representation require that correspondingly more work be put in to their defence.

A useful strategy, indeed a typical one, then, is to begin by trying to provide an account of fairly basic cases of representation, and, only when this is done, to worry about extending the account to more complex cases. This is the strategy that will be adopted in the following chapters. A corollary of the arguments developed in Part I is that basic cases of representation will be of a strongly action-guiding character. Basic cases of representation, at least, will be representation of affordances of the environment, not of objects and substances in the environment. This point, which will be defended in a later chapter, is, I shall argue, of profound importance, allowing us to solve, or at least dissolve, some of the more tenacious objections to naturalistic accounts of representation.

The other central claim defended in Part I is that cognitive processes are things achieved by organisms as a whole and not simply by internal mechanisms possessed by such organisms. Cognitive processes are, at least in part, constituted by organisms acting upon the world around them, and, in doing so, manipulating environmental structures which carry information relevant to the success or efficacy of the cognitive process in question. While internal mechanisms may be essential to cognition, what is also essential is somatic or bodily manipulation of information-bearing environmental structures. It is the organism taken as a psychosomatic whole that is the primary *locus* of cognitive processes.

This has ramifications for the content we can attribute to cognitive states and processes. In particular, I shall argue that it is possible to attribute representational content to both internal mechanisms and organisms taken as a whole. That is, it is possible to make both what I shall call an *organismic* attribution of representational content, an attribution of content to the organism as a whole, and an *algorithmic* attribution of content, an attribution of content to some sub-doxastic mechanism or mechanisms. Answering some of the more difficult objections to naturalistic accounts of representation requires being clear about to which object – organism or mechanism – we are attributing content. I shall try to show how the distinction between organismic and algorithmic attributions of content combines with the claim that basic cases of representation are representation of affordances, to allow us to resolve what are perceived to be the most serious objections to the problem of naturalizing semantics.

The following chapter provides an introduction to the two principal naturalistic accounts of representation. Firstly, *informational* accounts of representation associated with Stampe (1977), Dretske (1981, 1988, 1991, 1995), Evans (1982), Barwise and Perry (1983), Fodor (1984; 1987), and Stalnaker (1984). Secondly, *teleological* accounts of representation, associated, in the main, with Millikan (1984, 1986, 1989a, 1989b, 1990a, 1990b, 1991, 1993). Various objections to each theory will be discussed and most, but not all, dealt with. In chapter 11, I develop my own solution to (or dissolution of) the remaining problems facing the project of naturalizing semantics. This solution will draw heavily on the concept of an affordance, and on the distinction between organismic and algorithmic attributions of representational content.

10

Two theories of representation

10.1 INFORMATIONAL THEORIES OF REPRESENTATION

Informational theories of representation, or informational semantics as they are sometimes called, are built around the idea that representation derives from informational relations obtaining between organisms and environments. The relevant notion of information involved here is, roughly, natural information in Grice's sense. The number of rings in a tree, for example, is said to carry information about the age of the tree. The height of a column of mercury in a thermometer carries information about the temperature of the surrounding medium. The turning red of a piece of litmus-paper carries information about the relative acidity of the surrounding liquid. The figure-of-eight dance of certain bees carries information about the distance and direction of a food source. A compass needle carries information about the direction of magnetic north. And so on.

It is important to realize that, in the above cases, the relevant notion of information is completely independent of the contents of any person's propositional attitudes or other mental states. Information is understood to be objectively present in the environment independently of the representational states of any subject. Indeed, information is objectively present in the environment even if there are no subjects of representational states. This feature of the concept of information is crucial. The goal of informational semantics is to provide an account of representation in terms of the concept of information. Propositional attitudes, however, are representational states. Therefore, if information depended on the propositional attitudes of a subject of mental states, then information would itself depend on representational states. And then the project of informational semantics would become a matter of using the concept of representation to explain the concept of representation. It would, in other words, be circular. While such circularity would not necessarily be vicious, it would undermine the goal of informational semantics to reduce intentionality to the natural order. Informational accounts of representation are essentially reductionist in character. This goal is to show how semantic, intentional concepts and locutions can be reduced to non-semantic, non-intentional ones. To use representational states such as propositional attitudes in this reductive explanation would, effectively, be to abandon this project. Therefore, the concept of information, the concept in terms of which representation is to be explained, must be divested of the intentional, representational associations it sometimes has in everyday discourse. The informational relation must, therefore, be understood as objective in the sense that it holds independently of whether any cognitive system, any subject of intentional states, detects or processes it. In what, then, does this informational relation consist?

The concept of information is typically captured in terms of the concept of *nomic dependency*. The general idea is something like this. The fact that the litmus-paper turns red when immersed in a certain liquid carries the information that the liquid is acidic because, and only because, it is nomically necessary that the liquid is acidic when the litmus-paper turns red. The fact that the height of the column of mercury in the thermometer coincides with the numeral 21 indicates that the medium in which the thermometer is immersed is 21°K because, and only because, it is nomically necessary that the temperature of the medium is 21°K when the height of the column coincides with the numeral 21. The number of rings in the trunk of a tree carries information about the age of the tree because, and only because, there is a nomic covariation between the age of the tree in years and the number of rings in the trunk. More generally, suppose we have a source s and a receptor r. From the standpoint of information theory, the informational relation obtains not between s and r themselves, but between s's being a certain way and r's being a certain way. Suppose, then, that the source s is F, and the receptor r is G. Then, the fact that r is G carries the information that s is F if and only if it is nomically necessary that s is F given that r is G.

The topic of nomic dependency is, as is well known, a problematic one. I shall assume, along with Dretske, the fairly standard view that nomic connections can be distinguished from accidental generalizations by the facts that (i) the former, but not the latter, are referentially

213

opaque, that is, they create non-extensional contexts, (ii) the former but not the latter are supported by their instances, and (iii) the former, but not the latter, support subjunctive conditionals. It is also generally assumed that nomic dependencies can be *ceteris paribus*. In the above cases, the dependencies clearly are *ceteris paribus*. If the thermometer is broken, for example, the height of the column of mercury need carry no information whatsoever about the temperature of the surrounding medium.

The informational relation must be distinguished from any type of causal relation. Causation, on this construal of the informational relation, is not sufficient for information. Suppose s is F and this causes r to be G. Despite the causal relation connecting the two states of affairs, there can still be information carried by s's being F that is not transmitted to r's being G (this is known as the equivocation of r). Focusing on an actual causal relation reveals nothing of the alternative causal processes that might lead to the tokening of G in r. And these possible causal relations themselves generate information. An actual causal relation, then, is not sufficient to account for the information contained in a receptor.

Information, then, is to be explained in terms of the concept of nomic dependency, where this is distinct from that of causation. However, it would be a misleading oversimplification to think of the information contained in r's being G simply on the basis of a one-to-one nomic dependency between r's being G and s's being F. The reason is that what information r's being G carries about s's being F depends on what other information H is already available to the receptor. Dretske illustrates this point with the following example. Consider four shells with a peanut located under one of them. Suppose Smith has already turned over shells 1 and 2 and found both of them empty. Jones, however, is not party to this information. Then Smith and Jones both turn over shell 3 and find it empty. Finding shell 3 empty does not, it seems, supply each person with the same information. Finding shell 3 empty informs Smith that the peanut is under shell 4. It tells Jones only that the peanut is under shells 1, 2, or 4. Exactly what information is carried by one and the same signal varies according to what information is already available.

This indicates that the criterion for when a receptor carries information about a source must be amended to incorporate the relativity of information. The general idea would then be that expressed as follows. The fact that *r* is G carries, *relative to information H*, the information that *s* is F just in case it is nomically necessary that *s* is F if *r* is G, and it is not nomically necessary that *s* is F simply if H.

Adopting this amendment, however, may seem tantamount to abandoning the project of providing an informational account of representation. What accounts for the difference in the information gleaned by Smith and Jones from one and the same signal is that, prior to turning over the shells, there are things that Smith knew but Jones did not. But knowledge is itself a representational state. Therefore, once again, it seems that the informational account can explain representation only by tacitly appealing to it. If information presupposes knowledge, then one cannot use information to provide a naturalistic reduction of representation.

The correct response to this problem has, I believe, already been outlined by Dretske. The informational semanticist can claim, while the information contained in a signal is relative, what it is in fact relative to is simply further information. This suggestion is of a piece with the concept of information implicated in Gibson's ecological model of perception (chapter 5). On this view, the information contained in the turning over of shell 3 varies between Smith and Jones because there is further information of which Smith, but not Jones, is in possession. Thus, while the information contained in any signal is relative, it is not ultimately relative to the representational states of cognizers. It is relative to further information that cognizers, in virtue of their representational states may, or may not, have picked up. If then, it is possible to give an account of informational pick-up or detection in non-representational terms, the representation-independence of the concept of information will have been secured.

10.2 PROBLEMS FOR INFORMATIONAL ACCOUNTS OF REPRESENTATION

The project of providing an informational account of representation faces three well-known problems: (i) the problem of *intensionality*, (ii) the problem of *misrepresentation*, and (iii) the problem of *indeterminacy*. In fact, the presence of the definite article in the above titles may be unwarranted. There are, for example, two distinct types of intensionality problem, and several different forms the problem of misrepresentation may take. In this section, I shall outline each type of problem, distinguishing between their variant forms whenever appropriate.

The problem of intensionality

One of the constitutive features of representational states is that sentences used to ascribe them are *intensional*. One of the ways of telling that we are ascribing a representational state is by noting that the sentences we use in such ascription may change from true to false if, in the words we use to pick out the object of representation, we substitute for some referring expression another expression that refers to the same thing. An intensional context is one where substitution of co-referential terms in a sentence can alter the truth-value of that sentence. And representational contexts are paradigmatically intensional ones. Thus, to use the sort of example made famous by Quine (1960), The sentence 'Smith believes that Jones is a spy' can be true, while the sentence 'Smith believes that the tallest man in the room is a spy' can be false even if Jones is the tallest man in the room. The latter sentence will be false, for example, if Smith does not know that the tallest man in the room is Jones. Any account of representation must, it is claimed, respect and account for the intensionality of representational locutions and attributions.

The problem intensionality poses for informational accounts of representation can be stated as follows. If a signal that r is G carries the information that s is F, and if s is F because s is H, then, it might be thought, the signal r is G also carries the information that s is H. And, if this is true, informational semantics will have difficulties accounting for the intensionality of representational ascriptions, or so it is claimed. For example, suppose r's being G carries the information that s is water. This means that r's being G nomically depends on s's being water. Given that the properties F (being water) and H (being a substance composed of H_2O molecules) are co-extensional, then it seems that r's being G carries the information that s is H_2O also. But, it is argued, a person might believe that s is water without believing that it is H_2O, perhaps because she has no concept of H_2O, or does not know that water is made up of hydrogen and oxygen. A person can believe that s is water without believing that s is H_2O. And this intensionality of representational ascriptions is, it is claimed, something for which informational accounts of representation cannot account.

Following Jacob (1997:86) it is useful, in this context, to distinguish two levels or degrees of intensionality. A sentence, or ascription made by way of a sentence, is *weakly* intensional if replacement of one constituent 'F' by some co-extensional constituent 'H' alters its truth-value. A sentence, or ascription made by way of a sentence, is, on the other hand, *strongly* extensional if replacement of one constituent 'F' by a *nomologically* or otherwise *necessarily* co-extensive constituent 'H' alters its truth-value. If informational accounts of representation face a problem of intensionality, it is not a problem of accounting for weak intensionality. On the contrary, the informational account provides an elegant explanation of weak intensionality. The reason is that r's being G carries the information that s is F only if the former is nomically dependent on the latter. On the informational account, information is a matter of nomic dependence. But if F and H are merely co-extensional, then even if r's being G nomically depends on s's being F, it does not follow that r's being G nomically depends on s's being H. Thus, r's being G can carry the information that s is F without carrying the information that s is H, even though, as a matter of fact, all Fs are H. Mere co-extension between properties does not entail nomic dependence. And without nomic dependence there is no information. The informational account of representation, thus, is not only compatible with weak intensionality, it, in fact, explains why representational ascriptions should be weakly intensional.

Strong intensionality, however, is more of a problem. If F and H are nomically connected, as are water and H_2O in the above example, then if r's being G is nomically dependent on s's being F, then, by the transitivity of nomic dependence, r's being G is also nomically dependent on s's being H. Thus, it seems that if r's being G carries the information that s is F in virtue of the nomic dependence of the former on the latter, then it must also carry the information that s is H. If information follows nomic dependence, and if nomic dependence is transitive, then the information carried by a signal must also, in the above sense, be transitive. And this means that informational accounts of representation will have a difficult time handling the *strong* intensionality of representational locutions and ascriptions. If we assume, then, that representational locutions and ascriptions are strongly intensional (I can, prima facie, believe that there is water in the glass without believing that there is H_2O in the glass, despite the nomic co-extension of water and H_2O), then we have identified the first problem facing informational accounts of representation.

Jacob (1997) suggests the following solution to the problem of strong intensionality. The solution appeals to the well-known notion of a *mode of presentation*. Just as we can speak of different modes of presentation of one and the same object, so, according to Jacob, we can speak of different modes of presentation of one and the same piece of information. Alternatively, just as we can think of the same object or property under different concepts, so too, according to Jacob, we can talk of different thoughts encoding the same piece of information under different concepts. Thus, the suggestion is that the concept WATER differs from the concept SUBSTANCE COMPOSED OF H_2O MOLECULES. And, according to Jacob, this solves the problem of strong intensionality. In cases of strongly intensional ascriptions and locutions, we simply have cases of one and the same piece of information being encoded under different concepts or modes of presentation.

Even if it makes sense to talk of information, as opposed to objects and properties, being represented under different concepts, or encoded under different modes of presentation, it should be fairly clear that this suggestion is inadequate. Whatever else a mode of presentation, or concept, is, it is something that is composed of representational elements. And, if the informational account of representation is to be vindicated, these elements have to be given an informational explanation. To appeal to concepts or modes of presentation here, then, is simply to push the problem back a step. The same problem of strong intensionality will now arise for the representational elements of the mode of presentation. If there is a solution to the problem posed by strong intensionality, then, it will have to be found in other than an appeal to concepts or modes of presentation.

The problem of misrepresentation

According to the informational account of representation, the representational properties of a signal *r*'s being G arise out of the nomic dependency of this signal on a source *s*'s being F. What we can call the problem of misrepresentation arises because of a perceived difference between the notion of meaning, as commonly understood, and the notion of information understood in terms of nomic dependency.

Information, it is argued, is tied to aetiology in a way that meaning is not (Fodor 1990:90). That is, if the tokens of a symbol have two kinds of causal aetiology, then it follows that there are two kinds of information that tokens of that symbol carry. The meaning of a symbol, on the other hand, is something that all its tokens have in common, however, these tokens may happen to be caused. Information follows causal aetiology, and meaning does not.

As with the problem of intensionality, the problem of misrepresentation can be developed in two distinct ways. The first way takes the form of a *disjunction problem*. The second takes the form of a *problem of error*. Let us consider, first, the disjunction problem.

Consider a mental representation of a horse. Adopting common practice, I shall refer to this by way of the capitalized HORSE to show that we are talking about the representation and not the horse itself. The representation HORSE, it seems, means 'horse'. This is what makes it the particular representation it is. However, it also seems possible, indeed likely, that the representation HORSE can be caused by things that are not horses. Donkeys in the distance, and cows on a dark night, might, in certain circumstances, be equally efficacious in causing a tokening of the HORSE representation. Now, according to the informational account, representation is to be explained in terms of nomic dependence. And nomic dependence is cashed out, roughly, in terms of a signal *r*'s being G being nomically dependent on a source *s*'s being F. That is, the former is nomically dependent on the latter if, again roughly, *r* could not be G unless *s* was F. However, the representation HORSE can be tokened in the absence of horses. Therefore, HORSE is not nomically dependent on horses in the relevant sense. In fact, what HORSE does seem nomically dependent on is not the property of being a horse but the property of being a horse-or-a-donkey-in-the-distance-or-a-cow-on-a-dark-night. That is, HORSE seems nomically dependent not on the property of being a horse but on the disjunctive property [horse v donkey-in-the-distance v cow-on-a-dark-night]. (This disjunctive property can obviously be expanded to cover everything that does, in fact, cause a tokening of HORSE.) Thus, if information is a matter of nomic dependence, and if representation is a matter of information, then we seem forced to say that what HORSE represents is not the property of being a horse, but the above disjunctive property. But, fairly obviously, when we think, for example, that Arkle was a horse, and thus token the representation

HORSE, we do not regard ourselves as thinking that Arkle was either a horse or a donkey-in-the-distance or a cow-on-a-dark-night. We think that Arkle was a horse. And if I am inclined to have a flutter on the 2.45 at Uttoxeter, still less do I think of myself as betting on something that is either a horse or a donkey-in-the-distance or a cow-on-a-dark-night. There is thus a divergence between the meaning of a representation and the information carried by that information. The information is disjunctive in a way that the meaning is not. This is the disjunction problem.

The second problem, the problem of error, is closely connected. According to the informational approach, representational content is a matter of nomic dependency between a signal and a source. But this seems to entail that a signal cannot *misinform* about its source. We want to say, for example, that when the HORSE representation is tokened in the presence of a cow-on-a-dark-night, this is a case of misrepresentation. The cow is misrepresented as a horse. But the view that representation consists in nomic dependence precludes us saying this. For what the HORSE representation seems nomically dependent on is the disjunctive property of being a horse or being a donkey-in-the-distance or being a cow-on-a-dark-night. The cow satisfies this disjunction, and therefore we seem to be committed to the view that the tokening of HORSE in the presence of the cow is *not* a case of misrepresentation. Indeed, and even more troubling, nothing could ever count as a case of misrepresentation. Whatever causes the tokening of HORSE, for example, would be included in the disjunctive property upon which HORSE is nomically dependent. Thus, whatever causes the tokening of HORSE is what HORSE represents, and misrepresentation is therefore impossible. Thus informational semantics seems incapable of accounting for what is a manifest property of representational states: their tendency to misrepresent.

The problem of indeterminacy

The third major problem facing informational accounts of representation is the problem of indeterminacy. This problem is, in fact, closely related to the problem of transparency, and can be stated as follows. Suppose a signal r is G carries the information that s is F. And suppose s is F because s is H; that is, there is a nomological connection between s being F and s being H. Then, on the informational account, *r*'s being G must also carry the information that *s* is H. But, then, what is the representational content of the signal *r* is G? Does it represent that *s* is F? Or does it represent that *s* is H? On the informational account, there seems to be no basis for choosing between the two representational contents. That is, given the informational account, there seems to be no fact of the matter that could determine whether the representational content of the signal *r* is G is that *s* is F or that *s* is H. If we accept the reduction of representation to information, then, the representational content of the signal *r* is G seems indeterminate.

Dretske (1986:26) illustrates this problem of indeterminacy by way of the following, by now very well-known, example. Some marine bacteria have internal magnets, called magnetosomes, that function like compass needles; they align the bacteria parallel to the earth's magnetic field. The result is that bacteria in the northern hemisphere propel themselves in the direction of geomagnetic north. In the southern hemisphere, the magnetosomes are reversed, and southern bacteria propel themselves towards geomagnetic south. The survival value of these magnetosomes, it seems likely, consists in their allowing the bacteria to avoid the oxygen-rich surface water that would be lethal to them. In the northern hemisphere, for example, movement towards geomagnetic north will take the bacteria away from oxygen-rich surface water towards the comparatively oxygen-free water lower down. And movement towards geomagnetic south has the same effect in the southern hemisphere.

The question then arises: what do the magnetosomes of these bacteria represent. Do they represent the direction of geomagnetic north? Or do they represent the direction of oxygen-free water? Indeed, since they will align themselves with any ambient magnetic field, as for example would be supplied by a bar magnet, perhaps they represent only the direction of magnetic north, and not geomagnetic north. The problem is that the magnetosomes carry information about all three. Therefore, on the informational account, there seems to be no fact of the matter that could determine which of the three the magnetosomes (or, more precisely, an appropriate state of the magnetosomes) represent. If we adopt the informational reduction of representation to information, then, what the magnetosomes represent, their representational content, seems indeterminate.

It is useful to clearly distinguish the problem of indeterminacy from the problem of misrepresentation, since they are frequently run together. The problem of misrepresentation has the following form: even though *r*'s being G is maximally correlated with the disjunctive property of (*s* is F or *s* is H), we, none the less, want to count tokenings of *r* is G caused by *s* is H as *false* tokenings. The problem of indeterminacy, on the other hand, has the following form: *r*'s being G is correlated with both *s* is F and *s* is H, and there is no basis for saying that *r*'s being G represents one of these rather than the other. In the problem of misrepresentation, our intuitions tell us that *r*'s being G does *not* carry the information that *s* is H, and we are simply looking for a justification for our intuitions. In the problem of indeterminacy, our intuitions tell us that we have as much reason to believe that *r* is G carries the information that *s* is H as it does the information that *s* is F.

In the context of informational semantics, the problem of indeterminacy arises whenever an organism, or mechanism, detects one item of information in virtue of detecting another. In Dretske's example of the marine bacteria, the magnetosome, it is plausible to suppose, detects the direction of anaerobic water in virtue of detecting the direction of geomagnetic north. Since the two informational items are nomically correlated, and since nomic dependence is a transitive relation, the informational account seems committed to claiming that the magnetosome represents both the direction of anaerobic water and the direction of geomagnetic north. The problem of indeterminacy is, in this sense, a problem of transitivity. The problem of misrepresentation is quite different. There is no temptation to suppose, for example, that the HORSE representation represents horses *in virtue of* representing donkeys-in-the-distance, or in virtue of representing cows-on-a-dark-night. Ultimately, the difference between the two problems amounts to this. The problem of indeterminacy is a *conjunction* problem: *r*'s being G carries the information both that *s* is F and that *s* is H, and it carries the former information (say) in virtue of carrying the latter. The problem of misrepresentation is a *disjunction* problem: *r*'s being G carries the information that *s* is F but does not carry the information that either *s* is F or *s* is H.

To see the difference between these two problems, it will be instructive to see how they are commonly run together. Consider another stock example in these sorts of discussions; the case of the frog's sight–strike–feed mechanism. Frogs catch flies by way of a rapid strike with their tongues. Thus, it is plausible to suppose, mediating between the environmental presence of a fly and the motor response of the tongue strike is some sort of neural mechanism that registers the fly's presence in the vicinity and causes the strike of the frog's tongue. In more detail, we might suppose the presence of the fly causes the relevant mechanism to go into state S, and its being in state S causes (via various motor intermediaries) the tongue to strike. From this point, however, the example can be developed in two quite different ways; the first leading to a problem of indeterminacy, the second leading to a problem of misrepresentation.

The first way of developing the example points out that it is highly likely that the mechanism responsible for the frog's tongue strike is sensitive not to flies as such but to the presence of any appropriately sized ambient airborne entities. Evidence for this comes from the fact that frog's are reported to be relatively indiscriminate in their striking habits; striking not only at flies but at, notoriously, lead pellets or 'BB's lobbed at them. Thus, it seems likely that the relevant mechanism of the frog detects both flies and ambient black dots, and, crucially, that it detects the former in virtue of detecting the latter. Developed in this way, the example gives us a problem of indeterminacy. Does the mechanism represent flies, or does it represent ambient black dots? If we adopt the informational approach, there seems no basis for deciding; no fact of the matter that could favour one interpretation of the mechanism's representational content over the other. The representational content is, thus, indeterminate.

The second way of developing the example leads to a problem of misrepresentation. This development points out that what the frog's tongue strikes are maximally correlated with are not flies but the disjunctive property of being a fly or a BB (for example; the disjunction can, of course, be sufficiently open-ended to subsume all those things which do, in fact, cause the frog's tongue to strike). Of course, we want to say that strikes at BBs are, in some sense at least, mistakes: that the mechanism does not represent lead pellets. But the problem, then, is to detach what the mechanism carries information about, and hence what it represents, from the property with which it is maximally correlated. This is the problem of misrepresentation.

These problems are distinct but frequently run together. It is important to distinguish them, however, because, as we shall see, the problem of indeterminacy proves a lot more tenacious than the problem of misrepresentation.

A purely informational approach to representation, then, faces at least three problems. There is the problem of accounting for *strongly* (as opposed to *weakly*) intensional contexts; the problem of accounting for misrepresentation (understood as a conjunction of the disjunction problem and the problem of error), and the problem of indeterminacy. These problems, and, in particular, the problem of misrepresentation, have typically led proponents of the informational approach to supplement their account with principles derived from a quite distinct theory. This is the so called *teleological* theory of representation. And it is to this theory that we shall now turn.

10.3 THE TELEOLOGICAL THEORY OF REPRESENTATION

A teleological theory of representation will employ, as a pivotal concept, what Millikan calls *proper function*. The proper function of some mechanism, trait, or process is what it is *supposed* to do, what it has been *designed* to do, what it *ought* to do. More precisely, the following provides a simplified version of Millikan's already simplified version of her definition of proper function given in *Language, Thought, and Other Biological Categories*:

> An item X has proper function F only if: (i) X is a reproduction of some prior item that, because of possession of certain reproduced properties, actually performed F in the past, and X exists because of this performance; or (ii) X is the product of a device that had the performance of F as a proper function and normally performs F by way of producing an item like X.   (adapted from Millikan 1993:13)

This definition takes some unpacking. Firstly, the concept of a proper function is a normative concept. The proper function of an item is defined in terms of what an item *should* do, not what it actually does or is disposed to do. The concept of proper function, being normative, cannot be defined in causal or dispositional terms. What something does, or is disposed to do, is not always what it is supposed to do. This is for three reasons. Firstly, any mechanism, trait, or process will do many things, not all of which are part of its proper function. A heart, for example, pumps blood; it also makes a thumping noise, and produces wiggly lines on electrocardiograms. But only the first of these is its proper function since only pumping blood is something performed by hearts in the past that explains the existence of hearts in the present. Secondly, a process, trait, or mechanism can have a proper function

224

even if it never, or hardly ever, performs it. To use a flagship example of Millikan's, the proper function of the tail of a sperm cell is to propel the cell to the ovum. The vast majority of sperm tails, however, do not accomplish this task. Third, a process, trait, or mechanism may have a proper function and yet not be able to perform it properly – if, for example, it is malformed. A person's heart may be malformed and, thus, not be able to pump blood properly. Nevertheless, pumping blood is its proper function because ancestors of the person whose heart it is had hearts which pumped blood and this (in part) explains why they survived and proliferated. The concept of proper function is, thus, a normative concept. The proper function of an item is its *Normal* function, where, following Millikan, the capitalized 'N' indicates that this is a normative sense of normal as opposed to a causal or dispositional one.

What underlies the normativity of the concept of a proper function is the fact that the concept is essentially *historical* in character. The proper function of an item is determined not by the present characteristics or dispositions of that item, but by its history. In particular, the possession of a proper function F by an item depends on that item existing because it possesses certain characteristics that have been selected for because of the role they play in performing F. This is the import of (i). Condition (i) is a necessary condition of possessing what Millikan calls a *direct* proper function. Such possession is essentially a matter of history. There are no first-generation direct proper functions.

There is, however, an important distinction to be observed between direct and *derived* proper functions. The idea of a derived proper function is communicated by condition (ii). Consider the distinction between the particular pattern of pigmentation distributed across the skin of a chameleon and the mechanism that produces this distribution. Only the mechanism itself possesses a direct proper function, roughly the function of distributing pigmentation in such a way that the chameleon will match its immediate environment. However, the state of the chameleon's skin – the particular distribution of pigmentation – also possesses a proper function; a function it derives from the mechanism that produces it. A derived proper function of the 'Pollockian' arrangement of pigmentation in the chameleon's skin is to match the chameleon to the Jackson Pollock No. 4, upon which the poor chameleon has been placed. And, unlike direct proper functions, there can be first-generation derived proper functions. The Pollockian arrangement of the chameleon's pigmentation has the proper function it has even if no chameleon has ever been placed on a Pollock No. 4 before, consequently even if no chameleon has ever produced this particular pattern before.

The proper or Normal function, direct or derived, of many evolved items is *relational* in character. Generally this means that the characteristic has evolved to enable the organism to cope with its environment; to locate food, evade predators, protect itself against heat or cold, and so on. It is here that the relationality of Normal or proper function arises. Normal functions are often defined relative to some environmental object or feature: the function of the chameleon's skin is to make the chameleon the same colour as its immediate environment; the function of the lion's curved claws is to catch and hold onto prey; the function of the bee's dance is to indicate to other bees the distance and direction of nectar, and so on. In each case, the function of the characteristic is specified in terms of a relation it bears to an environmental item. And the reason for this is that the very reason the characteristic in question exists is that it has evolved to meet certain environmental pressures.

The core idea of the teleological theory of representation is that the mechanisms responsible for mental representation are evolutionary products also. As such, they will have (direct) relational proper functions. The idea, then, is that the representational capacities of a given cognitive mechanism derive from the environmental objects, properties, or relations that are incorporated into that mechanism's (direct) relational proper function. That is, if a cognitive mechanism M has evolved in order to detect environmental feature E, then this is what makes an appropriate state S of M about E; this is what gives the state S the content that E. In this way, the representational content of cognitive state S derives from the (direct) relational proper function of the mechanism M that produces S.

This account requires a clear distinction to be drawn between a cognitive state and a cognitive mechanism. Roughly, the distinction will be implemented in the following way. An organism's cognitive state tokens are (often) caused by events occurring in that organism's environment. And there are mechanisms, typically neuronal, that mediate those causal transactions. Each of these mechanisms will, presumably, have an evolutionary history and, therefore, will possess a (direct) proper function. Moreover, it is plausible to suppose, this proper function will be precisely to mediate the tokenings of cognitive states. That is, on the teleological view, there are various neural mechanisms whose (direct) proper or Normal function is to produce tokenings of cognitive states in environmentally appropriate circumstances. According to the teleological theory, the content of these cognitive states derives from the environmental features that are incorporated into the (direct) proper functions of the mechanisms that produce those states. Thus, if cognitive state S is produced by mechanism M, and if the direct proper function of M is to produce S in environmental circumstances E, then, according to the teleological theory, S represents, or is about, E. In this way the content of a cognitive state derives from the direct relational proper function of the mechanism that produces it.

10.4 TELEOLOGICAL SEMANTICS AND THE PROBLEM OF MISREPRESENTATION

One great strength of the teleological account of representation is that it yields a simple and immediate solution to the problem of misrepresentation, understood as a conjunction of the disjunction problem and the problem of error. Consider, first, the disjunction problem.

The problem was this. Given that the representation HORSE, for example, is maximally correlated not with the property of being a horse but with the disjunctive property of being a (horse v a donkey-in-the-distance v a cow-on-a-dark-night), how is it that HORSE represents the former property and not the latter? The answer supplied by the teleological account is that HORSE represents the property of being a horse and not the above sort of disjunctive property because the direct relational proper function of the mechanism that produces HORSE is to represent the property of being a horse. That is, the HORSE representation, we are to suppose, is a state of a mechanism M. And this mechanism M has the direct proper function of producing HORSE in the presence of horses (or instantiations of the property of being a horse). It does not have the proper function of producing HORSE in the presence of donkeys-in-the-distance or in the presence of cows-on-a-dark-night. But, on the teleological account, the content of a state S of mechanism M derives from the proper function of M. Thus, HORSE is about horses, and not about donkeys, cows, or disjunctions of the three. Providing a solution to the disjunction problem requires, in effect, detaching the content of a representation from the property with which it is maximally correlated. And this is precisely what the teleological theory allows us to do. Representation, on this view, derives from proper function. And the concept of proper function, being normative, cannot be defined in causal or dispositional terms. The fact that HORSE is tokened not only in the presence of horses but also in that of donkeys and cows, and is thus maximally correlated with a disjunction of the three is, therefore, irrelevant. What determines the representational content of HORSE is not what environmental item in fact *does* causally produce it, but what *should* causally produce it. And this is determined by the direct relational proper function of its producing mechanism.

Consider, now, the problem of error. The problem of error was that, given the informational account, it seems impossible for a signal to misinform about its source. We want to say that, when the HORSE representation is tokened in the presence of a donkey-in-the-distance, this is a case of misrepresentation. The donkey is misrepresented as a horse. But the informational account precludes us from saying this. For, what the HORSE representation seems nomically dependent on is the disjunctive property of being a horse or a donkey-in-the-distance or a cow-on-a-dark-night; and this disjunctive property is satisfied by the donkey. So, after all, we do not have a case of misrepresentation. Indeed, we never could have a case of misrepresentation. Whatever causes the tokening of HORSE, for example, would be included in the disjunctive property upon which HORSE is nomically dependent. Thus, whatever causes the tokening of HORSE is what HORSE represents, and misrepresentation is, therefore, impossible.

Providing a solution to this problem again requires us to be able to detach the meaning or content of a representation from what causes tokenings of it. And, as with the disjunction problem, this is precisely what the teleological theory allows us to do. According to the teleological account, the reason the HORSE representation misrepresents when it is tokened in the presence of a donkey or cow is due to the fact that the mechanism that produces HORSE has been designed, by natural selection, to do so in the presence of horses, not in that of donkeys or cows. The direct relational proper function of the mechanism, that is, is to produce HORSE in the presence of horses, and not in the presence of donkeys or cows. Thus, the teleological theory gives us a distinction between what *actually* causes tokenings of HORSE and what is *supposed* to cause tokenings of HORSE. This is a distinction that the informational account does not allow us to draw. And this is what allows the teleological theory to solve the problem of error.

In this way, then, the teleological theory yields a simple and elegant solution to the problem of misrepresentation. This is one of the great strengths of the teleological theory, one of the problems it was, one might say, designed to solve. With regard to the other problems, in particular the problem of indeterminacy, the teleological theory is commonly perceived to be less successful. In the next chapter, I try to show how, by combining the teleological theory with the environmentalist position developed in Part I, it is possible to solve the remaining problems of indeterminacy and (strong) intensionality.

11

Environmentalism and teleological semantics

While providing a simple and elegant solution to the problem of misrepresentation, teleological theories of representation are thought to suffer from the two remaining difficulties that plagued the informational account. Firstly, the teleological account is thought to suffer from a problem of indeterminacy. In the specific context of the teleological theory, this problem takes the following form. Biological function, it is argued, is indeterminate in the sense that in the case of two or more competing interpretations of the function of an adapted biological mechanism, there is often no fact of the matter that could determine which interpretation is the correct one. Therefore, any attempt to ground mental content in biological function seems to entail the indeterminacy of content. The second problem, the problem of intensionality, arises with the teleological theory because, it is argued, statements of biological function are transparent, or extensional, in that a statement of the form 'the function of evolved mechanism M is to represent Fs' can be substituted *salva veritate* by a statement of the form 'the function of evolved mechanism M is to represent Gs', provided that the statement 'F iff G' is counterfactual supporting. Therefore, statements of biological function are transparent, and any attempt to construct content out of biological function must fail to capture the intensionality of psychological ascriptions.

These problems, as we shall see, are related and often run together. It is, however, useful to distinguish them since, even if one problem does not bother you, the other one might. Dennett (1987), for example, is unperturbed by the problem of indeterminacy, indeed, he embraces the conclusion that mental content is indeterminate. Dennett, however, also thinks that intensionality is a hallmark of the mental (Dennett 1969). Therefore, he should be concerned by the problem of transparency.

In this chapter, I shall try to show how a teleological theory can

230

resolve these two problems. The argument I shall develop draws on the arguments defended in Part I of this book, and, in particular, on the connection between cognition and action emphasized there. I shall argue that the problems of indeterminacy and transparency stem *not* from the fact that the concept of biological function is inadequate for capturing the concept of content but, rather, from two related misunderstandings: (i) a confusion of the different levels of description at which biological function can be specified, and (ii) a confusion over the objects to which the contents underwritten by these functions can be attributed. These misunderstandings reinforce each other in several ways. Once they are cleared up, however, the problems of indeterminacy and transparency dissolve.

11.1 THE PROBLEM OF INDETERMINACY

The teleological theory attempts to ground mental content in Normal function. The content of a cognitive state S, on this view, derives from the direct relational proper function of a cognitive mechanism M. And this function of M is to produce, or go into, state S in environmentally appropriate circumstances. One prominent objection to this project is that it entails the indeterminacy of mental content. It does this because, it is claimed, the biological function of a mechanism is itself indeterminate. The stock example used to make this point is one we have already encountered: the sight–strike–feed mechanism of the frog.

To recapitulate somewhat, frogs catch flies by way of a rapid strike with their tongue. Thus, it is plausible to suppose, mediating between the environmental presence of a fly and the motor response of the tongue strike is some sort of neural mechanism that registers the fly's presence in the vicinity and causes the strike of the frog's tongue. In more detail, we might suppose the presence of a fly causes the relevant mechanism to go into state S, and its being in state S causes (via various motor intermediaries) the tongue to strike. According to the teleological approach, the content of state S is roughly 'fly' or 'fly, there', and it derives this content from the fact that the proper or Normal function of its underlying mechanism is to detect the presence of flies (or to go into state S when flies are present).

There is, however, a well-known problem with this sort of story. The above account assumed that the proper function of the mechanism was to register the presence of flies in the vicinity. If so, then the state that the mechanism enters into when flies are present is *about* flies, and thus *means* that there are flies in the vicinity. However, there is an alternative construal of the function of the internal mechanism. On this construal, what the mechanism in question has been selected to respond to are little ambient black things. (To avoid becoming entangled in a completely different issue, let me make it clear that the little ambient black things are environmental entities and not dots on a retinal image.) The proper function of the mechanism, on this construal, is to mediate between little ambient black things and tokenings of a state that causes the frog's tongue to strike. This state will, then, be *about* little ambient black things and will, therefore, *mean* that there are little ambient black things in the vicinity. The Normal function of the mechanism is different in each case and, hence, the content is distinct in each case (Fodor 1990:70–2). The content is obviously distinct in each case since not all little ambient black things are flies. And the proper function is also different. In the latter case, but not the former, the frog's mechanism is functioning Normally when the frog strikes at a little ambient black thing that is, in fact, not a fly but a lead pellet (a 'BB') that happens to be passing through.

The problem of indeterminacy arises because there seems to be no fact of the matter that could determine which of these interpretations is the correct one. Evolutionary theory, it is argued, does not provide any means of adjudicating between these interpretations. That is, evolutionary theory, by itself, is neutral between the claim that the neural mechanism Normally mediates fly strikes, in which case strikes at BBs are errors, and the claim that the mechanism Normally mediates ambient black thing strikes that are situated in an environment in which little black things are Normally flies (Fodor 1990:72). Since, so the argument goes, there is no fact of the matter favouring one interpretation over the other, the function of the mechanism is, to this extent, indeterminate. Therefore, whether the mechanism is about, and hence means that there are, flies in the vicinity or that there are little ambient black things in the vicinity is also indeterminate. In this way, the teleological approach is thought to entail the indeterminacy of mental content. And so, to use Fodor's colourful expression: it is most unlikely that Darwin is going to pull Brentano's chestnuts out of the fire.

This problem, in fact, proves surprisingly resistant to solution. To

232

begin with, and contrary to some assertions (e.g., Sterelny 1990:127), Sober's (1984) otherwise useful distinction between *selection of* and *selection for* does not, by itself, provide a solution. Sober's distinction works something like this. Consider a filter that will allow only balls of 1 cm or less in diameter to pass. Suppose that all such balls are green. In the group that passes through the filter there is selection *for* size, but selection *of* both size and colour. The moral underlying this distinction, of course, is that in the above case of the frog's sight–strike–feed mechanism, the relevant sense of selection is selection *for*. This, however, does not solve our problem, since it is possible to reformulate the issue in terms of the notion of selection for. That is, evolutionary theory provides us with no principled way of deciding whether the mechanism has been selected *for* the detection of flies or *for* the detection of little ambient black things in an environment where all the little ambient black things happen to be flies. Given that both strategies would be equally successful from the standpoint of survival, there seems to be no basis, from within evolutionary theory, for saying that the mechanism has been selected for the detection of flies rather than the detection of ambient black things. The reasons for this should become clearer as the chapter progresses.

Secondly, an appeal to counterfactuals will not help the teleological theory here. The counterfactuals in question would, presumably, be of the following sort. Had flies changed so that their retinal projections were not dot-like, natural selection would tend to construct mechanisms that tracked the changing shape of flies; had the frog's ancestral environment been from the start BB infested, natural selection would have tended to construct mechanisms that could discriminate flies from pellets, etc. There are two reasons why the teleological theory cannot appeal to counterfactuals in this way. Firstly, and most importantly, the teleological theory is an *actualist* account of representation (Fodor 1990:77). What gives a state the representational content it has is the *actual* evolutionary history of the mechanism that produces it. Counterfactual evolutionary history is simply irrelevant to content. Thus, standard teleological theory cannot appeal to these sorts of counterfactuals. Secondly, appeal to such counterfactuals would probably commit the teleological theory to a crude Panglossian interpretation of evolutionary theory, for, without some fairly controversial Panglossian assumptions, the relevant counterfactuals are likely to turn out false. For example, it simply is not true that, had the frog's ancestral environment been from the start BB infested, natural selection would have tended to construct mechanisms that could discriminate flies from pellets. For this would only be so given various assumptions about the relative evolutionary cost of developing the more sophisticated mechanisms. Perhaps the cost involved in developing the more sophisticated mechanisms would outweigh the benefits gained from them (see chapter 4). As we saw earlier, the ancestral environment of the reed-warbler, for example, was cuckoo infested. However, it is still not true that the reed-warbler developed the more sophisticated mechanisms necessary to detect the young cuckoo in its nest. So, even if the appeal to counterfactuals was, for the teleological theory, legitimate, the sort of counterfactuals to which it would, in fact, need to appeal are quite likely to turn out to be false.

The problem of indeterminacy, then, is fairly tenacious. It is worth noting, I suppose, that, even if the teleological theory does entail the indeterminacy of content, this is not necessarily an objection to it. While Fodor, for example, objects to the teleological theory on precisely these grounds, Dennett (1987), on the other hand, embraces semantic indeterminacy and sees this entailment as, if anything, a strength of the teleological approach. None the less, if the teleological theory does entail the indeterminacy of content, then it is not clear that the teleological theory has any distinctive value as an approach to naturalizing semantics. As Fodor puts it, if all we want to do is *not* solve the disjunction problem, then it is not clear that the teleological theory buys us anything that a straightforward causal theory would not (Fodor 1987:75). Similarly, if all we want to do is *not* solve the problem of indeterminacy, then it is not clear that we are embarked on the project of naturalizing semantics at all. Ignoring semantics, or eliminating semantics, is a very different project from naturalizing it. In order for the teleological theory to have any distinctive contribution to make towards a naturalistic reduction of representation, some solution to the problem of indeterminacy needs to be found.

In any event, I shall argue that the teleological account does *not* entail semantic or representational indeterminacy. The suggestion that it does, I shall try to show, stems from (i) a confusion of the different levels at which we can specify the proper function of an evolved mechanism, and (ii) a consequent conflation of the different objects to which the contents underwritten by such functions apply.

And, in particular, I shall try to show that a multiplicity of proper functions of an evolved mechanism does *not* add up to the indeterminacy of content.

11.2 THE PROBLEM OF TRANSPARENCY

The problem of transparency is that appeals to the proper function of a selected mechanism will not decide between reliably equivalent content ascriptions; that is, they will not decide between any pair of equivalent content ascriptions where the equivalence is counterfactual supporting. To put things in the formal mode: the context, *was selected for representing things as F*, is transparent to the substitution of predicates reliably coextensive with F. A fortiori, it is transparent to the substitution of predicates necessarily coextensive with F. In consequence, teleological ascriptions offer no hope of constructing contexts that are as intensional as 'believes that . . .'. If this is so, then it is difficult to see how appeals to teleology can reconstruct the intensionality of mental ascriptions (Fodor 1990:73).

This may seem counterintuitive. After all, it is clearly true that frogs do not strike at flies under the description 'fly or BB'. This is true, but it does not affect the present issue. From the standpoint of evolutionary biology, it is argued, it does not matter how you describe the object of fly strikes so long as it is reliable (i.e., counterfactual supporting) that all local flies-or-BBs are flies. If all the local flies-or-BBs are flies, then, from the point of view of selection, the frog that strikes at one does neither better nor worse than the frog that strikes at the other (Fodor 1990:74).

There is, fairly clearly, a close connection between the problem of indeterminacy and the problem of transparency. The problem of indeterminacy arises because there seems to be no fact of the matter that could favour one interpretation of biological function, for example, detecting flies, over another, such as detecting little ambient black things. But the difference in interpretation stems solely from a difference between the environmental objects that the function is thought to incorporate. Therefore, the problem of indeterminacy derives from there being no fact of the matter that could determine which of two distinct types of environmental object a given function incorporates. If this is so, then, since there is no fact of the matter distinguishing the environmental correlates of a cognitive mechanism's proper function, these environmental correlates can, in any specification of this proper function, be substituted interchangeably. Thus, the problem of indeterminacy entails the problem of transparency.

In the following sections, I shall argue that both the problem of indeterminacy and the problem of transparency can be solved broadly within the framework of the teleological approach. To show this, however, it is necessary to introduce two things. The first of these is a concept, the second a distinction (Rowlands 1997).

11.3 REPRESENTATION, ACTION, AND THE CONCEPT OF AN AFFORDANCE

Part I outlined a certain conception of cognitive processes, a conception that emphasized the connection between cognition and *action*. Acting on the world, manipulating information-bearing structures in the environment, is not, it was argued, tangential or peripheral to cognition; on the contrary, it is an essential part of it. In the understanding of cognitive processes, there are no deep theoretical reasons for separating off internal forms of information processing – effected by the transformation of internal information-bearing structures – from external forms of such processing – consisting in the manipulation of external information-bearing structures. Action, in this way, is constitutive of cognition. And, if this is correct, it will have important consequences for our understanding of mental representation. If cognitive processes are representational, and if action is constitutive of cognitive processes, then this suggests that there will also be important links between representation and action. It is this idea that will be explored in the present section. I shall argue that basic cases of representation at least are closely connected with the capacity of organisms to act on the world. Thus, representation is best understood as a phenomenon which emerges from out of a background of action. For cases of basic representation at least, the capacity of an organism to represent cannot be understood in isolation from its capacity to act. And precisely what an organism is capable of representing, and what on any occasion it does in fact represent, cannot be understood in isolation from the way in which it acts in the world.

The claim that there is an important connection between representation and action has clear historical precedents. The connection was emphasized, for example, by Merleau-Ponty (1962). According to Merleau-Ponty, representation must be understood in relation firstly to our embodiment, to the fact that we have bodies, and, secondly, to our possession of certain basic skills, skills that we inevitably acquire because of our embodiment. He points out, in his critique of Sartre's extreme view of freedom, that mountains are tall for us, and that where they are passable and where they are not is not up to us but is a function of the capacities we possess in virtue of our embodiment. Our embodiment means that we will represent certain things in certain ways:

> In so far as I have hands, feet, a body, I sustain around me intentions which are not dependent upon my decisions and which affect my surroundings in a way which I do not choose. These intentions are general ... they originate from other than myself, and I am not surprised to find them in all psycho-physical subjects organized as I am. (1962:440)

Our bodily nature, then, entails that we will inevitably represent things in a certain way – mountains as tall, or impassable, for example – rather than in another. The reason this is so is that representation is closely bound up with our capacity for action. Because of our bodies, we find ourselves with certain capacities for action rather than others, and representation is a phenomenon that emerges from these capacities. Moreover, for Merleau-Ponty, as we acquire new skills, as we increase our behavioural repertoire, so we increase our representational capacities. As we increase our behavioural repertoire, new things show up, new aspects get represented, aspects of the world that were hidden before we acquired our new skills.

The close connection between representation and action is, as we have seen, also emphasized by Gibson. To emphasize the connection, Gibson introduces the useful idea of an *affordance*. The affordances of the environment are, for a given creature, what it *offers* that creature, what it *furnishes* or *provides*, whether this benefits or harms the creature. A relatively flat, horizontal, rigid, and sufficiently extended surface, for example, affords locomotion for many animals. It is stand-on-able, permitting an upright posture for quadrupeds and bipeds. It is therefore also walk-on-able and run-on-able. A non-rigid surface, like the surface of a lake, however, does not afford support or easy locomotion for medium-sized mammals. It is not stand-on-able, but sink-into-able.

Affordances are relational properties of things; they have to be specified relative to the creature in question. Thus, the surface of a lake affords neither support nor easy locomotion for a horse, but it offers both of these things for a water-bug. Thus, to speak of an affordance is to speak elliptically; an affordance exists only in relation to particular organisms.

Different substances of the environment have different affordances for nutrition and manufacture. Different objects of the environment have different affordances for manipulation, exploitation, circumventing, etc. In addition to substances and inanimate objects, the environment is also made up of other animals, and these afford a rich and complex set of interactions – sexual, predatory, nurturing, fighting, playing, co-operating, and communicating.

From the point of view of survival, what is of immediate importance to an organism is not so much the substances and objects *in* its environment, but the affordances *of* its environment. That is, what is of immediate importance to an organism is not what an object or substance is but what it affords. From the point of view of survival, the identity of an object is important only to the extent that this identity can be associated with certain types of affordance. Any organism that can recognize objects but not detect the affordances of those objects would not survive. However, any organism that can detect the affordances of objects, even though it was incapable of recognizing those objects, could survive. From the point of view of survival, then, it is the affordances of the environment, and not the objects in the environment, that are of paramount importance.

If this is true, then it should not be assumed that an organism should be primarily sensitive to objects in its environment. On the contrary, it is far more likely that the sensitivities of organisms will have evolved to track the affordances, for that organism, of its environment. Thus, at least at some level of functional specification, the function of a particular perceptual mechanism will be to enable the organism to detect a particular affordance of its environment.

11.4 ORGANISMIC AND ALGORITHMIC PROPER FUNCTIONS

In emphasizing the connection between cognition and action, the environmentalist position is led to conceive of cognitive processes as items accomplished not just by internal mechanisms but, rather, by the organism as a whole. If action is constitutive of cognition, and if it is the organism as a whole that manipulates and exploits environmental structures, then it is the organism as a whole that is responsible for cognition, and not just certain internal mechanisms of that organism. This will carry over and infect our attributions of content to cognitive states. In this section, I shall argue that combining this basic insight of the environmentalist position with the concept of an affordance allows us to distinguish two, importantly distinct, levels of functional specification, consequently two distinct levels at which content may be attributed. I shall call these the *organismic* and *algorithmic* levels of description.

In the *Philosophical Investigations* no. 281, Wittgenstein makes the following, characteristically insightful, point:

> It comes to this: only of a living human being and what resembles (behaves like) a living human being can one say: it has sensations; it sees; is blind; is deaf; is conscious or unconscious.

Unlike Wittgenstein, I do not wish to argue that content cannot be attributed at the sub-personal, or sub-organismic, level. However, when we do talk of the attribution of content, we must be very clear about which level we are talking. That is, we must be very clear about to which object – the organism, or a sub-organismic mechanism – we are attributing the content. Generally, the content we can attribute at the organismic level does not coincide with the content we can attribute at the sub-organismic level.

Consider, for example, the attribution of perceptual content to an organism. The attribution might typically proceed via a locution of the form '. . . sees that P'. Suppose the organism in question is a particular human being, Jones. Jones will, of course, have a particular mechanism that underwrites, or makes true, this sort of attribution, namely, the eye. (Given the arguments developed in Part I, the claim will, of course, be that mechanisms of this sort *in part* underwrite or make true this sort of attribution. I shall take this as given but, for ease of exposition, shall henceforth omit the qualifier 'in part'.) So, if Jones sees that P and therefore makes the content attribution true, what underwrites this content attribution will be Jones's eye or eyes (or, more precisely, his whole visual apparatus). However, it does *not* follow that we can attribute the same content to the eye (or visual apparatus). The eye does not see, and the attribution of these sorts of

239

visual contents to eyes would be misguided. Rather, the eye is what allows the *person* or *organism* to see, and we can attribute visual contents to a person because (in part) of the proper functioning of their eyes.

Generalizing, the moral seems to be this. Suppose we have an organism O, sensitive to (i.e., able to detect) some feature of the environment. On the basis of this sensitivity, let us suppose, we can attribute the perceptual content C_O to the organism. However, O's sensitivity to this feature of the environment is underwritten or realized by mechanism M. And M, let us suppose, has this role because of its evolutionary history and the corresponding proper or Normal function with which this evolutionary history has endowed it. Because of this proper function, we can, according to the teleological approach, attribute the content C_M to M. It does not follow, however, and, indeed, it is usually false, that $C_O = C_M$. This is true even though it is M that allows O to be sensitive to its environment in a way that warrants the attribution of content C_O to it. That is, even though it is the proper function of M that warrants the attribution of content C_M to it, and even though it is the fulfilling by M of its proper function that allows the content C_O to be attributed to O, it does not follow, and, indeed, is almost always false, that $C_O = C_M$. The content attributable to a mechanism M and the content attributable to an organism O do not generally coincide, *even where it is the mechanism M that underwrites the attribution of content to O* (Rowlands 1997).

Therefore, content can be attributed both at the organismic level and the sub-organismic level, and the contents attributable at each level do not generally coincide. So, in talking of the teleological theory of content, we have to be very clear whether the content in question is attributable to an organism or to a mechanism possessed by that organism. If we are to adopt the teleological theory, we shall need a teleological account of both forms of content attribution.

The above case seems to require us to distinguish two proper functions of the mechanism M. These proper functions underwrite two importantly distinct levels of content attribution. At what I shall call the *algorithmic* level of description, we might get the following sort of account: the proper function of mechanism M is to detect Gs. For example, a proper function of one component of the visual system might be to detect texture density gradients in the structure of light surrounding the organism (the *optic array*). For any system that could do this, the content attribution of the form 'detects that d', where d represents the density gradient, would be warranted. This is content that we attribute not to the organism as a whole, but to a mechanism possessed by an organism. It is content attributable at the sub-organismic level. On the other hand, at what I shall call the *organismic* level of description, we might get the following sort of account: the proper function of M is to enable O to detect Fs. For example, a proper function of the component of the visual system responsible for detecting texture density gradients might be to enable the organism to perceive a roughly horizontal ground receding away from it into the distance. Thus, a content attribution of the form 'detects that g', where g represents this ground, would be warranted.

Organismic descriptions of the proper function of a mechanism underwrite attributions of content to the organism taken as a whole. Algorithmic descriptions of the proper function of that mechanism underwrite attributions of content to the mechanism itself. Organismic descriptions and algorithmic descriptions are clearly non-equivalent, and we can allow that they designate distinct proper functions of the mechanism. We can allow that the organismic description designates a function of the mechanism, the organismic proper function, that is distinct from, and irreducible to, the function, the algorithmic proper function, designated by the algorithmic description. These distinct functions underwrite attributions of content that are clearly distinct. However, even though both proper functions apply to, or are possessed by, the same object (i.e., the mechanism), *the content attributions that these functions warrant do not apply to the same object*. The organismic proper function underwrites attributions of content to an organism, whereas the algorithmic proper function underwrites attributions of content to a mechanism possessed by that organism. This point will be central to the solution I shall propose to the problems of indeterminacy and transparency.

To see how this distinction works, let us again consider a fairly basic case of perceptual representation. To avoid tedium, let us switch the example from the frog's representation of flies to the rattlesnake's representation of its prey.

The rattlesnake has certain cells that fire only if two conditions are satisfied. Firstly, the snake's infra-red detectors, situated in its nose, must be stimulated. Secondly, the visual system must get positive input. The former condition is satisfied when there is a localized source of warmth in the environment, the latter when there is localized source of movement. When these two systems are stimulated, the rattlesnake's hunting routines are engaged. In the snake's ancestral home there will indeed be food about, since the combined input is typically caused by a fieldmouse, the snake's usual prey. Of course, the rattlesnake can easily be fooled. An artificially warmed imitation mouse on the end of a stick would do the trick. So what is the proper function of the prey's detection system? What does it represent? If the above arguments are correct, we must distinguish between the organismic and algorithmic proper functions of the snake's mechanism (for ease of exposition, I shall henceforth assume that both infra-red and movement detectors are parts of the same mechanism).

Firstly, there is the organismic proper function of the mechanism. This is best specified in terms of the affordances of the environment to which the mechanism gives the snake sensitivity. Thus, the organismic proper function of the mechanism is to enable the rattlesnake to detect a certain affordance of the environment, namely *eatability*. This allows the attribution of content such as 'eatability!', or 'eatability, there!' to the rattlesnake.

Eatability, as an affordance, should be clearly distinguished from *edibility*. Many things are edible but not eatable. Roughly, something is edible for an organism simply if it can be eaten by that organism. Pieces of paper, twigs, small stones are all edible for humans, and BBs are, notoriously, edible for frogs. However, pieces of paper, twigs, and small stones are not eatable for humans, and BBs are not eatable for frogs. The concept of eatability, as an affordance, entails the concept of nutrition or nourishment, and means, roughly, 'good to eat', or 'nourishing to eat'. Eatability is edibility plus nourishment. So, the organismic proper function of the rattlesnake's prey detection mechanism is to detect the presence of eatability in this sense, not the presence of edibility.

Secondly, there is the algorithmic proper function of the mechanism. The mechanism enables the rattlesnake to detect when the environment affords eating. It achieves this, however, by way of a certain algorithm, namely, the detection of warmth and movement. The method 'chosen' by the mechanism to detect eatability is to detect warmth and movement. Therefore, the organismic proper function of the mechanism is to enable the rattlesnake to detect eatability, but the algorithmic proper function of that mechanism is to detect warmth and movement. The former proper function allows content attributions such as 'eatability, there!' to the *rattlesnake*. The latter proper function, however, warrants content attributions such as 'warmth, there!' or 'movement, there!' to the *mechanism*. Again, what is crucial is that, although both proper functions are possessed by the same object, i.e., the mechanism, the content attributions that these proper functions warrant do not attach to the same object. One attaches to the mechanism, but the other attaches to the rattlesnake as a whole.

The mechanism also seems to detect, hence represent, mice. However, detection of mice should, I think, be seen not as a proper function of the mechanism but as a Normal *consequence* of the mechanism fulfilling its organismic and algorithmic proper functions. That is, it is a consequence of the mechanism functioning Normally in a Normal environment. The claim that one of the proper functions of the mechanism is to detect mice does not survive serious scrutiny. In particular, two pressures, one 'from above', the other 'from below', undermine this interpretation. Firstly, at the organismic level of description, what is important is that the rattlesnake gets to eat, not that it gets to eat mice. Any similar source of food is equally satisfactory. From the point of view of the rattlesnake's survival, what is of primary importance is whether or not the environment is eatable. Whether or not the environment contains a mouse is important only to the extent that the mouse is eatable. Any relevantly similar thing, rat, mole, vole, frog, etc., will be equally satisfactory. These objects *in* the environment will be important only to the extent that they can be associated with an affordance *of* the environment. The primary organismic function of the mechanism is to enable the snake to detect the eatability of the environment because that is the *raison d'être* of the mechanism. The mechanism has evolved in order to allow the snake to survive (and thus to pass on its genetic material) by obtaining food. The mechanism will allow the snake to detect mice only in the derivative sense that mice are typically eatable. Exactly the same point can be made against the claim that the function of the mechanism is to enable the rattlesnake to detect the *edibility* of the environment. What is crucial to the organism is not whether the environment is edible but whether it is eatable.

Secondly, the pressure exerted from below by the algorithmic level is even more serious. The mechanism employed by the rattlesnake is sensitive to warmth/movement. It cannot distinguish between a warm, moving mouse, and any other similar warm, moving creature. Thus, it is not able to distinguish between mice, small rats, voles, small moles, baby squirrels, young birds, etc. Nor need it distinguish between these things, since they are all eatable, therefore all equally important in the survival stakes. Therefore, to attribute to the mechanism the content 'mouse!', or 'mouse, there!', would be to attribute more semantic detail than is really there. This will also go on to affect our interpretation of organismic proper function. At the organismic level, we cannot claim that the proper function of the mechanism is to enable the organism to detect the presence of mice if the mechanism itself is incapable of distinguishing between mice and other small mammals or birds. Again, this would be to attribute more detail than is really there, more detail than possibly could be there. Therefore, the proper functions of the mechanism are (i) to enable the rattlesnake to detect when the environment affords eating, and (ii) to detect when the environment exhibits warmth and movement. It also makes sense to talk of the mechanism detecting mice, but such detection is clearly secondary and derivative. Detection of mice should be understood not as a proper function of the mechanism but as a consequence of the mechanism performing its proper function in a Normal environment.

In the remainder of this chapter, I shall argue that, once we clearly distinguish the organismic from the algorithmic proper functions of a mechanism, the problems of indeterminacy and transparency vanish.

11.5 ORGANISMS, ALGORITHMS, AND THE PROBLEM OF INDETERMINACY

The problem of indeterminacy arises as follows. We have two or more possible interpretations of the proper or Normal function of an evolved mechanism. There is, it is argued, no fact of the matter that could support one interpretation over the other. Therefore, which interpretation of function is the correct one is indeterminate. Therefore, the Normal or proper function of the mechanism is indeterminate. Thus, in the case of the frog's sight–strike–feed mechanism, we have competing interpretations of proper function:

(1) The proper function of the mechanism is to represent the presence of flies in the environment.

(2) The proper function of the mechanism is to represent the presence of little black things in the environment.

There is, it is argued, no fact of the matter that could decide between these two distinct interpretations. Therefore, the proper function of the mechanism is indeterminate.

The distinction between organismic and algorithmic proper functions allows us to solve this problem. What is crucial, here, is that, although both sorts of proper function attach to the same object, i.e., the relevant mechanism, the attributions of content that these mechanisms warrant do not attach to the same object. Attributions of content warranted by the algorithmic proper function of a mechanism attach to that mechanism, but attributions of content warranted by the organismic proper function of a mechanism attach not to the mechanism itself but to the organism which possesses that mechanism. However, for there to be a problem of indeterminacy, both attributions of content must attach to the same object.

To see this, consider again the following example. Suppose we have a visual mechanism M whose algorithmic proper function is to detect texture density gradients, and whose organismic proper function is to enable the organism that possesses it to detect the presence of a horizontal receding ground. The algorithmic proper function warrants content attributions of the form 'detects density gradient d' to the mechanism, and the organismic proper function warrants content attributions of the form 'detects distance s' to the organism. No one would, or should, want to suggest that the content attribution 'detects distance s' to the organism is, therefore, indeterminate simply because we can also attribute the content 'detects density gradient d' to some mechanism possessed by the organism. The point is that the content attributions are *non-competing* because they attach to distinct objects. No consequences concerning the indeterminacy of content, or content attribution, can be obtained from statements of the form 'X represents that P' and 'Y represents that Q' if X is not identical to Y. Far from being an example of indeterminacy, what we have here is simply a case of two, perfectly determinate, contents being attributed to distinct things.

If this is correct, then in order for there to be genuine worry about indeterminacy, it would have to be shown either that (i) there is more than one legitimate interpretation of the organismic proper function of a mechanism, or (ii) there is more than one legitimate interpretation of the algorithmic proper function of the mechanism. Only then would we have a case of distinct and legitimate attributions of content being made to the same object.

According to the arguments developed in the previous pages, the correct interpretation of the organismic proper function of the frog's sight–strike–feed mechanism is this:

(3) The organismic proper function of the mechanism is to enable the frog to detect that the environment affords eating (i.e., to represent the eatability of the environment).

Are there any other plausible interpretations of the organismic proper function of the mechanism? The suggestion that the proper function of the mechanism is to represent the presence of little ambient black things in the environment can be dismissed. This is an interpretation not of the organismic proper function of the mechanism, but of its algorithmic proper function. As such, the content attributions it warrants attach to the mechanism itself and not to the frog. Hence, they in no way compete with the content attributions attaching to the frog. The only other possible suggestion seems to be that the proper function of the mechanism is to represent the presence of flies in the environment. This suggestion, however, can be ruled out for the same sorts of reasons that ruled out the interpretation of the proper function of the rattlesnake's mechanism in terms of the detection of mice. Firstly, from above, what is important for the frog's survival is not that it should strike at flies *per se*; but that it should strike at eatable things – gnats, midges, mosquitoes, etc. will all do perfectly nicely. Whether the environment contains flies is important to the frog only to the extent that flies are eatable. The *raison d'être* of the mechanism is to enable the frog to detect eatability, not flies. Secondly, from below, the claim that the proper function of the mechanism is to detect flies is not true to what we know of the algorithmic details of the frog's mechanism. Thus we know that the algorithm chosen by the mechanism involves the detection of small moving dots. As such, the frog is unable to distinguish between flies, gnats, midges and, notoriously, BBs. Thus, to attribute the proper function of detecting the presence of flies to the mechanism would be to impute more detail than is really there.

According to the argument developed in the previous pages, the algorithmic proper function of the frog's sight–strike–feed mechanism is best understood as follows:

(4) The algorithmic proper function of the mechanism is to represent the presence of little black dots in the environment.

Are there any plausible competing interpretations of the algorithmic proper function of the mechanism? The suggestion that the algorithmic proper function is to detect the presence of eatability can be dismissed. This description pertains to the organismic proper function of the mechanism, and has consequences for the content attributed not to the mechanism but to the frog itself. The only other possible suggestion seems to be that the algorithmic proper function of the mechanism is to represent the presence of flies in the environment. Thus, the content attributable to the mechanism would be of the form 'fly', or 'fly, there'. However, for the reasons described above, this does not cohere with what we know of the algorithmic details of the mechanism. We know that the mechanism works by tracking small black dots. As such, the mechanism is unable to distinguish between flies, gnats, midges, and so on. Therefore, to attribute content such as 'fly' to the mechanism would be to impute more detail than is really there.

There is a sense in which the mechanism both detects flies and allows the frog to detect flies. However, for the reasons described above, this cannot be understood as a proper function of the mechanism. Instead, it should be understood as a consequence of the mechanism functioning Normally, i.e., fulfilling its Normal function in a Normal environment. One can, therefore, speak of the mechanism detecting flies, but this is only in a secondary and derivative sense, and reflects neither the algorithmic nor the organismic proper function of the mechanism.

The problem of indeterminacy, I have argued, arises through a confusion of two distinct proper functions that a mechanism (such as the frog's sight–strike–feed mechanism) possesses. These proper functions – the organismic and algorithmic – are genuinely distinct proper functions and underwrite distinct forms of content attribution. However, this does not entail the indeterminacy of content since the content attribution licensed by each proper function attaches to distinct objects. In order for there to be a genuine problem of indeterminacy, the content in question would have to attach to the same object. Therefore, there would have to be equally legitimate competing interpretations either of organismic proper function or of algorithmic proper function, or both. However, there do not seem to be equally legitimate and competing interpretations of either the organismic proper function of the frog's mechanism or the algorithmic proper function of that mechanism. Therefore, there is no real problem of indeterminacy, at least none that is derivable from the teleological approach (Rowlands 1997).

11.6 THE PROBLEM OF TRANSPARENCY REVISITED

The transparency problem is that biological contexts such as *was selected for representing things as F* are transparent to the substitutions of expressions reliably coextensive with F, where reliable coextension can be cashed out in terms of the notion of counterfactual support. Therefore, appeal to a selected mechanism with a Normal function is not adequate to distinguish between extensionally equivalent ascriptions of content. Thus, the teleological approach seems to slice contents too thickly, and there seems to be little hope in accounting for the intensionality of content ascriptions. In the case of the frog, the statement 'the function of the mechanism is to register the presence of flies' and the statement 'the function of the mechanism is to represent the presence of little ambient black things' can be substituted *salva veritate* if we assume that (in the environment of the frog) the statement 'all the little ambient black things are flies' is counterfactual supporting.

The distinction between organismic and algorithmic proper functions gives us a way out of this problem. The organismic proper function of the mechanism is not to register the presence of flies, but to detect an affordance of the environment, i.e., eatability. The algorithmic proper function of the mechanism is to detect small ambient black things. These distinct functions attach to the same object, the frog's sight–strike–feed mechanism. However, the fact that these functions attach to the same object does not entail that the content they underwrite can be ascribed to the same object. Rather, the content that is underwritten by the organismic proper function of the mechanism attaches to the frog, while the content underwritten by the algorithmic proper function attaches to the mechanism itself. The content 'eatability, there' attaches to the frog, while the content 'small ambient black thing, there' attaches to the mechanism. Once we realize that algorithmic and organismic proper functions underwrite content attributions to distinct objects, the problem of transparency fails to materialize. In order for there to be a genuine problem of transparency, the following conditions must be met. Firstly, there have to be two competing attributions of content, such as 'X means that P' and 'X means that Q'. Secondly, P and Q have to be reliably covariant. Then, it is argued that the teleological theory does not have the resources to distinguish between these content attributions. However, the teleological theory does not, in fact, entail competing attributions of content of this form. It entails attributions of content of the following sort: 'X means that P' and 'Y means that Q', where X and Y are distinct objects. Therefore, the problem of transparency does not arise.

If there is to be a genuine problem of transparency, then the teleological theory must be shown to be incapable of distinguishing between attributions of content attaching to the same object. However, if we clearly distinguish between organismic and algorithmic proper functions, we see that there is little plausibility in the claim that the teleological theory is lacking in this respect. For example, if we confine our attention to the organismic proper function of the mechanism, then we will specify this function in terms of the affordances of the environment. And there is little reason to suppose that it is possible to substitute the following expressions *salva veritate*: (1) the proper function of the mechanism is to enable the frog to detect eatability, and (2) the proper function of the mechanism is to enable the frog to detect affordance X, where X is any affordance distinct from eatability. Similarly, at the algorithmic level, the function of the mechanism is unambiguous; the algorithmic proper function of the mechanism is to detect small ambient black things (and, as has been argued, not to detect flies). Therefore, since at each level the proper function of the frog's mechanism is unambiguous, then, at each level, the content underwritten by this function is also unambiguous. Therefore, the teleological theory can show that the content we are able to attribute to the frog is unambiguous, and the content we are able to attribute to the frog's mechanism is also unambiguous. Thus, there is no problem of transparency for the teleological theory.

11.7 COMPARISON WITH MILLIKAN

It might be useful at this point to compare the position developed above with that of Millikan. Millikan has, of course, virtually single-handedly developed the teleological theory into the prominent naturalistic approach to semantics that it is today. And any variant of this approach must, of necessity, define itself in relation to Millikan's position.

Two distinctions play a fundamental role in Millikan's approach to the disambiguation problem. The first is the distinction between the *producers* and *consumers* of representations, the second between *proximal* and *distal* stimuli. To see how these distinctions operate, consider again the example Millikan uses to discuss the disambiguation problem: the example of the bacterial magnetosomes first discussed by Dretske (1986). Some marine bacteria of the northern hemisphere orient themselves away from toxic oxygen-rich surface water by way of magnetosomes, tiny inner magnets, which orient themselves towards geomagnetic north and thus guide the bacteria into deeper, relatively oxygen-free, water. (In the southern hemisphere the bacteria have their magnetosomes reversed.) What, then, is the function of the magnetosomes? Is it to indicate the whereabouts of oxygen-free water? Or is it to indicate the direction of geomagnetic north? Indeed, since, when under the influence of a bar magnet, magnetosomes can lead their possessors into toxic oxygen-rich water, perhaps the proper function of the mechanism is simply to indicate the direction of magnetic, and not geomagnetic, north. We appear to have a problem of disambiguation.

Millikan's solution is to distinguish between the *producers* of representations and the *consumers* of representations. In order to identify the function of the magnetosome, and so, in order to identify what the magnetosome represents, we have to focus on what the *consumers* require that it correspond to in order to perform *their* tasks. Thus, we should ignore how the representation is normally produced, and concentrate instead on how the systems that react to that representation work. What *they* need, according to Millikan, is only that the pull be in the direction of oxygen-free water at the time. Thus, what the magnetosome represents is unambiguous: it represents the direction of oxygen-free water, for it is the absence of this which would disrupt the functioning of those mechanisms which rely on the magnetosomes for guidance. The consequence of this, and this brings us to the second distinction, is that what is represented by the magnetosome is its distal, and not its proximal, stimulus; and this conclusion, for Millikan, applies quite generally.

There is, I think, a certain amount of common ground between this type of argument and the ones which figured earlier in this book. In particular, the emphasis on what is required for the continued operation of the consumers of the representation is strongly reminiscent of the argument for the claim that the proper function of the rattlesnake's or frog's mechanism is to indicate an affordance of the environment rather than an object in the environment, since this is what matters to its continued survival. If we identify the rattlesnake or frog with the consumer of the representation, then the common ground with Millikan's argument is very clear.

However, I do not think that the distinction between the consumers and producers of representations will, by itself, do the work Millikan requires of it. This is because the notion of a consumer of a representation is crucially ambiguous; just as ambiguous, in fact, as the notion of a producer of a representation. Just as we can distinguish between organismic and algorithmic proper functions of a mechanism, so, too, we can distinguish between the organismic and algorithmic consumer of a representation.

At the organismic level, the consumer of the representation is the organism itself. Thus, the organismic consumer of the magnetosome is the bacterium itself. What the organism needs in order to do its job (roughly, survival and procreation) is to move in the direction of oxygen-free water. More generally, when we focus on the organismic consumer of a representation, we will generally specify what is required in order for that consumer to accomplish its required tasks in terms of a distal stimulus.

As Millikan would agree, however, it also makes sense to speak of the *algorithmic* consumer of a representation. That this is so is significantly obscured by Millikan's choice of example. In the case of the marine bacteria, the magnetosome functions by using the earth's magnetic field to literally pull the bacteria in the direction of geomagnetic north, hence in the direction of oxygen-free water. There is no mechanism internal to the bacterium, for example, which reads off the information detected by the magnetosome, and there are no locomotory structures which this mechanism could then direct to propel the bacterium in a given direction. In other words, in the case of the bacterium, we are dealing with an extremely simple case of transduction. This is one of the reasons why, in the case of the bacterium, there is no genuinely representational level of description. Thus, the only user of what the magnetosome indicates is the bacterium itself. Other examples employed by Millikan in this context are all cases where the organism is the only, or at least by far the most obvious, user of the representation in question. Thus, to illustrate the notion of a consumer of a representation, Millikan uses the example of the beaver's tail splash, employed to indicate the presence of danger (Millikan 1989). In this case, by far the most obvious user of the representation – the tail splash – is the organism itself, i.e., other beavers.

However, in many cases, we can also identify the algorithmic consumer of a representation. Suppose, for example, that bacteria were more complicated organisms than they in fact are. Instead of being pulled along by its magnetosomes, each bacterium possessed a device sensitive to the various states of the magnetosome, and thus sensitive to the information embodied in those states. On the basis of this, it sent messages to the various locomotory structures which, in this hypothetical example, we will suppose the bacterium to possess. If this were the case, then we could speak not only of a bacterium being the consumer of the representation, but also of the relevant internal device being a consumer of the same representation: it would make sense to speak of not only the organismic consumer of a representation, but also its algorithmic consumer.

Furthermore, what marks the difference between an organism which possesses only transductive capacities and one which possesses genuinely representational capacities is, in part, the possession of an internal mechanism sensitive to the states of a distinct mechanism which represents features of the world. The presence of this sort of device is necessary for the sort of multiple deployability (that is, its deployability in a variety of contexts and in order to accomplish a variety of tasks) of mental representations that is characteristic of a fully-fledged representational system.

Therefore, in the case of a fully-fledged representational system, an internal representation will have not only an organismic consumer but also an algorithmic consumer. What the algorithmic consumer requires to do *its* job will be very different from what is required by an organismic consumer. What our imagined algorithmic consumer of the representational states of the magnetosome requires to do its job is that these states correspond in a reliable way with the earth's magnetic field. After all, the algorithmic consumer of the representation will have been designed to register the effect that a magnetic field has on the magnetosome. Thus, its design presupposes a reliable connection between a certain orientation of magnetic field and a certain state of the magnetosome. To the extent that we can talk of what the algorithmic consumer *cares about*, it cares about the magnetic field and the effects this has on the magnetosome. For it is this and this alone which is relevant to the algorithmic consumer doing *its* job.

Therefore, just as there are two levels at which we can specify the proper function of a mechanism, so there are also two levels at which we can specify the consumers of states of those mechanisms (i.e., representations). At the algorithmic level, the consumer of the representation is an internal mechanism. It consumes this representation in the sense that its proper function is to correlate the state of the representational mechanism with the (proximal) state of the world which causes it. What is required for our (imagined) algorithmic consumer of the magnetosomal representations to do its job is that it be capable of detecting the state of the magnetosome, and that the state of the magnetosome be reliably correlated with the direction of magnetic north. At the organismic level, however, the consumer of the state of the magnetosome is the bacterium itself. At this level, what the consumer needs in order to do its job is to travel in the direction of oxygen-free water. Thus, the function of the state of the mechanism is to enable the organism to move in the direction of oxygen-free water, and the organism consumes the state of the magnetosome in precisely this way. Therefore, at least roughly, what the organismic consumer of a representation cares about is the representation's distal stimulus, since it is this which is relevant to the organism's doing its job. But the algorithmic consumer of a representation cares about that representation's proximal stimulus, since it is this that is relevant to its job.

The difference between Millikan's position and the one developed in this chapter, therefore, derives from the fact that Millikan does not distinguish between organismic and algorithmic proper functions. Because of this, she fails to distinguish between organismic and algorithmic consumers of representations. Without these distinctions, she sees the problem of disambiguation as one of coming down in favour of one interpretation of what a state represents. This interpretation focuses on distal causes of representations. This chapter, on the other hand, argues that there is no need to favour one interpretation of representational content over another in this way. We can specify the content of a representational state in terms of both its distal *and* proximal causes. This is because a representational mechanism will have both an organismic and an algorithmic proper function and, consequently, both an organismic and an algorithmic consumer. However, this does not entail that the disambiguation problem has been unresolved because, as argued earlier, the two types of proper function underwrite attribution of content to distinct entities. Because of the ambiguity of the notion of a consumer, Millikan's distinction between producers and consumers of representations does not significantly advance the disambiguation issue. But this, I have argued, is not a major hindrance to the teleological theory; the problem of disambiguation can be solved in another way.

11.8 STIMULUS–BASED AND BENEFIT–BASED ACCOUNTS OF REPRESENTATION

The distinction between organismic and algorithmic proper functions of an evolved mechanism also allows us to resolve another dispute that is absolutely central to recent discussions of representation. The dispute is between *stimulus-based* and *benefit-based* approaches to representation. Indeed, that the distinction between organismic and algorithmic proper functions should be employable in this context is not surprising: the dispute between stimulus- and benefit-based approaches to representation is, as we shall see, simply another manifestation of the problem of indeterminacy.

It is commonly thought that any attempt to naturalize semantics must be forced to choose between two accounts. On the one hand, there are stimulus-based accounts of representation, on the other, there are benefit-based accounts. Dretske endorses a version of the former. He writes:

> when an indicator, C, indicates both F and G, and its indication of G is via its indication of F . . . then despite the fact that it is the existence of G that is most directly relevant to explaining C's recruitment as a cause of M (F is relevant only in so far as it indicates that G exists), C acquires the function of indicating that F. It is F – the (as it were) maximally indicated state – that C comes to represent. (1990:826)

Thus, to return to his flagship example, the magnetosome possessed by certain marine bacteria represents the direction of geomagnetic north and not the direction of oxygen-free water. It does so even though the purpose of the magnetosome – the reason the magnetosome has been selected – is to direct the bacteria away from the lethal oxygen-rich surface water. Geomagnetic north is the stimulus for the magnetosome, and representation, for Dretske, follows or tracks stimulus, not benefit.

Millikan, on the other hand, as we would expect given her, broadly speaking, consumerist account of representation described above, endorses a benefit-based approach. Commenting on Dretske's example, she writes:

> What the magnetosome represents is only what its *consumers* require that it correspond to in order to perform *their* tasks. Ignore, then, how the representation . . . is normally produced. Concentrate instead on how the systems that react to the representation work, on what these systems need in order to do their job. What they need is only that the pull be in the direction of oxygen-free water at the time. For example, they care not at all how it came about that the pull is in that direction. . . . What the magnetosome represents, then, is univocal; it represents only the direction of oxygen-free water. For that is the only thing that corresponds . . . to it, the absence of which would matter, the absence of which would disrupt the function of those mechanisms that rely on the magnetosome for guidance.   (1989b:93)

To adopt a stimulus-based account of representation is to view the content of a state of a mechanism as being determined by what produces it. To adopt a benefit-based approach is to view the content of a representation as being determined by the purpose of the representation; the reason the representation exists. The former sees content as ultimately a function of cause; the latter sees it as ultimately a function of purpose.

It is worth noting that the distinction between stimulus- and benefit-based accounts of representation does not correspond to the difference between informational and teleological semantics. The former distinction cuts across the latter. Whether or not one adopts a teleological account of representation depends on whether or not one believes representation should be explained in terms of function. But this leaves it completely open whether one thinks the function of a mechanism is to track stimulus or benefit. Thus Dretske, for example, while supplementing his earlier purely informational account of representation with several crucial teleological claims, none the less, still endorses a stimulus-based account.

It is thought necessary to make a choice between stimulus-based and benefit-based accounts of representation precisely because of the threat of indeterminacy. If we do not choose between stimulus and benefit as the determinant of representation, then we seem forced to say, of an appropriate state of a bacterium's magnetosome, that it *detects* both geomagnetic north and oxygen-free water; hence that it is *about* both geomagnetic north and oxygen-free water; hence that it *means* both geomagnetic north and oxygen-free water. We must, so it is commonly thought, choose between stimulus and benefit or be committed to the indeterminacy of representational content.

Hopefully, the arguments developed in this chapter make clear exactly why we do not have to make this choice. Applied to the dispute between stimulus- and benefit-based approaches, the distinction between organismic and algorithmic proper functions can be applied as follows. Firstly, we adopt a stimulus-based account of the representational capacities of mechanisms. That is, we associate the stimulus-based approach with the algorithmic proper function of evolved mechanisms. The algorithmic proper function of an evolved mechanism is to detect, or track, a certain stimulus – geomagnetic north in the above example. Secondly, we adopt a benefit-based account of what an evolved mechanism allows an organism to detect. That is, we associate the benefit-based approach with the organismic proper function of a mechanism. The organismic proper function of a mechanism is to enable the organism to detect, or track, a certain environmental benefit – oxygen-free water in the above example. Thus, the content underwritten by the algorithmic proper function of a mechanism will incorporate a certain environmental stimulus, and will be of the form 'stimulus, there!'. And the content underwritten by the organismic proper function of the mechanism will incorporate a certain environmental benefit, and will be of the form 'benefit, there!'. However, as the arguments of the previous sections hopefully make clear, we are not obliged to choose between these attributions of content. The attributions attach to distinct objects; the former to a mechanism, the latter to an organism. Therefore, the attributions are non-competing. But, therefore, we are also not obliged to choose between organismic and algorithmic proper functions. And, therefore, we are not obliged to choose between stimulus- and benefit-based accounts of representation. The debate currently raging between proponents of the two approaches is misconceived.

11.9 CONCLUSION

I have argued that the teleological theory of representation has the resources to handle what are perceived as serious problems for it. The theory is, thus, undermined neither by the problem of indeterminacy nor by the problem of transparency. Failure to appreciate this point stems from a conflation of two types of proper function – organismic and algorithmic – possessed by an evolved mechanism. The reason these functions must be distinguished is that they underwrite attributions of content to distinct objects. The algorithmic proper function of a mechanism underwrites attributions of content to the mechanism itself, while the organismic proper function underwrites attribution of content to the organism that possesses the mechanism. However, the problems of indeterminacy and transparency arise only if the attributions of content attach to the same object. Therefore, the teleological theory is committed neither to the indeterminacy of content nor to the transparency of content ascriptions. Moreover, the distinction between organismic and algorithmic proper functions allows us to see, firstly, that Millikan's distinction between producers and consumers of representations will not do the disambiguating work required of it, and, secondly, that the debate between stimulus- and benefit-based approaches to representation is, in any event, misconceived.

257

References

Anderson, J. R. (1983) *The Architecture of Cognition*, Cambridge, MA, Harvard University Press.

Barrand, A. (1978) 'An ecological approach to binocular perception: the neglected facts of occlusion', Ph.D. dissertation, Cornell University.

Barwise, J. & Perry, J. (1983) *Situations and Attitudes*, Cambridge, MA, MIT Press.

Bechtel, W. (1993) 'What knowledge must be in the head in order to acquire language', in W. Durham & B. Velichovsky eds., *Biological and Cultural Aspects of Language Development*, New Jersey, Lawrence Erlbaum.

Bechtel, W. & Abrahamsen A. (1991) *Connectionism and the Mind*, Massachusetts, Basil Blackwell.

Bethel, W. M. & Holmes, J. C. (1973) 'Altered evasive behaviour and responses to light in amphipods harbouring acanthocephalan cystacanths', *Journal of Parasitology*, 59, 945–56.

(1977) 'Increased vulnerability of amphipods to predation owing to altered behaviour induced by larval acanthocephalans', *Canadian Journal of Zoology*, 55, 110–15.

Block, Ned (1986) 'Advertisement for a semantics for psychology', in *Midwest Studies in Philosophy*, 10, 615–78.

Bower, G. H. & Bolton, L. S. (1969) 'Why are rhymes easier to learn?', *Journal of Experimental Psychology*, 82, 453–61.

Broadbent, D. E. (1958) *Perception and Communication*, London, Pergamon.

Bruce, V. & Green, P. (1985) *Visual Perception*, London, Lawrence Erlbaum.

Buckout, R. (1982) 'Eyewitness testimony', in Ulric Neisser ed., *Memory Observed*, San Francisco, W. H. Freeman.

Burge, Tyler (1979) 'Individualism and the mental', in P. A. French, T. E. Uehling & H. K. Wettstein eds., *Midwest Studies in Philosophy*, 4, Minneapolis, University of Minnesota Press.

(1982) 'Other bodies', in A. Woodfield ed., *Thought and Object*, Oxford University Press, 97–120.

References

(1986) 'Individualism and psychology', *The Philosophical Review*, 94, 1, 3–45.

Callicott, J. Baird (1989) *In Defense of the Land Ethic*, New York, State University of New York Press.

Carson, H. L. (1961) 'Heterosis and fitness in experimental populations of *Drosophila Melanogaster*', *Evolution*, 15, 496–509.

Chisholm, Roderick (1966) *Theory of Knowledge*, New York, Prentice Hall.

Chomsky, N. (1957) *Syntactic Structures*, The Hague, Mouton.

(1959) 'Review of Skinner's *Verbal Behavior*', *Language*, 35, 26–58.

(1968) *Language and Mind*, New York, Harcourt, Brace & World.

Claringbold, P. J. & Barker, J. S. F. (1961) 'The estimation of relative fitness of *Drosophila* populations', *Journal of Theoretical Biology*, 1, 190–203.

Clark, Andy (1989) *Microcognition*, Cambridge, MA, MIT Press.

(1993) *Associative Engines*, Cambridge, MA, MIT Press.

(1997) *Being-There*, Cambridge, MA, MIT Press.

Cole, Hood, & McDermott (1982) 'Ecological niche picking', in Ulric Neisser, *Memory Observed*, San Francisco, W. H. Freeman.

Croft, W. (1991) *Syntactic Categories and Grammatical Relations: The Cognitive Organization of Information*, University of Chicago Press.

Cummins, R. (1989) *Meaning and Mental Representation*, Cambridge, MA, MIT Press.

Davidson, Donald (1970) 'Mental events', in L. Foster & J. W. Swanson eds., *Experience and Theory*, University of Massachusetts Press, 79–101.

Dawkins, R. (1976) *The Selfish Gene*, Oxford University Press.

(1982) *The Extended Phenotype*, Oxford University Press.

Dawkins, R. & Krebs, J. R. (1978) 'Animal signals: information or manipulation?' in J. R. Krebs & N. B. Davies eds., *Behavioural Ecology*, Oxford, Blackwell Scientific Publications, 282–309.

Dennett, Daniel (1978a) *Brainstorms*, Montgomery, VT, Bradford Books.

(1978b) 'Towards a cognitive theory of consciousness', reprinted in Daniel Dennett, *Brainstorms*, Cambridge, MA, MIT Press, 149–73.

(1987) *The Intentional Stance*, Cambridge, MA, MIT Press.

Derrida, J. (1976) *Of Grammatology*, Baltimore, Johns Hopkins University Press (trans. G. C. Spivak).

(1977) 'Signature event context', *Glyph*, 1, 1–23.

Donald, Merlin (1991) *Origins of the Modern Mind*, Cambridge, MA, Harvard University Press.

Dretske, Fred (1981) *Knowledge and the Flow of Information*, Cambridge, MA, MIT Press.

References

(1986) 'Misrepresentation', in R. Bogdan ed., *Belief*, Oxford University Press.

(1988) *Explaining Behavior*, Cambridge, MA, MIT Press.

(1990) 'Reply to reviewers', *Philosophy and Phenomenological Research*, 1, 4, 819–39.

(1991) 'Dretske's replies', in B. McLaughlin ed., *Dretske and His Critics*, Oxford, Basil Blackwell.

(1995) *Naturalizing the Mind*, Cambridge, MA, MIT Press.

Elman, J. (1991a) 'Incremental learning, or the importance of starting small'. Technical Report 9101. Center for Research in Language, University of California, San Diego.

(1991b) 'Distributed representations, simple recurrent networks and grammatical structure', *Machine Learning*, 7, 195–225.

(1991c) 'Representation and structure in connectionist models', in G. Altmann ed., *Cognitive Models of Speech Processing*, Cambridge, MA, MIT Press.

Evans, G. (1982) *The Varieties of Reference*, Oxford University Press.

Feyerabend, Paul (1975) *Against Method*, London, Verso.

Field, Hartry (1978) 'Mental representation', *Erkenntnis*, 13, 9–61.

Fodor, Jerry (1974) 'Special sciences', *Synthese*, 28, 97–115.

(1975) *The Language of Thought*, New York, Crowell.

(1981) *Representations*, Brighton, The Harvester Press.

(1984) 'Semantics, Wisconsin style', *Synthese*, 59, 231–50.

(1987) *Psychosemantics*, Cambridge, MA, MIT Press.

(1990) *A Theory of Content and Other Essays*, Cambridge, MA, MIT Press.

Fodor, Jerry & Pylyshyn, Zenon (1988) 'Connectionism and cognitive architecture: a critical analysis', *Cognition*, 28, 3–71.

Foley, J. M. (1990) *Traditional Oral Epic: The Odyssey, Beowulf, and the Serbo-Croatian Return Song*, Berkeley, University of California Press.

Gibson, James. J (1950) *The Perception of the Visual World*, Boston, Houghton-Mifflin.

(1966) *The Senses Considered as Perceptual Systems*, Boston, Houghton-Mifflin.

(1977) 'The theory of affordances', in R. Shaw & J. Bransford eds., *Perceiving, Acting and Knowing: Towards an Ecological Psychology*, New Jersey, Lawrence Erlbaum.

(1979) *The Ecological Approach to Visual Perception*, Boston, Houghton-Mifflin.

(1982) *Reasons for Realism: The Selected Essays of James J. Gibson*, New

Jersey, Lawrence Erlbaum.

Goody, Jack (1977) *The Domestication of the Savage Mind*, Cambridge University Press.

Gopnik, A. & Meltzoff, A. (1993) 'Words and thoughts in infancy: the specificity hypothesis and the development of categorization and naming', in C. Rovee-Collier & L. Lipsitt eds., *Advances in Infancy Research*, Norwood, Ablex.

Gould, S. J. & Vrba, E. S. (1982) 'Exaptation: A missing term in the science of form', *Paleobiology*, 8, 1, 4–15.

Grice, H. P. (1957) 'Meaning', *Philosophical Review*, 66, 377–88.

Hacker, P. M. S (1987) 'Languages, minds, and brains', in Colin Blakemore and Susan Greenfield eds., *Mindwaves*, Oxford, Basil Blackwell.

Hocutt, Max (1966) 'In defence of materialism', *Philosophy and Phenomenological Research*, 27, 366–85.

Holmes, J. C. & Bethel, W. M. (1972) 'Modification of intermediate host behaviour by parasites', in E. U. Canning & C. A. Wright eds., *Behavioural Aspects of Parasite Transmission*, London, Academic Press, 123–49.

Hornsby, Jennifer (1986) 'Physicalist thinking and conceptions of behaviour', in P. Pettit & J. McDowell eds., *Subject, Thought and Context*, Oxford University Press, 95–115.

Jacob, Pierre (1997) *What Minds Can Do*, Cambridge University Press.

Kaplan, David (1980) 'Demonstratives', The John Locke Lectures, Oxford University Press.

Kim, Jaegwon (1982) 'Psychophysical supervenience', *Philosophical Studies*, 41.

Kuhn, Thomas (1970) *The Structure of Scientific Revolutions*, University of Chicago Press.

Langacker, R. (1987) *Foundations of Cognitive Grammar*, Stanford University Press.

LePore, Ernest & Loewer, Barry (1986) 'Solipsistic semantics', *Midwest Studies in Philosophy*, 10, 595–614.

Lewontin, R. C. (1961) 'Evolution and the theory of games', *Journal of Theoretical Biology*, 1, 382–403.

(1968) 'The concept of evolution', *International Encyclopedia of Social Science*, 5, 202–10.

(1979) 'Sociobiology as an adaptationist program', *Behavioral Science*, 24, 5–14.

Loar, Brian (1981) *Mind and Meaning*, Cambridge University Press.

References

Love, M. (1980) 'The alien strategy', *Natural History*, 89, 30–2.

Luria, A. R. & Vygotsky, L. S. (1992) *Ape, Primitive Man, and Child*, Cambridge, MA, MIT Press.

MacArthur, R. H. (1962) 'Some generalized theorems of natural selection', *National Academy of Science, Proceedings*, 48, 1893–7.

Macdonald, Cynthia (1989) *Mind–Body Identity Theories*, London, Routledge.

(1990) 'Weak externalism and mind-body identity', *Mind*, 99, 387–404.

Maratsos, M. (1983) 'Some current issues in the study of the acquisition of grammar', in J. Flavell & E. Markman eds., *Handbook of Child Psychology*, 3, *Cognitive Development*, New York, Wiley, 707–86.

Maratsos, M. & Chalkeley, M. (1980) 'The internal language of children's syntax: the ontogenesis and representation of syntactic categories', in K. E. Nelson ed., *Children's Language*, New York, Gardner Press, 127–214.

Margolis, H. (1987) *Patterns, Thinking and Cognition. A Theory of Judgment*, University of Chicago Press.

Marr, David (1982) *Vision*, San Francisco, W. H. Freeman.

Marr, David & Nishihara, H. K. (1978) 'Representation and recognition of the spatial organization of three dimensional shapes', *Proceedings of the Royal Society of London*, Series B, 269–94.

Marr, David & Hildreth, E. (1980) 'Theory of edge detection', *Proceedings of the Royal Society of London*, Series B, 187–217.

Marr, David & Poggio, T. (1981) 'A computational theory of human stereo vision', *Proceedings of the Royal Society of London*, Series B, 301–28.

McClelland, J. L. & Rumelhart, D. E. (1981) 'An interactive activation model of context effects in letter perception: Part 1, an account of basic findings', *Psychological Review*, 88, 375–407.

McDowell, John (1986) 'Singular thought and the extent of inner space', in P. Pettit & J. McDowell eds., *Subject, Thought and Context*, Oxford University Press, 137–68.

McGinn, Colin (1982) 'The structure of content', in A. Woodfield ed., *Thought and Object*, 207–58.

(1989) *Mental Content*, Oxford, Basil Blackwell.

(1991) 'Consciousness and content', in McGinn, *The Problem of Consciousness*, Oxford, Basil Blackwell.

Merleau-Ponty, Maurice (1962) *The Phenomenology of Perception*, London, Routledge.

Michaels, C. F. & Carello, C. (1981) *Direct Perception*, New Jersey, Prentice Hall.

Miller, G. (1956) 'The magical number seven plus or minus two: some limits on our capacity to process information', *Psychological Review*, 63, 81–97.

Millikan, Ruth (1984) *Language, Thought and Other Biological Categories*, Cambridge, MA, MIT Press.

(1986) 'Thoughts without laws', in Millikan (1993) *White Queen Psychology*, 51–82.

(1989a) 'In defense of proper functions', in Millikan (1993) *White Queen Psychology*, 13–29.

(1989b) 'Biosemantics', in Millikan (1993) *White Queen Psychology*, 83–101.

(1990a) 'Compare and contrast Dretske, Fodor and Millikan', in Millikan (1993) *White Queen Psychology*, 123–33.

(1990b) 'Truth rules, hoverflies, and the Kripke–Wittgenstein paradox', in Millikan (1993) *White Queen Psychology*, 210–39.

(1991) 'Speaking up for Darwin', in B. Loewer & G. Rey eds., *Meaning in Mind: Fodor and his Critics*, Cambridge, MA, MIT Press.

(1993) *White Queen Psychology and Other Essays for Alice*, Cambridge, MA, MIT Press.

Milner, B. (1966) 'Amnesia following operations on the temporal lobes', in C. Whitty and O. Zangwill eds., *Amnesia*, London, Butterworth.

(1975) 'Psychological aspects of focal epilepsy and its neurosurgical treatment', in D. O. Prpura, J. K. Penry, & R. D. Walter eds., *Advances in Neurology*, 8, New York, Raven Press.

Newell A. & Simon, H. A. (1981) 'Computer science as empirical enquiry', in John Haugeland ed., *Mind Design*, Cambridge, MA, MIT Press, 35–66.

O'Neill, E. G. Jun. (1942) 'The localization of metrical word types in the Greek hexameter', *Yale Classical Studies*, 8, 105–77.

Papoušek, M. & Papoušek, H. (1991) 'The meanings of melodies in motherese in tone and stress language', *Infant Behavior and Development*, 14, 425–40.

Perry, John (1977) 'Frege on demonstratives', *The Philosophical Review*, 86. (1979) 'The problem of the essential indexical', *Nous*, 13, 3–12.

Pettit, Philip & McDowell, John (eds.) (1986) *Subject, Thought and Context*, Oxford University Press.

References

Pinker, S. (1984) *Language Learnability and Language Development*, Cambridge, MA, Harvard University Press.

(1989) *Learnability and Cognition: The Acquisition of Argument Structure*, Cambridge, MA, MIT Press.

Putnam, Hilary (1967) 'The mental life of some machines', in H. N. Castaneda ed., *Intentionality, Minds and Perception*, Detroit, Wayne State University Press, 177–213.

(1975) 'The meaning of "meaning"', in Keith Gunderson ed., *Language, Mind and Knowledge: Minnesota Studies in the Philosophy of Science*, 7, Minneapolis, University of Minnesota Press.

Pylyshyn, Zenon (1984) *Computation and Cognition: Toward a Foundation for Cognitive Science*, Cambridge, MA, MIT Press.

Quine, W. V. O. (1960) *Word and Object*, Cambridge, MA, MIT Press.

Reed, E. S. (1988) *James. J. Gibson and the Psychology of Perception*, New Haven, Yale University Press.

(1993) 'The intention to use a specific affordance: a conceptual framework for psychology', in R. H. Wozniak & K. Fischer eds., *Developments in Context: Acting and Thinking in Specific Environments*, New Jersey, Lawrence Erlbaum.

(1995) 'The ecological approach to language development: a radical solution to Chomsky's and Quine's problems', *Language and Communication*, 15, 1, 1–29.

Rogoff, B. (1990) *Apprenticeship in Thinking*, New York, Oxford University Press.

Rowlands, Mark (1991a) 'Towards a reasonable version of methodological solipsism', *Mind and Language*, 6, 1, 39–57.

(1991b) 'Narrow content', in B. Smith & H. Burckhardt eds., *Handbook of Metaphysics and Ontology*, Munich, Philosophia.

(1994) 'Connectionism and the language of thought', *British Journal for the Philosophy of Science*, 45, 485–503.

(1995a) *Supervenience and Materialism*, Aldershot, Avebury.

(1995b) 'Externalism and token–token identity', *Philosophia*, 24, 2, 359–75.

(1995c) 'Against methodological solipsism: The ecological approach', in *Philosophical Psychology*, 8, 1, 5–24.

(1997) 'Teleological semantics', *Mind*, 106, 422, 279–303.

Rubin, David (1995) *Remembering in Oral Traditions*, Oxford University Press.

References

Rumelhart, D. E., McClelland, J. L. & the PDP Research Group (1986) *Parallel Distributed Processing: Explorations in the Microstructure of Cognition*, 1, *Foundations*, Massachusetts, MIT Press.

Ryle, Gilbert (1949) *The Concept of Mind*, London, Hutchinson.

Sedgwick, H. A. (1973) 'The visible horizon: a potential source of information for the perception of size and distance', Ph.D. dissertation, Cornell University.

Simon, H. A. (1967) 'The logic of heuristic decision making', in N. Rescher ed., *The Logic of Decision and Action*, University of Pittsburgh Press, 1–20.

Slobodkin, L. B. (1972) 'On the inconstancy of ecological efficiency and the form of ecological theories', *Connecticut Academy of Arts and Sciences*, 44, 291–305.

Smolensky, P. (1987) 'The constituent structure of connectionist mental states; a reply to Fodor & Pylyshyn', *The Southern Journal of Philosophy*, 26, *Supplement*, 137–61.

 (1988) 'On the proper treatment of connectionism', *Behavioral and Brain Sciences*, 11, 1–74.

Snow, C. (1977) 'The development of conversation between mothers and babies', *Journal of Child Language*, 4, 1–22.

Sober, E. (1984) *The Nature of Selection*, Cambridge, MA, MIT Press.

Stalnaker, R. C. (1984) *Inquiry*, Cambridge, MA, MIT Press.

Stampe, D. W. (1977) 'Toward a causal theory of linguistic representation', in P. A. French, T. E. Uehling, & H. K. Wettstein eds., *Contemporary Perspectives in the Philosophy of Language*, Minneapolis, University of Minnesota Press.

Sterelny, K. (1990) *The Representational Theory of Mind*, Oxford, Basil Blackwell.

Stich, Stephen (1983) *From Folk Psychology to Cognitive Science*, Cambridge, MA, MIT Press.

Strawson, Peter (1959) *Individuals*, London, Methuen.

Studdert-Kennedy, M. (1991) 'Language development from an evolutionary perspective', in N. A. Krasnegor, D. M. Rumbaugh, R. L. Schiefelsbusch, and M. Studdert-Kennedy, eds., *Biological and Behavioural Determinants of Language Acquisition*, New Jersey, Lawrence Erlbaum.

Terrace H. & Bever, T. G. (1980) 'What might be learned from studying language in the chimpanzee? The importance of symbolizing oneself', in T. Sebeok & J. Sebeok eds., *Speaking of Apes*, New York, Plenum Press.

Thoday, J. M. (1953) 'Components of fitness', in *Society for Experimental Biology Symposium*, 7, 96–113.

Tomasello, M. (1992) *First Verbs: A Case Study in Early Grammatical Development*, New York, Cambridge University Press.

Tomasello, M., Farrar, J., & Dines, J. (1983) 'Young children's speech revisions for a familiar and unfamiliar adult', *Journal of Speech and Hearing Research*, 17, 359–62.

Tulving, E. (1983) *Elements of Semantic Memory*, New York, Oxford University Press.

Ullman, S. (1980) 'Against direct perception', *Behavioural and Brain Sciences*, 3, 373–415.

Van Valen, Leigh (1976) 'Energy and evolution', *Evolutionary Theory*, 1, 179–229.

(1980) 'Evolution as a zero-sum game for energy', *Evolutionary Theory*, 4, 289–300.

Vygotsky, L.S. (1989) *Thought and Language*, Massachusetts, MIT Press.

Wickler, W. (1968) *Mimicry*, London, Weidenfeld & Nicolson.

(1976) 'Evolution oriented ethology, kin selection, and altruistic parasites', *Zeitschrift für Tierpsychologie*, 43, 106–7.

Wittgenstein, Ludwig (1953) *Philosophical Investigations*, Oxford, Basil Blackwell.

(1978) *Remarks on Colour*, G. E. M. Anscombe ed., Berkeley, University of California Press.

(1979) *The Cambridge Lectures, 1932–35*, Oxford, Basil Blackwell.

Woodfield, Andrew (1982) *Thought and Object*, Oxford University Press.

Zuriff, Gregory (1987) *Behaviorism:A Conceptual Reconstruction*, New York, Columbia University Press.

Index